THE BEST
OF THE LAST TEN YEARS
IN AUSTRALIAN SPORT

THE BEST
OF THE LAST TEN YEARS
IN AUSTRALIAN SPORT

Edited by DAVID LORD

SAVVAS PUBLISHING

ACKNOWLEDGEMENT

This book is a collection of articles on a number of
sports. To cover this spectrum it has been necessary
to call on assistance from many people and
organisations to supply photographs and editorial.
Some credits have been given in the book but others
may have been missed.
We appreciate very much the help so willingly
given and express our gratitude to the many people
who have helped.

National Library of Australia ISBN 0 909216 02 9

Published by Savvas Publishing
172-174 Morphett Street, Adelaide, South Australia
First published 1978
Reprinted 1984
All rights reserved. Copyright ©

Printed and bound in Singapore
by Eurasia Press (Offset) Pte Ltd

Australia II sailed in to the history books in September, 1983, when she captured the Americas Cup from the New York Yacht Club which had held it for 132 years.

CONTENTS

1 HORSE RACING

By JOHN HOLLOWAY

JOHN HOLLOWAY is one of the younger brigade of Sydney's racing journalists, employed by the "Daily Mirror" newspaper. His list of contacts in the "sport of kings" spreads throughout Australia with a coverage of big races in three states—NSW, Victoria and Queensland.

Combine utter confusion with bitter disappointment in Australia's greatest race, the Melbourne Cup, and you have the most memorable drama in horse racing in the past decade, probably in the history of the Australian turf.

The scene was Flemington on the first Tuesday in November in 1969. Thirty-nine minutes remained before the Melbourne Cup was scheduled to be run for the 109th time when the crowd in excess of 80,000 received the shock of their racing lives.

"Attention ladies and gentlemen . . . the stewards have ordered the scratching of Big Philou from the Melbourne Cup at 2.01 p.m." was the message amplified to the crowd who listened in stunned silence.

Big Philou was the Melbourne Cup favourite at 4 to 1 at the time of his withdrawal. He was trained by Bart Cummings and was to be ridden by Roy Higgins.

Cummings had been quoted as saying "Big Philou is just about the greatest certainty I've ever had in my life".

Jockeys are not allowed to tip but Roy Higgins had also let it be known that he expected his third Melbourne Cup win in five years on Big Philou—and the win would be easier than the ones on Light Fingers and Red Handed.

I was covering my second Melbourne Cup as a racing journalist and the scratching left me dumbfounded. Within seconds the Flemington track was rife with rumours that Big Philou had been "got at".

Officials, pressmen and photographers were clambering around Big Philou's stall where the big horse was scouring badly and veterinary surgeons had examined him only minutes earlier.

It was a sorry and sickening state of affairs and one had to feel desperately sorry for Bart Cummings who had spent untold hours working Big Philou up to the great "two mile" race, known throughout the world.

And Roy Higgins, too, who watched the Melbourne Cup from the grandstands when every trainer with a runner in the race would have sought the services of Australia's number one jockey.

Investigations by the VRC a few days later revealed Big Philou had been nobbled with a purgative drug known as Danthron.

Cummings was at a loss to explain how the horse was drugged and who drugged him and part-owner Mr. Charles Gawith offered a $5,000 reward for information leading to a conviction.

The case went on for many months with a former stable employee of Cummings being charged with conspiracy with unknown persons to cheat and defraud, but he was later acquitted.

Big Philou certainly was the sensation horse in the spring of 1969.

Take his win—on protest—in the Caulfield Cup when Roy Higgins fired in a successful objection against Nausori, ridden by Des Lake, on the grounds of interference.

"Yes—I'll protest for sure" Roy Higgins told Bart Cummings "And I'm sure to get the race," Higgins said on his return to the Caulfield enclosure.

Big Philou, a 9-2 favourite, had been beaten a neck by Nausori with Tobermory a further three-quarters of a length back third.

It was a lengthy protest hearing which Higgins won with the jockey claiming Des Lake had taken his running by crossing too quickly to the inside fence after getting to the lead.

Roy Higgins' protest in the Caulfield Cup was the first successful one since 1893.

But back to the Melbourne Cup of 1969 and victory went to Rain Lover who emulated the feat of Archer in 1861 and 1862 by becoming the second horse to win successive Cups. Rain Lover was ridden by "Jerky" Jim Johnson and this was a race which was one of the most exciting I can recall.

I didn't back Rain Lover but I cheered myself hoarse in the final 400 metres when it was evident the gallant stayer was going to take a place in racing history under his huge impost of 60.5 kg. Alsop, a Victorian stayer, had joined Rain Lover at this stage of the race and it appeared certain he would cause a considerable upset under his light weight and win.

But Rain Lover produced a rare brand of stamina to stall off his rival and win in a photo finish by a head—a victory which was given a fitting reward as the dual Melbourne Cup winner was led back to the enclosure by his proud owner Mr. C. A. Reid.

The previous year Rain Lover won the Cup by eight lengths, but in the 12 months between the stayer had lost this form and consequently he was an 8 to 1 chance in 1969 after the withdrawal of Big Philou.

The past ten years of the Melbourne Cup has been practically the private property of Bart Cummings, known throughout Australia as the "Cup's King".

Think Big's two wins in 1974 and 1975 saw him equal the feat of Etienne De Mestre by training five winners of the Melbourne Cup.

But Cummings' performances undoubtedly overshadowed the efforts of De Mestre with his phenomenal "quinella" results in the Cups.

Cummings' "one-two" results in the rich race began as early as 1965 when he won his first Melbourne Cup with Light Fingers who beat her stablemate Ziema by a half head.

The following year Galilee was first and Light Fingers two lengths away second. In 1974 when Think Big won his first Melbourne Cup he beat Leilani into second place and at the presentation Bart Cummings told the crowd "the wrong horse won the Melbourne Cup".

And the following year Think Big relegated another of his stablemates, Holiday Waggon, into second place giving Cummings his fourth "quinella".

In the 1976 Melbourne Cup the champion trainer was beaten by the "big wet" with Flemington resembling a mud-heap after a freakish downpour only half an hour before the race was due to run.

Cummings saddled up Gold and Black who was beaten into second place by the New Zealander Van Der Hum the latter being a ten lengths better galloper on rain-affected ground.

But 12 months later Gold And Black had his moment of Melbourne Cup glory with Sydney jockey John Duggan going one better after a memorable duel with the crowd's favourite, Reckless.

The two singled out in the final 100 metres of the 3200 m race with Cummings' phenomenal training feats being the master and the stayer became his record sixth Melbourne Cup triumph.

Horses trained by Bart Cummings played a major role in races throughout Australia in the past decade with the trainer bringing out the best in a large number of great gallopers.

Another fantastic incident associated with Cummings was the 1974 AJC Doncaster Handicap, 1600 m, at Randwick won by Tontonan.

This was the day the male and female streakers "stole the show" with the pair causing a sensation as they emerged from the crowd of 52,000 at the flat and ran to the saddling enclosure just after the start of the $100,000 race. At first there were loud groans from thousands of people in the paddock enclosure.

Then roars of laughter broke out all over the course and the streakers stole the spotlight from the great Randwick "metric mile" race.

When jockey Roy Higgins brought Tontonan back to the enclosure the male streaker lifted his right hand high in the air.

Tontonan lugged out towards the outside fence in the last 400 metres of the race and Higgins quipped: "I wanted to get a close-up look of the action", referring to the woman streaker who was in her mid-twenties.

Tontonan, a splendid sprinter by the outstanding stallion Showdown, was a marvellous money-spinner for the Cummings stables, winning $245,150 in prizemoney in an injury-plagued career.

Tontonan won many feature races on the Australian turf calendar including the STC Golden Slipper Stakes, AJC Sires Produce Stakes, the VATC Oakleigh Plate as well as his Doncaster success.

LUSKIN STAR . . . a racing machine

IMAGELE ... with Kevin Langby aboard

But his win in the Golden Slipper was another sensational race in 1973, giving Cummings his second success in the fabulous two-year-old event.

This was the year Tommy Smith's marvellous chestnut Imagele was considered to have a mortgage on the race.

Imagele had carried all before him in his early two-year-old career and he had beaten Tontonan pointlessly in the final lead-up race to the Slipper a fortnight earlier.

As a result Imagele was a prohibitive odds-on favourite, Tontonan the second fancy.

Imagele was one of three gallopers involved in a spectacular fall at the 600 metres with Kevin Langby being taken to hospital after the incident and the horse being seriously injured.

Imagele, consequently, was out of action for several months but the galloper showed what a fighting heart he had by recovering and being brought back to training by Tommy Smith for the three-year-old classics.

Imagele contested the 1973 AJC Derby and this was another memorable event with three three-year-olds—Imagele, Leica Lover and Grand Cidium—flashing past the winning post practically on terms.

I'll never forget the anxious moments Tommy Smith spent waiting for the photo finish to come down.

This was one of Smith's greatest training triumphs, nursing Imagele back from a sick and sorry horse, to winning one of the feature races in Australia and he declared the chestnut as one of the best horses he had ever been associated with during his career.

Imagele retired to the stud after a career of 20 starts which saw him win 11 times and be placed five times earning $150,876.

But his life as a stallion was short-lived with Imagele passing away after serving only one season. His death was a great loss to Australian racing as he had given so much in a short space of time and he had the pedigree to be a wonderful asset to the breeding industry.

Racing in the past ten years has been spotlighted by people such as Bart Cummings, Tommy Smith and, of course, the fabulous jockey George Moore who retired in 1971 after winning the Victoria Derby on Classic Mission at Flemington. George Moore was the complete jockey—the best I've seen and am ever likely to see. Moore was incredibly temperamental; hardly the ideal type for a pressman to get on with, but his ability couldn't be ignored.

He "retired" on many occasions, but finally hung up his boots after winning the Victoria Derby with the jockey returning to riding only the previous February and taking out many of the big plums in the sport.

In the six weeks after his last comeback Moore won the VRC Newmarket Handicap on Baguette, the STC Golden Slipper for the second year in a row on Fairy Walk and the AJC Doncaster Handicap on Rajah Sahib.

Probably Moore's most outstanding performance was registered at the Sydney Easter carnival at Randwick in 1969.

There were 29 races conducted over the four days and Moore won 15 of them. He rode the final two winners on Doncaster day; the first four on Sydney Cup day and then another winner to give him five for the day.

Moore won many feature races overseas as well as Australia with the highlight being his English Derby win on Royal Palace.

The champion jockey didn't win a Melbourne Cup, or for that matter, a Caulfield Cup.

But he has a record in big races throughout Australia which will never be equalled.

Moore won the AJC Derby five times; the Epsom twice, Metropolitan once, Doncaster three times, AJC Sires Produce six times, Sydney Cup three times, AJC Oaks three times, the Champagne Stakes three times, the Rosehill Guineas four times and the Golden Slipper twice.

In Melbourne he won the Victoria Derby twice, the Oaks and Sires Produce Stakes once, the St Leger and Newmarket Handicap twice.

His big-race Brisbane wins included the Queensland Derby three times and the Stradbroke, Doomben Ten Thousand and Cup three times also. He won a Brisbane Cup on Tulloch in the champion's last run, the Oaks twice and the Sires Produce Stakes four times.

After his retirement from race riding Moore took up training in Hong Kong and quickly established himself as the number one trainer in the country.

His son, Gary, is the leading jockey and the pair are as dominant as Moore was when he rode as number one jockey for the Tommy Smith stable.

Moore has no plans to take up training in Australia.

The jockey won the AJC and Victoria Derbies on the New Zealander Classic Mission who was involved in one of the most controversial issues, the three-year-old with the "four-year-old teeth".

The Australian Jockey Club sent two officials to New Zealand to gain evidence to prove Classic Mission was a three-year-old in case he won the AJC Derby and a protest was lodged. Classic Mission, with Moore riding a masterful race, won the AJC Derby by the shortest possible margin from Latin Knight in another action-packed event.

Classic Mission was trained by Syd Brown, a former New Zealander who is now firmly established in Sydney with many big race wins to his credit also.

Baguette and George Moore were another formidable association with the champion galloper becoming the first horse to win the two-year-old "grand slam" in 1970.

The grand slam consisted of the Golden Slipper Stakes, the AJC Sires Produce Stakes and the Champagne Stakes.

Baguette was unbeaten as a two-year-old winning $103,110 in his first year of racing.

Baguette was by Rego from the extraordinary brood mare Dark Jewel, the dam of so many top gallopers, including Cabochon and Betelguese, and easily her most famous son.

BAGUETTE . . . a formidable combination with George Moore

When Baguette retired he'd won a total of 15 races and $195,000 in prize money and the other big-race wins collected by the sprinter included the Doomben Ten Thousand and the Newmarket Handicap at Flemington.

The horse is enjoying a successful career as a stallion and the name of Baguette will continue for many years in Australian racing.

Gunsynd was probably the horse which captured the imagination of racegoers throughout Australia in the past decade.

The "Goondiwindi grey" was trained early in his career by Bill Wehlow in Brisbane, but connections transferred him to Tommy Smith just prior to the running of the 1971 Epsom Handicap.

Under Smith's care Gunsynd was to become a true champion and the plucky grey with a wonderful will to win in the spotlight wherever he raced—and he certainly went around plenty of times.

Gunsynd was by Sunset Hue from Woodie Wonder and he was purchased for the meagre sum of $1,300 as a yearling.

At the end of his racing career Gunsynd amassed $280,455 being the greatest stakes winner in the history of the Australian turf at the time.

Gunsynd won 29 races and was placed 15 times with his wins ranging from 1000 metres to 2500 metres.

He won an Epsom and Doncaster Handicap, the W. S. Cox Plate, the Sandown Cup, the George Adams Memorial Mile and the Queen Elizabeth Stakes just to name a few.

SURROUND . . . weight for age "Queen"

Gunsynd contested the 1972 Melbourne Cup and although beaten into third place by Piping Lane and Magnifique the grey covered himself with glory.

The horse refused to give in under his top-weight and the crowd of nearly 103,000 gave him a tremendous ovation as he returned to the enclosure.

Gunsynd was involved in a superb "match" with another of Australia's exciting gallopers, Tails, in the Queen Elizabeth Stakes, 2400 m, at Randwick. That was in 1972 and the following year Gunsynd had his farewell race in the same event with another "match" being against the champion New Zealander Apollo Eleven.

Gunsynd had to be content in second place in both these races after stirring battles with Tails and then Apollo Eleven in the weight-for-age conditions.

More than 30,000 racegoers attended Randwick on Gunsynd's farewell day and the grey didn't let his followers down although he was beaten half a length by Apollo Eleven who the previous Monday won the Sydney Cup, 3200 m, as he liked.

Gunsynd was syndicated to stand at the Kia-Ora Stud in Scone for $270,000 and this on top of his winnings makes him one of the all-time greats in Australian turf.

The horse was farewelled in Sydney, Melbourne and Brisbane . . . then Goondiwindi before finally having his last racecourse appearance at Scone, 20 kilometres from where he was to stand at stud.

He had songs written about him, poems too, and probably was the most written about horse in the past decade.

Gunsynd's popularity at the stud continued

in his first year with the birth of his first foal receiving front-page attention in every paper throughout Australia.

Gunsynd won on every metropolitan race-track in Sydney, Melbourne and Brisbane which is an amazing feat in itself.

Tails, another former Queenslander, came of age for trainer Pat Murray and the flashy chestnut carved out a niche in the record books.

He won successive AJC Metropolitans, 2600 m, at Randwick in 1969 and 1970 and he failed narrowly in his third attempt in 1971 being beaten narrowly by the lightly weighted Tommy Smith charge, Oncidon.

Like Gunsynd, Tails is now standing at the stud with quite a few of his progeny showing the staying potential which won many races for the chestnut.

Sydney racing in the seventies saw the introduction of a new race, one which was to become an instant success during the Randwick autumn carnival.

This was the Australasian Champion Stakes run over the 2000 metres and it really lived up to its name with the best three-year-olds from Australia and New Zealand being at Randwick in quest of the $100,000 prize.

The race was run for the first time in 1971

TOMMY SMITH . . . 25 successive Sydney premiership wins

and the seven winners have shown that you have to be a good horse to win.

Gay Icarus was the inaugural winner of the Champion Stakes with the Victorian beating Baguette and Gunsynd into the minor placings.

Latin Knight, Gold Brick, Asgard, Taras Bulba, Cheyne Walk and last year Sir Silver Lad, the nuggety little N.Z. colt, were the winners in following years.

There have been sensational defeats in the Champion Stakes in the past two years involving two of the hottest racing stars in Australia and New Zealand.

Balmerino was beaten out of a place behind Cheyne Walk in the 1976 race while Surround, the freak filly trained by Geoff Murphy, performed similarly behind Sir Silver Lad last year.

Both started red-hot favourites after displaying brilliant form in the lead-up races, but in retrospect neither horse ever looked likely to win the race.

Balmerino and his youthful trainer Brian Smith were in the public's eye right from the time they arrived in Australia, and the New Zealander certainly gave the racing public their money's worth handing in some outstanding performances.

Balmerino won the 1976 Brisbane Cup, 3200 m, as a three-year-old. He was the first of his age to win the rich Queensland race for more than twenty years.

Balmerino was beaten out of a place in the 1977 Sydney Cup, but later went to America for the International Stakes. He was unplaced there, but later proved himself to the world by winning a feature race in the U.S.

Surround, a half-sister to another magnificent galloper in Purple Patch, was the weight-for-age "queen" of Australia when she won the W. S. Cox Plate at Moonee Valley in the spring of 1976.

This field brought together the best gallopers in Australia, but Peter Cook was able to bring the grey filly home the easiest of winners.

After her Champion Stakes defeat Surround more than acquitted herself with effortless wins in the AJC Oaks, the Queensland Oaks and the QTC Grand Prix Stakes.

Two-year-old racing in 1976-77 saw Luskin Star emerge as the brightest star on the horizon

GUNSYND . . . the Goondiwindi grey

with the Newcastle trained colt putting Max Lees and jockey John Wade on the "map".

Luskin Star did a Baguette by winning the "grand slam" in the autumn—the Slipper, Sires' Produce and Champagne Stakes—all with ridiculous ease.

Luskin Star races like a machine. He seems to win without any major effort and has tasted defeat only once, on a very heavy Newcastle track when he was resuming from a spell.

As a three-year-old Luskin Star was to become Australia's hottest racing property and barely was his name out of the headlines.

Lees worked out a programme, in between massive bids to buy the chestnut, which saw him beaten by Romantic Dream at wfa at Canterbury—failing by an "inch".

His next two starts saw him win the Newcastle Cameron Handicap as he liked and then the $60,000 Caulfield Guineas as his final lead-up to his spring goal, the richest wfa race in Australia, the W. S. Cox Plate.

Here Luskin Star clashed with the English grey Raffindale in what had been regarded as a "match" race. Raffindale had taken Australian racing by storm with paralysing displays in three states—South Australia, N.S.W. and Victoria. Prior to this race Luskin Star was involved in a track accident which resulted in blood streaming from his injured leg and it put a Cox Plate start in extreme doubt.

But as history showed it the injury didn't make any difference because Luskin Star proved himself a non-stayer when he finished

down the course behind Family of Man with Raffindale coming in second.

Then on November 1—Melbourne Cup Day — Luskin Star was purchased by English soccer pools magnate Robert Sangster for $1.2 million with quarter shares later being passed on to two Australian based syndicates and Bart Cummings was to become his trainer.

What the future holds in store for Luskin Star is exciting to say the least with a possible overseas campaign in store to prove himself against the best in the world.

He is easily the most breathtaking sprinter since Vain was annihilating his rivals as a two and three-year-old in 1969.

Vain must rate as one of the fastest horses ever to race in Australia. By Wilkes from Elated, Vain raced 14 times with his record being 12 wins and two seconds.

He won $145,335 before being forcefully retired to stud through injury, but Vain has proven as brilliant at the stud as he was on the racetracks. Vain's clash with Special Girl in the 1969 Golden Slipper was billed as the two-year-old championship of Australia.

Special Girl, at the time, was the fastest horse I had seen race, with the filly of Neville Begg's ridden by George Moore scoring as she liked in lead-up races to the Golden Slipper.

But the Golden Slipper wasn't a race—it was a walkover for Vain who went straight to the front and won by as far as jockey Pat Hyland wanted to.

Vain's two defeats were in the Sires' Produce Stakes by Beau Babylon and the Moonee Valley Stakes by the Syd Brown trained Daryl's Joy, who himself was a champion.

I saw Vain win the Craven "A" Stakes, 1200 m, at Flemington by 12 lengths in 1.9.8 as a three-year-old in the most amazing speed display one could ever imagine.

He was another fabulous crowd-pleaser and there are not many horses to race in Australia with a record equal to that of Vain.

Of course, when one mentions a crowd pleaser what horse comes to mind but the Victorian Reckless and his lovable 78 year-old trainer Tom Woodcock of Phar Lap fame.

Reckless couldn't win a race in his first 33 starts but came good with a vengeance in 1977.

In the space of two months Reckless performed a feat never previously accomplished with Sydney, Adelaide and Brisbane Cup wins — all over 3200 m — with Woodcock and Reckless flying to each state on the morning of the races from his Melbourne stables.

He was the sentimental favourite when second to Gold And Black in the Melbourne Cup and then on January 2 this year Reckless broke down when a gallant third in his finale race, the Perth Cup, with his jockey through his Cups campaign, Pat Trotter, being forced to lead him back to the enclosure.

Tommy Smith's dominance of Australian racing in the past 10 years continued with the champion trainer wrapping up his 25th successive premiership win in Sydney at the completion of the 1976-77 season.

What words can describe Smith? The "little master" runs his huge team with stop-watch precision and his success in feature races in the past decade has been flabbergasting.

In the past three years Smith has had to contend with Bart Cummings who has set up his mains stables in Sydney. There is nothing more that Smith likes than a challenge and he has excelled with Cummings bringing out the best of his rival's training talents.

Smith's wins in major races are too numerous to mention but there isn't a race on the Australian calendar to elude him.

His number of Derby wins total 23 during his career, a world record performance.

In the past ten years Smith has won three AJC Derbys with Silver Sharpe, Imagele and Great Lover with his other big-race wins at Randwick including the Epsom Handicap four times, the Doncaster Handicap five times, the Metropolitan five times, the Champagne Stakes three times, the AJC Oaks three times, the Sires' Produce twice and the Champion Stakes once.

He has also won the Golden Slipper four times making him the most successful trainer in the history of the two-year-old race.

Smith is a tireless worker and always available to his owners and the press, radio and television media.

The trainer's Tulloch Lodge stables have been in the news plenty of times in the past couple of years with several fire attempts as well as the recent "horse nobbling" incidents.

But Smith is strong enough and powerful enough to overcome these obstacles and he will remain number one in Sydney for as long as he continues to train.

On the jockey front, Malcolm Johnston,

ROY HIGGINS AND BART CUMMINGS . . . a tough combination to beat

the baby-faced apprentice from the Theo Green school of jockeys, became the biggest name in Australia.

Johnston is a natural and he beat the might of the Tommy Smith's stables in the 1975-76 racing season by winning the jockey's premiership as an apprentice.

Normally the number one rider for Tommy Smith is the premier jockey, but Malcolm Johnston, aided by his 1.5 kg allowance, scored a resounding win over Kevin Langby.

Last year Johnston went to England for three months on loan to trainer Ian Balding. He rode with distinction, learning important facts on his riding style from the likes of Lester Piggott, and he is destined to become one of the greats of his profession.

Then in 1978 Tommy Smith sealed Johnston's future as Australian biggest money earning jockey by appointing him as his stable rider—to ride any horse for him anywhere in Australia—which is a remarkable feat for the 21 year-old Johnston.

There were many tragedies regarding the breeding industry in that time also with the deaths of many recognised stallions.

Oncidium, Pakistan II, Sobig, Mellay and Hermes were tragic losses to the N.Z. breeding industry while in Australia the death of Wilkes was the most significant.

But other stallions which died included Todman, Agricola, Corinto, Triton, Imagele, Better Boy and the American-bred trio, Blue-scope, Swiftly Morgan and Dignitas who all had stood at the Dawson Stud, Cootamundra, of Fred Calvin.

Still on the breeding scene and the 1975-76 season saw the first of the progeny of Without Fear, who stood at Colin Hayes' Lindsay Park Stud in S.A., race in Australia.

Without Fear's two-year-old's rewrote the record books throughout the world, siring more winners in one season of racing than any previous stallion.

Colin Hayes, too, continued his tremendous success as a trainer and studmaster and he is firmly entrenched as one of Australia's "big three" in the training circles.

Jockey Roy Higgins was another record-breaker with the jockey winning his tenth Victorian premiership in 1976-77 breaking the previous best held by Bill Williamson.

There's been hardly a dull moment in racing in the past ten years. There has been excitement, scandal, marvellous horses, top-class jockeys and trainers combining and gambling being on a bigger basis as each year rolls by. If the next ten years is just half as interesting—and with horses like Luskin Star around it promises to be—then my task as a racing journalist won't be too hard at all.

Taras Bulba, Apollo Eleven, Divide and Rule, Irish Whip, Igloo, Black Onyx and the mighty filly Analie were other gallopers who reached considerable heights in the past ten years of racing.

RAIN LOVER . . . winning the 1969 Melbourne Cup

2 CRICKET

By PETER McFARLINE

PETER McFARLINE, is the Chief Cricket Writer for the "Age", Melbourne. He joined that newspaper as a sporting writer in 1969, after seven years on the Brisbane "Courier Mail", taking over the cricket job in 1976. He has made two tours to England—with the 1975 and 1977 teams and helped former Australian Captain Ian Chappell in his best-selling book "Chappelli". McFarline won the Victorian Cricket Association's Media Award for the 1976-77 season.

Cricket, probably more than any other team sport, lends itself to domination by extraordinary characters.

Despite its long history, its fine traditions, its strong links with the old school tie, it has been the individual magic that has been the main attraction, even to the most ardent followers, down the years.

Who, with even a marginal interest in the game, hasn't heard of Dr. W. G. Grace? Or Spofforth? Or Sir Jack Hobbs? Or Sobers? Or Bradman, who, despite his Royal accolade, had more affection attached to a surname than perhaps anybody in sport.

The decade 1967-77 was no different in Australian cricket.

After an ordinary start, in which many of the game's critics were still confidently predicting its demise, the game rose from the ashes, so to speak, to a zenith in 1974, 1975 and 1976 which was as exciting as any on the field—to torment in 1977.

That its very existence was threatened by the emergence in 1977 of a private promoter in television mogul Mr. Kerry Packer and the following bitter battle between his organisation and the established world cricket authorities will remain cricket's most ferocious argument.

But above the fires of Australia's on field rejuvenation rose the spectres of three men whose names will live as long as cricket exists.

It is indisputable, I believe, that Ian Chappell, his brother Greg Chappell and Dennis Lillee collectively, and apart, rode above that era in a manner that can never be ignored, scarcely forgotten.

All three were leading players in the breakaway movement, which led to their being banned from Test cricket and, at the time of writing, seemed destined never to play first-class, or Test cricket, again. The rights and wrongs of the affair, its politics and its effects, are not the subject for discussion here.

Of course, there were the Lawrys, the Thomsons, the McKenzies, the Marshs, the Massies, the Stackpoles, the Redpaths, the Walters. And others. But without being unfair, they either rode shotgun to the big three, were merely guiding influences on them, or were brief and passing highlights to the illustrious ones.

Cricket being what it is, a game that forever engenders arguments and few satisfactory conclusions, let us examine these three men and their influence on the game. Later, we will discuss some of the other names who graced the horizon of Australian cricket in the last 10 years—and the reader can draw his or her own conclusions, or, as often happens, draw a bead on the unfortunate writer.

Ian Michael Chappell, born September 26, 1943 in Adelaide, South Australia, must come first—not only because of his seniority in years, but also because of the degree of his influence on the game.

His maternal grandfather Victor York Richardson had captained Australia many years before, and his father, Martin was a successful Adelaide club cricketer who just failed to make the first-class scene. So there was much background for Ian, and later Greg, on which to build their cricket careers.

It is a sound commentary on their personalities that they did it with a minimum of blood-line help, Ian soon throwing off the tag of "Vic. Richardson's grandson" and Greg very quickly achieving his own name rather than that of "Ian's brother".

It is a proud family that can boast three Australian captains—prouder still that each left his own particular stamp on the game.

IAN CHAPPELL . . . fame and notoriety

[News Ltd.]

Ian made his debut for South Australia in the Sheffield Shield competition of 1961-62, a time which put him under the influence of the greatest all-rounder of them all, Sir Garfield Sobers, who was then playing for South Australia.

By the time he decided to end his first-class career, after the 1975-76 season, he had played 250 matches, scoring 18,790 runs at 48.80 with 56 centuries, a total exceeded only by three other Australian batsmen, Sir Donald Bradman (117), Neil Harvey (67) and Lindsay Hassett (59).

A Test career that began inauspiciously against Pakistan in Melbourne in 1964 had grown in stature until he finished with 72 Test matches, scoring 5,187 runs at 42.86 with 14 centuries. He was also a useful leg-spin bowler who took 173 wickets in first-class cricket, but whose enthusiasm for that job fell away over the years with his preoccupation of batting, fielding and later captaincy.

Enough of figures—or as he was wont to say "they mean nothing".

It was Chappell, the man, who put himself upon the game as batsman and captain in an undeniable fashion. A fighter, who was so often engaged in controversy he learned to laugh at it, Chappell became involved in a vigorous love-hate relationship with the game and those who form its every part.

Players to a man loved him—for his tenacity, his unwillingness to· fold under the greatest pressure, his vigorous pursuit of victory. Administrators and officials, in general, hated him for his forthrightness, his pig-headed attitude, his inability to understand that the old rules, which have run the game for more than a century, were good enough for the modern era.

When he became captain of Australia—in January 1971 after the unpleasant coup d'etat that ousted Bill Lawry—Chappell quickly emerged as the most controversial figure in Australian cricket since the 1930s.

It was as captain that Chappell gained most of his fame and notoriety. As a batsman who refused to be intimidated, who fought against his own bouts of poor form and who grafted or blasted according to the situation, he matured and blossomed under the various captaincies of Bob Simpson and Bill Lawry (for Australia) and Barry Jarman and Les Favell (for South Australia). From them he learnt and moulded his own character as a cricketer.

And when Lawry was purged after the sixth Test of the 1970-71 series against England in Australia, Chappell was ready for the challenge the selectors rather reluctantly threw at him.

Australia lost the Ashes 2-0 in that series as John Snow ran rampant with his fiery fast bowling. Chappell swore to himself it would· never happen again—not in his time anyway. It didn't.

By 1972, when he lead a young squad—described yet again as the worst-equipped ever to leave Australian shores to England—he was ready. He had around him a core of

[Australian Cricket]

GREG CHAPPELL . . . batsman extraordinary

talented young men who were to play a major part in Australia's triumphant rise back to the top of the international cricket heap.

There was brother Greg, destined to match and better all the dreams ever held for his marvellous ability; a wicketkeeper called Rodney Marsh who came from the ignominy of the nickname "Iron Gloves" to be his country's most successful guardian; an ageless maestro called Doug Walters and a young fast bowler with a recklessness matched only by his large heart — Dennis Lillee.

Between them, they fashioned a drawn series with Australian victories at Lords and The Oval negated only by the fusarium of a doctored Leeds wicket and an undeniable English pace attack at Old Trafford.

There were others, of course, . . . the roly-poly opening batsman Keith Stackpole who served Chappell faithfully as hitter and adviser and a shy Western Australian called Bob Massie, who captured 16 wickets in his Test debut at Lords — and died out of the game a year later a cricket pauper.

From England in 1972, it was all success for Chappell.

He led the side to victory over Pakistan in 1972-73, the West Indies (1973), New Zealand in 1973-74 and most satisfying, to an Ashes-regaining 4-1 triumph against England in 1974-75. By then, Australia had unearthed a lethal partner for Lillee — a young terror called Jeff Thomson whose speed and fire was a perfect foil for Chappell's main weapon.

Yet even in that controversial series when four-letter words and insults flew like shrapnel around the playing fields of the country, it was Chappell the batsman who set the pattern. In the first Test in Brisbane, when the England pace bowlers Peter Lever and Bob Willis launched a bumper barrage, it was Chappell's brave innings of 90 that set his side on the road to victory.

In 1975, he took his second Australian party to England to play in the inaugural Prudential World Cup and a four-Test series. Rising as ever to the challenge, this time that Australians were dullards at the one-day game, he conjured

ROD MARSH . . . agile record breaker

[News Ltd.]

his team into a memorable final at Lords, losing in the finish by 17 runs to the West Indies in a game that will live in cricket's Hall of Fame.

The Ashes were retained 1-0 in a disappointing series and then Chappell relinquished the captaincy after 30 Tests, 15 victories, 5 draws and not one full series in eight lost.

He had had enough, he said and had lost interest. There had been low points, the vast criticism heaped on the new elitism of the Australians, the tag "ugly Australians" which emerged after a series of Chaucerian performances by the hard-talking Australians.

There was also the tiresome burden of leading the fight for better pay and conditions for his players, a fight which the abrasive Chappell found most frustrating. The rewards of his work in that direction were to come later.

After one more series, playing under brother Greg, against the West Indies, he retired from the game to play club cricket with Melbourne side North Melbourne. But even his final first-class year 1975-76 was full of achievement.

He led his Shield team, South Australia, from last to first in the competition a remarkable triumph of leadership, on and off the field, of one of the youngest first-class sides ever assembled in the country, soured only by the ill-thought out strike which towards the end of the season threatened the future of some of the country's most promising cricketers.

If ever there was a contradiction in the word "brother", it came with the advent of Gregory Stephen Chappell as Australian batsman extraordinary and captain.

From the time Greg stepped onto the Test field to make a debut century at Perth in the second Test of the 1970-71 series against England, he was the complete antithesis of his brother. Introverted where Ian was gregarious, he nevertheless possessed a talent that set him above all other Australians of his time.

In an era that boasted three of the world's finest post-war batsmen, Greg was rated on a par with South African Barry Richards and West Indian Vivian Richards. As a close to the wicket fieldsman, there was none better and he was much under-rated as a medium pace bowler.

Born on August 7, 1948, he attended the same school, Prince Alfred College, Adelaide, as Ian, but his cricket apprenticeship differed in that he had two years with County side Somerset before making his Australian debut.

Possessing a classical, upright stance at the wicket, Greg was undoubtedly the strongest leg-side player seen in this country for many years, No cricket situation seems to bother him unduly—every answer comes straight out of the copybook as if he had written it.

He scored his 14th Test century, 112, against England at Old Trafford in July, 1977—a feat that took 23 more Tests for Ian to achieve. Where Ian often struggled, grafted and suffered trial by discomfort at the crease, Greg rarely did.

When he retired from Test cricket, after The Oval Test of the ill-fated 1977 tour, he had scored 4,097 runs at 53.20, from 52 Test matches.

He moved to Queensland at the start of the 1973-74 season to take up the position as State captain, an ambition he felt would be a long time coming during Ian's reign in Adelaide.

Although he failed to lead the State to its maiden Shield title, he achieved prodigious batting feats for his adopted home. The mantle of Australian captain fell easily on his shoulders upon Ian's retirement. In his first Test as his country's leader in Brisbane, 1975, he made the unfortunate West Indian bowlers suffer to the tune of a century in each innings— the first time such a feat has been achieved by a debutant captain.

That series was won 5-1 by Chappell's Australians. In the summer of 1976-77, the decline of the all-powerful Australian side which had ruled the world since 1973 began as the Pakistan visitors drew a three-Test series 1-all. In New Zealand, a short time later, Chappell lashed, drove and cajoled his men into a 1-0 victory in the two Test series.

[Australian Cricket]

DENNIS LILLEE . . . a great agitator

JEFF THOMSON . . . fire and brimstone

But the signs were there. His party to England in 1977 was sadly without Lillee and included a Jeff Thomson whose fitness was in doubt following a serious shoulder accident in the summer. Despite an awe-inspiring century in the second innings at Manchester, Chappell could not lift his players past the English challenge.

And with the future of Test cricket very much in upheaval from the challenge of the ambitious Kerry Packer, Greg Chappell passed from the Test match scene with his captaincy unproven and his batsmanship somewhat unfulfilled.

No resume of the last decade in Australian cricket would be complete without Dennis Lillee. If the two Chappells were the brains and the batting power behind the country's rise, Lillee was the big gun forever cutting down the opposition.

Most of his greatness was achieved in the shadow of a severe back injury that had doctors declaring at one stage he would never bowl again.

Dennis Keith Lillee, born in Perth on July 18, 1949, made his debut for Western Australia in the 1969-70 season against Queensland in Perth. One season later, he made his test debut for Australia against England in Adelaide. His 26 pace run, his unharnessed hostility and unbridled speed were a frightening sight—especially if you happened to be less than 22 yards away tapping your bat nervously in the blockhole.

The name Lillee shot to everyone's lips when, in an amazing burst, he took 8-29, the last 6 for 0, when Australia played the Rest of the World XI in Perth in October, 1971. His victims included such names as Sobers, Kallicharran, Kanhai and Gavaskar.

Australians, having suffered badly at the hands of Snow the year before, and Procter and Pollock two years earlier, rubbed their hands together and waited. They didn't have to wait long. Lillee was the cornerstone of the attack when Australia visited England and his speed, fitness and willingness to work long stints at the crease was instrumental in the series being drawn.

The first doubts about his fitness appeared in the 1972-73 series against Pakistan. Ian Chappell, at times, was forced to work Lillee

rather harder than he wished. In the third Test in Sydney, Lillee went down with a bad back and Australia, with him. A last wicket stand between Bob Massie and John Watkins gave the side a slight hope.

Lillee, the indefatigable saw it, got off his sick bed, and joined Max Walker in an assault on the Pakistan batsmen that saw Australia win by 59 runs. Ian Chappell says to this day that the sight of Lillee coming onto the Sydney Cricket Ground for the last innings gave the Pakistanis such a shock it was worth two or three wickets to Australia.

That Test was a memorable victory, but severe damage had been done to Lillee's spine. He broke down before the first Test against the West Indies, bowled in only one more game and returned home to discover three stress fractures of the vertebrae and a plaster cast waiting to encase his back.

"It will be" doctors at the University of Western Australia told him, "at the very least a matter of 18 months and no bowling if you are to recover,"

No-one had reckoned on Lillee's determination. He gave up his job, settled down to a long summer of exercise and careful rehabilitation and turned himself into an opening batsman for his Perth club side.

By the time England arrived in Australia, Lillee was ready. So too was a new ally, an unlikely looking Sydney lad with a javelin-thrower's action and a fiery temperament. The visitors were not impressed. Lillee, they said, could not have recovered and Thomson could not be anywhere near as fast as was rumoured.

Brisbane proved all that Chappell wanted to know. Lillee was not only fit, but with the warning his back had given him, was now a thinking bowler, with clever variation and a heart that bowed to no batsman. Thomson was now the terror-monger. In a bitter series, Thomson took 33 wickets and Lillee 29. The bruises they caused and the ribs they buckled completely broke the spirit of the visitors.

The pair carried on in harness in the 1975-76 series against the West Indies answering the pace challenge with more pace.

There was still doubt about Lillee's back and its ability to carry on under the tremendous physical load he gave it.

Throughout the 1976-77 season, he bowled, swallowing pain-killing tablets and suffering injections in the cause—21 wickets in three Tests against the Pakistanis, 15 in two against New Zealand, and a match-winning 11—6-26 and 5-139—were his rewards. When Lillee announced his unavailability for the 1977 tour of England, he had captured 171 wickets in only 32 Test matches, a striking rate never before achieved by any bowler—fast or slow.

The dominance of Lillee, and in later seasons Thomson, set up a kind of cricket subculture. They drew the game's popularity to unparalleled heights in Australia where the cry "Lilleee, Lilleee, Lilleee" burst from thousands of throats every time he charged to the wicket to deliver hapless batsmen their poison.

They revived the memories of Lindwall and Miller, Tyson and Statham, Larwood and Voce, Gregory and MacDonald. Yet Lillee, always a great agitator for better pay for players, had gone through purgatory for 18 months without an income, because he wanted to play again for his country.

No wonder Australia's Test players boiled with anger when a senior Australian Cricket Board official once said publicly, after a player's call for more money: "If they don't want to play for Australia, there are 500,000 others who do".

If Lillee was the main strike force, then mention must be made of his partner in many dismissals, the chunky Western Australian wicket-keeper Rodney Marsh. Marsh came into the Australian team at the start of the 1970-71 series against England.

On his own admission he had much to learn, and made many mistakes, so many he earned the unhappy soubriquet "Iron Gloves". When he ventured onto the SCG for the first time that season, he was booed. That only made the brother of international golfer Graham Marsh more determined.

By March, 1977, in his 47th Test match, he had claimed an Australian record of 188 victims. Marsh also chose that match to score 110 not out in Australia's second innings of the Centenary Test, the first time the

[Australian Cricket]

DOUG WALTERS . . . *unpredictable*

feat had been achieved in an Anglo-Australian Test match. He had already done the same trick against Pakistan four seasons previously.

Marsh's agility at times had to be seen to be believed. He spent most of his time standing more than 20 yards behind the stumps, having his hands turned red raw by the continuous thumping of the ball into his gloves—a ball delivered at speeds of up to 100 mph by a pair of bowlers, generally recognised as the fastest two in the world.

Apart from his batting and "keeping", Marsh was recognised by both Chappells as an expert tactician, leading Western Australia to an easy victory in the 1976-77 Sheffield Shield competition.

There have been others in the last decade who have blazoned Australia's cricket map with glory. The stoical Victorians Ian Redpath and Bill Lawry, took the brunt of the opening batting jobs that went during Australia's low period prior to 1972. Both became the butt of the selectors' ire, Lawry's removal from the Australian side in 1971 being regarded as one

IAN REDPATH . . . bore the brunt

[News Ltd.]

[News Ltd.]

KEITH STACKPOLE . . . attacking batsman

of the worst selection blunders in the country's sporting history.

Redpath, a right-hander of similar mould to Lawry, was moved up and down the order so often he used to regard himself as a utility.

There was Keith Stackpole, the bulky Victorian right-hander who was transformed into an opening batsman and whose attacking style earned him 2,807 runs at 37.42 in 43 Test matches.

One cannot forget the unpredictable Doug Walters, who crashed into Test cricket with centuries in his first two matches in the 1965-66 series against England and who 12 years later was making 250 for Australia against New Zealand.

The nerveless Walters is worth a chapter by himself, but the editor has only given me 3,000 words. And that is scarcely enough to do justice to a marvellous decade in Australian cricket.

3 TENNIS

By ROD HUMPHRIES

ROD HUMPHRIES — a former player who has also coached professionally and written about international tennis for 15 years, both here and overseas, and last year was one of six nominations from around the world as "International Tennis Writer of the Year". Humphries was tennis writer for the "Sydney Morning Herald" for 13 years and now head-writer for Australia's top television show, "This Is Your Life".

Rodney George Laver, the "Rocket" from Rockhampton, is not only the best Australian tennis player of the last 10 years . . . but the best the world has ever seen.

That is a very provocative statement. It is not only my considered opinion, but the opinion of many of the great tennis judges around the world.

The question invariably comes up whenever sportsmen meet and no matter how you look at world tennis, the "Rocket" wins every time.

Four Wimbledons and two Grand Slams of the Australian, French, Wimbledon and United States titles is quite an amazing record.

No male player has won more singles titles since the beginning of the modern era of lawn tennis after World War 1. Everybody placed Donald Budge on a pedestal when he won the Grand Slam in 1938. Laver did it twice . . . as an amateur and later in the more competitive world of Open tennis.

The Grand Slam takes on more significance today because most of the world's top players can perform at their best on only one surface . . . some cannot handle grass . . . others slow clay courts.

To take the Grand Slam a player has to win 28 consecutive matches on the fast Australian grass, the slow red clay of Roland Garros, and survive the pressure and the grass of Wimbledon and Forest Hills. Forest Hills has now been converted to clay.

Laver was runner-up at Wimbledon to Alex Olmedo in 1959 and Neale Fraser in 1960 —and then came into his own. He beat American Chuck McKinley and fellow-Australian Martin Mulligan in the next two finals without losing a set—and with the loss of only 13 games over the two finals.

The year 1962 was his Grand Slam year. He beat Roy Emerson 8-6, 0-6, 6-4, 6-4 to win the Australian title and then was two sets down to Emerson before winning the French final 3-6, 2-6, 6-3, 9-7, 6-2.

After beating another old foe in former champion Fraser in the semi-finals of Wimbledon, Laver whipped Mulligan 6-2, 6-2, 6-1. All that was left was the U.S. Open at Forest Hills.

The pressure on Laver was enormous, but he equalled the feat of another red-head named Budge and cleaned up the fourth title by again beating Emerson, 6-2, 6-4, 5-7, 6-4.

Who will forget the whipping Laver got at the hands of Lew Hoad and Ken Rosewall when he first turned professional in 1963? Hoad, in particular, made him look like a real amateur, so to speak.

But he did not take long to learn the percentage game and he was soon the world's number one professional.

Goodness knows how many Wimbledons he would have won between 1963 and 1968—or his sparring partner Ken Rosewall from 1957 to 1968 for that matter—but they both came back with a vengeance when the game was thrown open in 1968.

Laver won the historic first Open Wimbledon by beating Arthur Ashe in the semi-finals and fellow-Australian southpaw, Tony Roche 6-3, 6-4, 6-2 in the final.

But 1969 was the year I remember as Laver's best. The game had been thrown open, everybody was hungry for the new dollars and the depth of talent was deeper than ever before.

Laver had a tough hurdle to get over in the first Australian Open at the Milton courts in Brisbane. Roche, then heir-apparent to Laver's crown of World number one until injury crippled his career, played one of the longest matches in tennis history in forcing Laver to five sets in the semi-finals. Laver

ROD LAVER . . . the best the world has ever seen

finally won 7-5, 22-20, 9-11, 1-6, 6-3. The final against the Spaniard Andres Gimeno was easy compared to the semi-final. Laver won 6-3, 6-4, 7-5.

Then came the red dust of Roland Garros where Laver had to contend with defending champion Rosewall in the final. He won 6-4, 6-3, 6-4. Another young lion, the 1967 Wimbledon champion, John Newcombe stood in Laver's way in the Wimbledon final of 1969. Laver had toppled Arthur Ashe in one semi and Newcombe had downed Roche in the other. Laver, almost 31 and seven years older than his opponent, finally subdued Newcombe 6-4, 5-7, 6-4, 6-4.

The same foursome lined up for the semi-finals of Forest Hills . . . only this time Laver beat Ashe and Roche beat Newcombe.

Roche looked like he might thwart Rocket's grand slam when he sneaked away with the first set 7-9. Laver lifted his game to win the last three sets 6-1, 6-3, 6-2.

It is doubtful that any player can win the Grand Slam again, let alone twice. And because of the way tennis is set up today it is doubtful if any player can dominate the game to the extent Laver did in his prime years.

Laver had everything. He was a sharp-shooter from both wings and his top-spin shots on both forehand and backhand were his main attacking weapons. His serve was solid without being a dynamic weapon like that of Newcombe and Ashe. But it was the deceptive spin and curve that made it so effective.

Laver had an unbelievable eye and reflexes and pulled off the "impossible" just when you thought he was beaten. Many thought his shots too "flashy", but he always managed to whip a baseline winner across court when there appeared only an inch of room to move.

But above all he had a winner's mind . . . cold and calculating. He never believed he was beaten, even when trailing two sets and a break in so many important matches.

He was the first tennis player to make a million dollars from prize money alone . . . and one doubts whether we will see the likes of him again.

And when you talk of Laver you invariably speak of little "Muscles" Rosewall.

When you look at Rosewall's career it is not 10 years, but a quarter of a century. He is a sports phenomenon at 43 years of age (43 on November 2, 1977) and still ranked in the top 12 or 15 players in the world on the official Association of Tennis Professional computer rankings.

Rosewall never won Wimbledon. But so what? His best years—from 1957 to 1965-66 were spent in the wilderness of the then-professional tennis set-up. He and Hoad, Gonzales, Segura, Sedgman and company were outcasts. I truly believe that Rosewall would have won Wimbledon five or six times in the early 1960s . . . but it was not to be.

But the man's record is quite unbelievable anyway. He played two Wimbledon finals before turning professional . . . against Czech Jan Drobny in 1954 and Hoad in 1956.

Drobny was the crowd's favourite after being around for so long and being runner-up in two previous finals. The bias by the English crowd was so strong that many observers felt it seriously affected the 19-year-old Rosewall. Hoad blasted Rosewall in four in 1956 . . . but Muscles stopped Hoad from winning a Grand Slam by taking the U.S. Open final from him in four sets.

Rosewall turned professional and soon climbed over Gonzales and Hoad to win the World professional championship in Britain in 1957, 1960, 1961, 1962 and 1963. He was fading by the end of the 1960s. However, the advent of Open tennis gave him new life.

He won the first French Open title in 1968, beating Laver in a four-set final. It had been 15 years since he first won the title by beating American Vic Seixas.

JOHN NEWCOMBE . . . dedication won through

Then came the Australian Open at Kooyong in 1971 and 1972 with wins over Arthur Ashe and Mal Anderson. This time it was 16 years since his last Australian title victory.

But more important were Rosewall's last flings at winning the elusive Wimbledon title in his 36th and 40th years.

First he lined up against the young Newcombe in 1970. This time the crowd was right behind Rosewall, but a long five-setter took its toll and Newcombe ran out the winner 5-7, 6-3, 6-2, 3-6, 6-1. Newcombe said later it was the most difficult match of his career . . . "it is hard to beat a legend."

And who will forget Rosewall's last ditch effort to win in 1974. Down two sets to love and 3-5 against previous champion, American Stan Smith, Rosewall came back from an impossible position to beat Smith in five sets, 6-8, 4-6, 9-8, 6-1, 6-3 in the semi-final.

Then it was the two-fisted Jimmy Connors, who stood between him and the ultimate victory.

Connors, hitting the ball as hard as any of Rosewall's opponents since his "twin" Lew Hoad, climbed on top of his ageing opponent and clubbed him 6-1, 6-1, 6-4.

Rosewall, who had won the U.S. Open by beating Tony Roche in the 1970 final—also 14 years since his previous victory—then faced Connors again in the 1974 final. But the experience at Wimbledon had given Connors a great psychological advantage over Rosewall and his victory was even more convincing—6-1, 6-0, 6-1.

With Father Time tapping him on the shoulder, Rosewall found indoor tennis—without the treacherous elements—and the acceptance of the tie-breaker system which kept matches shorter, much to his advantage.

Tennis buffs still rate his performances in beating Laver in Lamar Hunt's World Championship of Tennis finals in Dallas in 1971 and 1972 as two of the highlights of his illustrious career.

Rosewall beat Laver 6-4, 1-6, 7-6, 7-6 in 1971 while his victory in 1972—to the tune of 4-6, 6-0, 6-3, 6-7, 7-6—is quoted by many experts as the greatest tennis match ever played.

But while Laver and Rosewall are my picks as the two best players in the last 10 years, John Newcombe is close on their heels.

Newcombe was what I call a "made" player. He had a big serve and dangerous forehand drive, but he worked extremely hard on the rest of his game to make him a great performer. His backhand, in particular, was a much lesser stroke in his amateur days, but Newcombe perfected the chip and later the top-spin backhand to measure up with the rest of his game.

Newcombe had the right mental attitude to be a great champion. He too was never beaten and could always be counted on to pull a match out of the fire from seemingly hopeless positions.

He was the last amateur champion at Wimbledon . . . beating a depleted field and crushing German Willie Bungert 6-3, 6-1, 6-1 in a lop-sided final.

But his wins over Rosewall in 1970 and Stan Smith in 1971 proved beyond doubt that he was one of the all-time greats of the game.

KEN ROSEWALL . . . a champion for a quarter of a century

Newcombe's last Wimbledon win in 1971 was a particularly emotional affair as his long-time friend and business manager, John Parker, who was dying of cancer, made his first and last trip to Wimbledon to see his friend.

When he was down two sets to one, Newcombe said to himself that "this one is for John" . . . and he came back to win a thrilling five-setter 6-3, 5-7, 2-6, 6-4, 6-4.

Newcombe also won the World Champion-

TONY ROCHE . . . thwarted by injury

MARGARET COURT . . . the greatest winner in the history of women's tennis

ship of Tennis, beating Bjorn Borg 4-6, 6-3, 6-3, 6-2 in 1974 . . . but it was his win in the Australian Open the following January that had the critics raving once more.

He came from an impossible position in the quarter-final against Geoff Masters before scraping home in five sets . . . and then survived several match points before beating his partner, Tony Roche in the semi-final.

The brash American, Jimmy Connors, was defending champion and had won 98 of 102 matches leading up to the final. Newcombe called on all his guile, experience and great strength to topple Connors 7-5, 3-6, 6-4, 7-5 in a memorable final.

The great disappointment of the last decade has undoubtedly been Newcombe's friend and doubles partner, Tony Roche.

He was probably endowed with more natural ability than Newcombe, but was constantly plagued by injuries just when he looked set to take over Laver's mantle as the world's number one.

Roche had a form of "tennis elbow" which was operated on several times . . . an injury which restricted his serving power and thus thwarted his chances of taking big titles.

Roche burst onto the scene with wins in the German and French Opens in 1966. It wasn't long before he was in the Wimbledon final against Laver in the first Open title in 1968.

He was again knocking at the door as a finalist in the U.S. Open against Laver in 1969 and Rosewall in 1970.

But he was destined to spend long periods out of the game with injury and thus did not fulfil his great potential. Like so many southpaws, Roche could do tricks with the ball that an orthodox right hander could not do. But it has always been my contention that the unorthodox strokes place enormous pressure on muscles and cause injury in the long term.

John Alexander and Phil Dent were the obvious pair to take over from Newcombe and Roche . . . but the big tournaments did not eventuate.

Alexander, a big server and strong hitter in the Newcombe mould, did not have the dedication to reach the top that his predecessors had. However, in all fairness, Alexander and Dent did not have the discipline and training under wizard Harry Hopman that helped to make the other players so great.

The change in tennis that came with the game being thrown open brought new waves of players and schedules that were exacting and difficult for the young professionals. Money was much easier than the early days and the drive was not always there.

Dent is the type of player who needs to be disciplined under a strict manager . . . and without it he has been one of the also-rans of world tennis.

Australia has had some very talented players like Ross Case and Geoff Masters in recent years, but they do not have the authority of their predecessors in Australian tennis.

EVONNE CAWLEY . . . the darling of Australian tennis

The great Australian tennis machine has ground to a halt. With the way world tennis is set up today it is most unlikely this country will ever approach the glory of the 1950 s and 1960 s when champions like Sedgman, McGregor, Hoad, Rosewall, Cooper, Anderson, Fraser, Laver, Emerson, Stolle, Newcombe and Roche rolled off the assembly line every time there was a gap to be filled.

On the women's side, again there is no argument as to the best player of the last decade . . . for all-time, actually.

Margaret Court is the greatest winner of women's tennis tournaments in the history of the game and she and the late Maureen Connolly are the only players to achieve a Grand Slam of the Australian, French, Wimbledon and United States titles.

Margaret, who always appeared to have

vultures on her shoulders in the early days of her international tennis, matured into a great champion

She won three Wimbledon titles—beating her nemesis Billie Jean King in 1963, defending champion Maria Bueno in 1965 and Mrs King again in 1970.

To many the 1970 final was the classic women's tennis match. Margaret battled for what seemed an eternity before the Australian added the third leg of her Grand Slam 14-12, 11-9.

Margaret could see her dream of the Grand Slam slipping away when little American Rosie Casals took the second set to level at 6-2, 2-6 in the U.S. Open final. But Margaret "went for broke" and ran out a 6-1 winner in the third set.

The only other Wimbledon winner among

**KERRY REID... captured the 1977
Australian title**

the Australian women is Evonne Goolagong-Cawley in 1971. She was a surprise winner over Margaret 6-4, 6-1. All due respects to Margaret . . . she was three months pregnant with her first child at the time.

But Evonne has proved a marvellous cham-pion. She never did win Wimbledon a second time and one wonders whether that opportunity has passed her forever.

Chris Evert is the dominating force these days and despite her lapse to Virginia Wade in the last Wimbledon, she will be a winner at the Mecca of tennis for a few years to come. Evonne just cannot climb over Miss Evert, but the arrival of her first baby certainly seems to have matured her play, something that could well prove a massive plus feature in the coming years.

When assessing the best women of the last decade, one has to mention the likes of Judy Tegart-Dalton, Lesley Turner-Bowrey and Kerry Melville-Reid.

Mrs Dalton came closest to pulling off the big one . . . losing 9-7, 7-5 to Billie Jean King in the first Open Wimbledon in 1968.

Lesley Bowrey won the French Open in 1963 and 1965, beating Ann Jones the first time and Margaret Court for her second title.

Kerry Reid has been somewhat of a "brides-maid" in a decade at the top of world tennis . . . but she did win the last Australian Open.

The boom in the United States and the emergence of the European and South American players will make it extremely difficult for Australia to regain the high position it once held on the world tennis scene, despite recapturing the Davis Cup in 1977, highlighted by a never-to-be-forgotten, five-set marathon between John Alexander and Italy's Adriano Pannatta.

4 GOLF

By TERRY SMITH

TERRY SMITH writes brightly on golf for the "Sydney Sun" and "Sun Herald". Author of "The Complete Book of Australian Golf" he is Australian golf correspondent for "The London Daily Telegraph" and a former Editor of "Australian Golf" magazine. Smith has covered several British, U.S. and French Opens. A member of Manly Golf Club, he is a happy hacker whose golf swing is described by Peter Thomson as "excellent for killing snakes".

Everyone knows that the golf rainbow ends in the United States with a $9 million pot of gold labelled P.G.A. tour. That's the place where everybody lines up behind Tom Watson and Jack Nicklaus and, once Tom and Jack have filled their pockets, the others share what is left.

Other rainbows have developed all over the world. The treasure is smaller, but so are the fields—and the competition is not so fierce.

But combined with a record in the world's four major championships, the real test of a golfer's technical excellence of striking, character and application is the American tour.

So without the aid of a sophisticated computer, I hail Bruce Crampton as Australia's top golfer of the past decade. No, don't applaud now, the hard part comes later.

Playing with a chilling consistency, Crampton was runner-up to Nicklaus in the U.S. Masters and Open championships of 1972 and finished second to the great man in the American P.G.A. title in both 1973 and 1975.

And in 1973, in his 37th year, he became only the fifth player—joining Nicklaus, Arnold Palmer, Billy Casper and Lee Trevino—to reach his millionth dollar in prize money on the U.S. tour.

Failing to win one of the world's major championships must be a big disappointment to Crampton. "That's ordained," he says, with a bit of mystery. "It's just another chapter in my book of fate. If I was meant to win, it would have happened. I'm just proud to finish second to Jack, the greatest player in the world."

Now for the difficult part of my act. Without the aid of a safety net, mirrors, accomplices, electronic devices or even a shapely assistant in fish-net tights, I will take the plunge and attempt to rate Australia's top golfers of the past 10 years.

They are Bruce Crampton (1), Bruce Devlin (2), David Graham (3), Graham Marsh (4), Jan Stephenson (5), Billy Dunk (6), Kel Nagle and Peter Thomson (eq. 7).

Before the male chauvinists start bristling, I have no qualms about slipping Miss Stephenson ahead of Dunk in the rankings following her rapid rise into the super league of the world's women professional golfers.

In 1976 this impulsive lass from Sydney won two big tournaments in America, voted by her peers as the best short-iron player and second best putter on the U.S. tour. The "New York Times" gushed: "Jan's sinuous movements are reminiscent of Marilyn Monroe."

A year later Jan returned home and captured the Australian Women's Open by squeezing out America's Pat Bradley at the fourth hole of a sudden death play off at Manly (Sydney).

Gone was the cheeky schoolgirl who not so long before had upset staid officials of the Ladies Golf Union by wearing psychedelic panties under the briefest of mini skirts. Jan had grown into a golfer of ice cool skills with the ability to beat the best in the world.

Now I'm not saying Dunk isn't a potential world-beater. Far from it. Any man who can break more than 70 course records and finish with seven straight birdies to shoot a 10 under par 60 at Merewether in Newcastle in 1970 is capable of winning anything.

It's just that Billy prefers to potter about in his vegetable garden, or wine cellar, and go fishing with his three young sons rather than go to America and become rich and miserable. He is a reluctant hero.

"If there was a pill which made people invisible, Dunk would probably take an overdose," claimed an English writer. A sad thing, because with his brave wedge shots and deadly putting, he can make bigger men look foolish.

It is a fine debating point, but I think Miss Stephenson pips Dunk by the narrowest margin because she has won her spurs in the super-competitive cauldron of American golf, while Billy opted to stay home.

The past decade has seen Crampton's clockwork swing pave the way for one money-making triumph after another for this lonely mercenary. For eight years in a row he topped the $100,000 mark in prize-money.

He reached his peak in 1973 when he won four tournaments and was runner up five times on the U.S. tour to have earnings of $281,640 for the year, despite dropping off the circuit from mid-August to November.

Crampton's prickly manner won him few friends on the American tour, but his fellow professionals respect him as a true craftsman whose swing tempo never varies from a driver to a wedge, from the first hole of a tournament to the last.

He always swings well within himself, using only 80 per cent of his strength, and his ability to hole crucial 10-footers to save his par at times can border on the incredible.

One of Crampton's greatest rounds was a tournament and course record 63 at the extremely demanding Firestone Country Club in Akron,

BRUCE CRAMPTON . . . Australia's best player in the last decade

Ohio on the way to finishing second to Nicklaus in the 1975 P.G.A. championship.

Bruce sadly has a grumpy image as a result of bawling out marshals and photographers and glaring and snapping at fans in the gallery who dare to move while he is preparing to make a shot.

There is a famous story of how he played in stony silence with three millionaire weekend golfers who paid $1,000 for a round with him . . . except when he caught them teeing up ahead of the markers.

And a tale of another famous Australian player asking Crampton's help to read the line of a putt in the first round of the Canada Cup. "Can't you work it out for yourself?" Bruce snapped to his partner. Needless to say, not a word was exchanged between the pair for the remainder of the tournament.

Those close to Crampton say he can be warm, kind and helpful, but once he steps onto a golf course he becomes cold and officious. Bruce explains: "It's my business I'm going about. You don't see the captain of a 747 jet making jokes when he's flying, do you?"

He stunned his peers in May, 1977 by suddenly announcing his retirement at the age of 41. Admittedly there had been whispers for several years that Crampton's marriage was on the rocks. "I need to spend more time with with my family," he said. "I want to get to know them and have them get to know me."

Bruce Devlin plays the American tour about half time nowadays, devoting the remainder of his time to golf course designing, but his deeds during the past decade rank him second only to Crampton in a rating of Australia's golfers.

He vies with Nagle and Dunk as the most popular Australian player of the lot, and his followers rejoiced in Bruce's golden year of 1970 when he won the Bob Hope Classic, Cleveland Open, Alcan tournament in Ireland—which had a first prize of $55,000—and World Cup with David Graham in Buenos Aires.

Easy-going, tanned and lean, Devlin looks like he should be playing in Western movies and he stays friendly at all times, regardless of how he plays.

His opening 69 playing the big ball in a gale in the Alcan at mighty Portmarnock was unquestionably the greatest round of his career.

BILLY DUNK . . . a reluctant hero

At his best Devlin sets up countless birdie chances with superb driving and long irons that are hit boldly right to the flag, but far too often he puts the ball as close with a 5-iron as he can with a 9-iron.

He came home in 1968 and provided some drama charged moments by tying with America's Lee Trevino in the Dunlop tournament at Yarra Yarra in Melbourne. Trevino poured on the pressure with five birdies in the last seven holes to force a play off, but it didn't go past the first extra hole where Devlin planted a 7-iron approach shot stone dead for the decisive birdie.

Australia's third victory in what is now the World Cup—changed from the Canada Cup in 1967—occurred in Buenos Aires in 1970 when Devlin and Graham shocked everybody by waltzing away to a 10-stroke victory with a record score of 544, 32 under par.

There is a funny story about the tyro Graham being picked as Devlin's partner. The International Golf Association wanted Crampton as Devlin's companion, but the Australian P.G.A. dug in their heels and said if the comparatively unknown Graham wasn't wanted, then Australia wouldn't send a team.

Thank heavens they did. "Que hombre," screamed the gallery as Graham opened with some exquisite golf in posting 65, 67, 65 to Devlin's 66, 69, 66.

Disgraceful scenes on the last day robbed Graham, who surprisingly had failed to win a player's card at the U.S. rookie school a week earlier, of the individual trophy. Roberto de Vicenzo's unruly supporters several times threw his ball into a favourable lie to enable the local hero to pip the Australian by a stroke.

Graham is a fierce competitor who continued to prove he can beat the best in the world,

GRAHAM MARSH . . . a broken arm successfully switched his first love from cricket to golf

when he toppled Nicklaus and Co. to capture the 1977 Australian Open by three shots with rounds of 74, 71, 68, 71—284. In 1976 he capped an astounding year by winning the $40,000 first prize in the Piccadilly World Match Play championship at Wentworth. In the first round, Graham beat Hubert Green 3 and 2, and then gained a spot in the final with an enthralling fight back to pip Ray Floyd on the 36th green. In an event famous for stirring matches, few have compared with the final, in which Graham squeezed out title-holder Hale Irwin by holing a 10-foot putt for a birdie two at the 38th.

This lifted his prize-money to more than $280,000, which included $40,000 and a car for his victory in the Chunichi Crowns event in Japan. Two months later Graham opened with 63 and led throughout to win the $60,000 first prize in the $300,000 Westchester Classic. He posted the fourth major victory of easily his most profitable year by playing with ruthless consistency to capture the $200,000 American Golf Classic with rounds of 69, 67, 69, 69.

DAVID GRAHAM . . . a fierce competitor to capture the 1977 Australian Open from a class field

There is an electric quality about Graham at his best, and he has a consuming desire to succeed as a result of much frustration and disappointment in his youth. One of the few club-making experts among modern-day professionals, he is poised to become a wealthy man from his partnership with Nicklaus in a club-manufacturing business. Nicklaus says, "What David can do in making a club is a lost art these days."

The world outside America continued to remain Graham Marsh's oyster until 1977 when he took up a player's card for the U.S. tour. He promptly shot rounds of 65, 72, 67, 69 to win the Heritage Classic by a stroke from Tom Watson, so his climb into the world super league was complete.

But if there was any doubt about Marsh's right to be ranked as one of the world's great players, he erased it later in the year by winning the World Match Play championship at Wentworth. He could hardly have had a tougher draw, having to dispose of Hubert Green, Manuel Pinero and Hale Irwin before brushing aside Ray Floyd 5 and 3 in the final.

Marsh might have taken up cricket as his younger brother Rodney, Australia's Test

with a strong belief that golf is a game for highly trained athletes. Surely it is only a matter of time before he wins one of the world's accepted classics. Peter Thomson predicts Marsh will be the first Australian to capture the British Open since he himself triumphed at Royal Birkdale in 1965.

There have been many mighty feats by Australian golfers in the last decade, but never in the history of the game has there been a finish at the Old Course at St Andrews to equal Marsh's thundering 4, 3, 4, 3, 2 (birdie, birdie, par, birdie, eagle) in the third round of the Scottish Open in 1973. "I love the challenge of playing the Old Course," he declared.

The memories come flooding back. Thomson's superlative birdie at Kooyonga's final hole to force a play-off with Graham in the 1972 Australian Open is among the sharpest. Amid great excitement, Thomson eased a three-quarter power 7-iron into the tight corner where the flag was stuck, and it stopped eight inches short.

The next day Thomson won his third Aus-

PETER THOMSON . . . memories flood back

KEL NAGLE . . . ranks with Bruce Devlin and Billy Dunk as Australia's most popular players

wicket-keeper, has done if a broken arm hadn't kept him out of that game at the start of a season. To build it up, he turned to golf and rapidly fell in love with its individuality.

Marsh was beaten at the last hole by John Muller in the final of the 1967 Australian Amateur title. A year later, at 24, he somewhat hesitantly swapped the security of a schoolmaster's desk in Perth for the gamble of a professional golfing career. His rise was rapid. In 1973 Marsh became the first player to win more than $100,000 without setting foot in America, and he fared even better in 1976 when he captured seven tournaments, including four big events in golf-mad Japan where they have elevated him almost to the status of demi-god.

As befits a former mathematics master, Marsh is highly analytical and he combines the intellectual approach of a chess player

tralian Open by six strokes with a beautifully played 68 which included five birdies. His victory came 21 years after his first success— a tribute to the enduring quality of his swing and his skill. As it proved, Graham virtually surrendered with his opening stroke, which he angrily hooked out of bounds. He was upset when Thomson hit off without a coin being tossed. Thomson calmly holed a 20-footer for a birdie four, while Graham took seven.

And who can forget Dunk stepping into a small island of grass, bullrushes and gorse in the huge bunker beside the 18th green at Royal Melbourne on the final day of the 1975 Chrysler Classic? The green was lightning fast, his back swing was impeded by the reeds and he had to chop down to avoid a tiny tree. Dunk was looking at a bogey, even a double bogey. His one stroke lead over Graham looked extremely shaky.

Dunk will never play a more important shot. It landed short of the cup and rolled 12 feet past. He settled grimly over the putt . . . and bravely stroked it home to the accompaniment of a cheer that could be heard a mile away. "It was the most important putt of my life," Dunk said after his closing 68. "Not for the money, but because I don't like being called a choker." He had been deeply hurt by some dreadfully unfair criticism that inferred he had shown the intestinal fortitude of a chicken in taking 77 in the last round of the previous week's Australian Open.

I harked back to a chat with Thomson during the 1972 World Cup at Royal Melbourne. "There is nothing wrong with Dunk's courage," he said. "And I have never heard greater nonsense than somebody saying he has a mental block. The simple fact is all too clear—at critical times his technique is found wanting. His trouble is mechanical, not mental." For years Dunk has fought a hook, and sometimes in blocking it out he knocks his ball to the right.

Dunk and Crampton, far from our strongest team, finished third when the World Cup returned to Royal Melbourne's fearsome composite course in 1972. Reduced to 54 holes after a washout on the second day, Taiwan's Hsieh Min Nan and Mister Lu, a little charmer who weighs only 9.7 after a double helping of

BOB SHEARER . . . exciting prospect

JACK NEWTON . . . powerhouse player

egg rolls and chop suey, were the joyful victors. Hsieh completed a double by winning the individual trophy.

We have been lucky enough to see all the world's top players during the past decade, and the superstars rarely have failed to deliver the goods. Jack Nicklaus won the Australian Open in 1968, 71, 75, 76, but these deeds pale beside his astounding 10 under par 62 at Manly in Sydney during the 1971 Dunlop tournament. He summoned his game to its mightiest pitch to surge to nine under par after only 10 holes, and finished with a bag of an eagle and 10 birdies! Those of us who saw it didn't need a computer or record book to confirm Nicklaus as the greatest golfer who ever lived. No arguments. That's all there is to be said.

Gary Player tossed a nine under par 63 at his rivals on the way to winning his seventh Australian Open at Lake Karrinyup in Perth in 1974. But I prefer to recall the gritty South African's 65 (7 under par) at Kingston Heath in Melbourne during his 1970 Open triumph.

JAN STEPHENSON . . . sinuous movements
[Australian Golf Magazine]

After the first round Player declared the only man in the world who could stop him hooking was Ben Hogan. Yet the next day he stepped out wearing a handkerchief as a mask against Melbourne's pollen and broke the course record with his 65.

"I'm sure glad Hogan's not here," Devlin commented. Thomson came out firing from both barrels in the next morning's Melbourne Age, accusing Gary of "laughable emotionalism." But that's the Player way . . . he can be counted on to say something outrageous, and then stare you down with his wide eyes blazing their sincerity like headlamps on full beam.

He seems to have always just played the best or worst round of his life, putted on the trickiest greens, or never have struck a ball into such terrible winds. There is a Press-room joke, delivered in a mock South African accent, that goes as follows: "Fellas, this here must be the finest pencil I've ever used to mark down a score."

No matter how many titles Player may amass, he cannot go any higher in the esteem of Australian golf followers. They dote on this small, black-clad figure. "They can beat me to the ground, but I won't fight back", he vowed when threatened by anti-apartheid demonstrators during the 1974 Wills Masters at The Australian Golf Club. Saturday's play was continually disrupted by screaming demonstrators, but Player coolly notched a two under par 70. It was one of the finest rounds of golf he is ever likely to play.

Jack Newton, Bob Shearer and Greg Norman are exciting products of Australia's golfing conveyor belt in recent years, while Randall Vines finished fifth in the individual honours in the 1973 World Cup in Marbella, Spain, behind Johnny Miller, Player, Mister Lu and Nicklaus. Vines had an amazing run of birdie, birdie, albatross, birdie, birdie at Royal Hobart during the 1968 Tasmanian Open!

Newton was desperately unlucky not to win the 1975 British Open in which he lost a play-off to America's Tom Watson by a stroke — 72 to 71. So young Newton left Carnoustie with a course record 65 and his reputation for courage and pugnacity still intact. He bogied three of the last four holes for a tally of 279 to tie with Watson, who had holed a 25-footer for a birdie at the 72nd hole. "When young Jack gives it one, you can almost smell the rubber burning," declared a British writer.

The upset of the decade was provided by Geoff Parslow, the host professional at Yarra Yarra in toppling the mighty Johnny Miller to win the 1977 Victorian Open. Parslow equalled Tony Jacklin's course record 63 on the way to eclipsing the American who was being paid a whopping $180,000 to make two trips to Australia within three years.

Donna Young, of America, shot one of the great rounds of women's golf when she had a 64 including 8 birdies, and 10 pars, during the 1975 Australian Women's Open at Victoria, which certainly isn't a pitch and putt affair. "Prima Donna," trumpeted one Melbourne newspaper headline.

Tony Gresham struck a blow for Australia's amateurs by upsetting America's Ben Crenshaw by two strokes to win the individual honours in the 1972 Eisenhower Cup in Buenos Aires. His chipping and putting coupled with his courage under fire would have made the Sydney player a big money winner as a professional.

Gresham emphasised his skills by winning the NSW. Open from a strong field at Manly with rounds of 66, 69, 69, 71 — finally capping his career with a victory in the 1977 Australian Amateur Championship.

But probably the most significant happening in Australian golf occurred in 1976 when Kerry Packer gave the Australian Open the kiss of life by lifting the prize-money from $35,000 to a whopping $160,000. Inspired by his father Sir Frank Packer's deeds in America's Cup yachting and prompted by Jack Nicklaus, he has embarked on a crusade to lift the Australian Open into the world's fifth major championship.

I doubt if he can, but let's hope he never gives up trying.

GREG NORMAN . . . a future champion

5 BOWLS

By RUSS WAUGH

RUSS WAUGH was the bowls writer for the "Sun" Sydney for over 12 years. He played for NSW Interstate on many occasions in every position from lead to captain. He firmly believes it is necessary for all players aspiring for top honours to serve an apprenticeship, to become an expert in all positions and learn the game in all phases. He has played top bowls for 30 years, has won a NSW State triples, the tournament of champions, master singles and fours, group singles, and numerous club titles.

With bowls rating so highly among Australian sportsmen and women as a competitive game, it is well nigh impossible to fully cover the scene in a few hundred words . . . and my editor won't allow me the extra space.

I have, therefore, selected the top names from this era where the sport has enjoyed tremendous popularity . . . and some success at international level.

For years there has been a wealth of good singles players, even though every decade produces someone who dominates.

Names such as Glyn Bosisto (Vic), Garney Noble (City, NSW), George Makin (Canberra) and Bob Pinkerton (Camden) will always start tongues wagging.

That mantle now belongs to Frank Soars from the Currawong Club in NSW—and he more than just upholds the tradition.

Soars has an unbelievable record, with a remarkable string of successes over the past 10 years . . . winning over 70 titles including the State singles, State fours, State triples, Australian fours and a NSW Champion of Champion's success.

I rate him as possibly the best bowler I have played with or against. Formerly with the Mona Vale Club in Sydney, Soars is currently the undisputed star of the NSW South Coast where Phil Martin from Sussex Inlet hails from . . . the man Soars rates with a fatherly respect for another great champion who was so instrumental in the current champion's early bowling years. Soars, a regular interstate representative has, in turn, assisted many aspiring champions, adding yet another dimension to an already illustrious career.

I believe the game has produced an attacking flair in recent years, one that makes it a more attractive game for spectators and players alike.

Frank Soars exemplified the modern trend when his ability came to the fore back in 1966 in capturing the State fours title.

Barry Salter (Waratah NSW) is a young international who represented Australia in the singles and pairs at the World bowls championships at Worthing, England in 1972 and the 1973 South African Games in Pretoria.

Salter played third to win two Australian fours titles, has won a NSW State pairs and Newcastle District titles and is one of the finest thirds the game has produced. Many keen judges rate him as the greatest with his extensive knowledge of the game.

As a great advertisement for the sport, Salter calls his shots in an easy, authoritative way.

His delivery is copybook with a full follow through staying down for a second or two after delivery, playing all-paced greens with precision.

Newcastle has produced a long line of great bowlers—Dave Downie, "Tisha" McIntosh and Ken Porter, the list is endless. But the latest in the list of champions from Newcastle is Barry Salter.

Soars has an almost fatherly respect for Phil Martin (Sussex Inlet NSW) a great champion and admits Martin helped him no end. Soars, a regular interstate bowler in turn has helped many aspiring champions adding yet another dimension to an already illustrious career. I believe there is a more attacking flair now than there was in the old game. It's a more attractive game for the spectator. Soars exemplifies the modern trend. His real ability started to show when he won the State fours in 1966.

What is there to say about Peter Rheuben that hasn't already been said?

Rheuben represented Australia in the

FRANK SOARS . . . an unbelievable record

pairs at the 1974 Commonwealth Games, won an Australian fours in 1970, the NSW State singles in 1972—the State Champion of Champions the same year. He is a City masters winner and a regular interstate captain.

Rheuben built up a tremendous reputation in the space of five years. His record for his club Ryde (NSW) is second to none, producing his best when his side is not going well.

He also has the happy knack of getting everything out of his club players like Les Hewitt, Steve Bocksette and David Blumberg—Ryde winning the State No. I pennant three times in the last 10 years.

Rheuben, in my book, has come of age as a top class interstate captain and by the time the next World bowls team is chosen he should be right in the front line.

Asquith's (NSW) Bob King is an International bowler who made bowls history in

1977 when he won the famed City masters for a record third time.

King, who won a silver medal for Australia in the fours at the 1974 Commonwealth Games in New Zealand, has represented NSW on numerous occasions.

He is the only bowler to win the 27-year-old City masters three times, winning the event in successive years—1971 and 1972. He has put in some incredible performances in open tournaments and masters event during his outstanding career.

His performance for his club has won him lavish praise from present and past critics. He stuck with his club through thick and thin. It is nigh impossible to imagine him playing with any other club.

While he is on the green calling the shots, Asquith know they are in with a winning chance.

King has deep concentration. He never

complains and has proved he can play top flight bowls in any position. His reputation is such that top players could be excused for wanting to play any other player than King when he is in winning frame of mind.

In 1976 John Slater (St. George NSW) was rated the bowler of the year by many experts.

Slater, who won the NSW pairs title in 1964, and again the following year, took out the Australian pairs and had a bumper year in 1976.

Firstly he won the South Pacific singles conducted by the Illawarra District, then the City club's master of champions and the prestige masters.

Then followed the NSW State triples and the State pairs before going down in the final of the State singles by a single shot — 30-31.

Little wonder he was rated the "Don Bradman" of NSW bowls for that year.

Slater is the perfect stylist who plays every shot with confidence representing NSW on numerous occasions.

BARRY SALTER . . . *young international*

PETER RHEUBEN . . . *tremendous reputation*

BOB KING ... 1974 Commonwealth Games silver medal

St. George have won many No. 1 pennant games with him as captain, and he is regarded as the club's outstanding captain-player. It is unlikely his record to win two State titles and runner-up in the singles the same year will ever be equalled.

Keith Poole of Queensland was captain of the Australian fours team which won silver medals at the 1974 Commonwealth Games in Christchurch, NZ.

Poole won the Australian fours championship twice — 1959 and 1972 — and the Queensland State singles and fours, after taking up the game at 21-years-of-age.

Although Australia has participated in the bowls section of the Commonwealth games since 1934, its only successes have been minor ones.

Poole could have been regarded a little unlucky not to have walked off with the gold. Right up until the last round Poole's team was well in the running for gold medals.

Poole, who has represented Queensland on numerous occasions, is an exciting captain. He can play every shot in the book, thriving in any conditions. One of Poole's greatest attributes is his ability to boost his team's confidence with a never-say-die attitude.

He has the ability to wrap up a game when he gets a handy lead, seldom plays a dull game and never looks anything but a winning contender.

Poole is a big match player. Not even the most fanatical NSW supporter, and that means something, could ever predict a victory against Poole even in Sydney Town.

Les Shean, formerly with City Club, Sydney NSW, and currently with Queensland, has represented NSW as a captain.

He is widely respected for his generalship and as an ornament to the game, it is incredible how often he has given many players a new lease of bowls life.

Shean's keyboard is harmony, believing a happy team gives the players the will to win with confidence.

always keeps a cool head to achieve results. I'm afraid too many captains can't captain themselves, but Shean is one who escapes that category, and must qualify for the top 10.

Des Moran of South Australia is more than a run-of-the-mill bowler. He has a truly remarkable record having won all South Australia's major titles, the State fours (twice), State champion of champions (three times), the State pairs (twice) and the State singles—a record very few have equalled in any State.

In 1976 Moran won the coveted City of Sydney Club's master of champions, a tournament limited to State champions and masters winners only, turning in an impressive display against a hot field.

He is always a formidable opponent and is a perfect example of concentration on his game. He seldom puts in a mediocre performance and has been selected in the South Australian interstate side since 1959.

How can you go past Moran for a place in the top 10 in Australia? Over the years he has

JOHN SLATER . . . rated the "Don Bradman" of NSW bowls

Shean, a dual City masters singles winner, has been a NSW State singles and fours winner, and had a champion of club champions title to his credit before transferring to Palm Beach, Queensland.

He represented Australia in a series of tests against South Africa as a master of yard-on play—and seldom plays narrow bowls. He has the full variety of shots from dead-draw to fast drive, but his little on shots are copybook.

Shean doesn't fool around when he is down on the head, making sure he just reaches.

Widely regarded as a great captain, he

KEITH POOLE . . . plays every shot in the book

BRANCO KATUNA-RICH . . . five State titles in WA

LES SHEAN . . . represented Australia in tests against South Africa

unorthodox style with a rather quick walk on to the mat delivery and extreme accuracy with all shots.

I find it hard to leave out of my top 10 players of the calibre of Victorians Leigh Fitzpatrick and John Snell. Fitzpatrick has represented Australia as a singles player in Commonwealth Games plus an Australian pairs title in his bag, Victorian State fours and a Victorian Champion of Champions.

Stewart Shannon of Queensland has won the Queensland State singles and fours, a number of masters titles and has represented his State many times.

Shannon is a complete stylist. Having a perfect, constant delivery enables him to be a master of the dead-draw shot, but he also plays the delicate trail shot with ease.

In addition Shannon is just as accurate with

STEWART SHANNON . . . a complete stylist

won many titles through sheer determination. He plays every shot with authority and is an inspiration to any team.

Moran is a key player for South Australia and with him in full cry in the interstate side, you would have no option but to rate them a chance against any State.

Branco Katuna-Rich of Western Australia with his son Dennis were the sensation of the Australian Championships in Perth in 1974.

The father-son combination was beaten in the final of the national pairs by a single shot, 14-15 after a sensational extra end.

The performance was all the more remarkable because it was the first tournament the 24-year-old Dennis had ever played in.

Branco Katuna-Rich had won five State titles in Western Australia including singles, pairs and triples and represented Australia in a series of tests against South Africa and Rhodesia.

A regular Western Australian interstate captain for the past 10 years he is noted for his

his fast drive, a shot he plays with reluctance as he firmly believes in the axiom "draw to score, drive to destroy."

Shannon's approach to the game is to play the minimum weight for the maximum result, a belief that has proved him to be a match winner. When he is at his brilliant best he is more than a handful for any opponent.

His temperament is such that he can play the ideal shot under extreme pressure, a trait so vital to any successfull captain, and he always manages to produce the brand of bowls which excites the bowls fans. Shannon's ability to know when to drive and what weight to play is the cornerstone to success—a lesson to any budding champion.

DES MORAN . . . formidable opponent

6 SQUASH

By JIM WOODWARD

JIM WOODWOOD joined the "Sydney Daily Telegraph" in 1964 as a sports writer and has covered almost every game that is played. He is the paper's Rugby Union writer, back-up cricket writer and in 1971 spent 12 months in Vietnam as an Australian Army public relations correspondent.

While squash in Australia as it was a decade ago is almost unrecognisable today, one aspect of the game has remained constant.

Players have come and gone with many a storm in a tea cup as the sport adapted to the modern era, involving sponsorship and professionalism. But through all the upheavals one thing has stood rock solid — Heather McKay's relentless reign at the top.

The undisputed Queen of squash courts around the world, Mrs. McKay has weathered every adversity including the nonchalant attitude of the Australian sporting public and apathetic Governments to retain her crown.

Rarely in any sport in any country has one player so dominated the scene at an international level for such a long period of time as Mrs. McKay. Forced to take a second job in the early days to raise money for the honour of representing and bringing glory to her own country, Mrs. McKay has been at the top for an incredible 16 years.

She was there during the early days when Australian players gingerly entered the major overseas tournaments as amateur players. Just two losses later Mrs. McKay has seen the game develop in this country from almost an international experiment to the stage where Australian players rank amongst the best in the world.

Back in the 1960s the task of raising the necessary airfares was a massive task.

In 1962 the Australian team of 12 needed thirty-six thousand pounds to compete in the British amateur.

When approached for financial assistance three major sporting firms at the time offered a meagre £3,000 between them.

After threatening not to endorse their products a little more money was forthcoming, but that's what trailblazers like Ken Hiscoe and Dick Carter had to contend with.

Professional squash has changed the whole complexion of the game but Australia is still fiercely proud of the amateur side of the sport.

The Australian Squash Racquets Association is very strict in this regard.

Boasting the greatest number of active participants in Australia, there will obviously always be just the slightest percentage of players who are professionals.

But for those who have reached the top there is now a living to be made from squash.

Leading Australian player Geoff Hunt's decision to shelve a university degree and science career to turn professional in 1971 has paid off handsomely.

Hunt has very strong ideas on how the professional game should be run.

He advocates all glass courts, TV Coverage and a squash "Davis Cup."

In order to keep the game snowballing coaches have been eagerly sought to turn professional and are allowed to compete in pennant matches alongside amateurs.

The days of a bread and water existence are now over for Mrs. McKay who, having turned professional a couple of years ago, runs a squash court centre in Toronto (Canada) with her husband.

"Nowhere else in the world could offer us what we have now," Mrs. McKay says of her new venture.

"Brian and I can see no reason to return to Australia when we have exactly what we want here."

That's a different situation than in Australia where it became a case of "Ho-hum Heather's won again" as she built up what many would argue is the greatest sporting record of all time.

Heather McKay is one of the rare sportsmen, or women, who's headlines seem to get smaller every time she took out a major squash title.

It is unlikely any woman will ever again reach even half the 16 successive British Open titles Mrs. McKay has strung together since 1962.

So devastating has Mrs. McKay been in her reign at the top she has been beaten only twice in the last 17 years.

The last time her colours were lowered was in 1962 by England's Fran Marshall in the Scottish Final on the young Australian's first trip to Britain.

The time before that was to Yvonne West in the 1960 NSW Title.

In March 1977 Mrs. McKay dropped her first game in five years before beating England's No. 2 Sue Cogswell 9-5, 9-7, 5-9, 9-0 in a British Open semi-final.

Apart from being the greatest woman squash player on earth Mrs. McKay was also a star hockey player having represented NSW and Queensland and gaining selection in the Australian team in 1967.

She was born on July 31, 1941, one of 11 children of Mr. F. L. L. Blundell, a Queanbeyan baker.

By the time she had turned 18 Heather Blundell was already Queanbeyan senior, and junior, tennis champion.

A year later she took up squash and, showing remarkable aptitude for a girl who claimed she couldn't run fast at school captured her first Australian Title. That was from the back rankers' mark of an elimination match. She hasn't touched a tennis racquet since.

As Heather Blundell she took out the 1962-65 British Open titles before marrying Brian McKay on December 13, 1965.

Heather will never forget 1962, the year she played in her first Overseas tournament in Scotland.

Her opponent was Fran Marshall, Britain's No. 1, who beat her in five gruelling sets.

"It was a tremendously tough match. Neither of us gave an inch" she recalls.

"To give you an idea of how hard it was, I had taken two racquets away with me, and during the match, I broke both of them. The darn things just cracked."

"I had to borrow one from someone in the gallery to finish".

HEATHER McKAY . . . unbeatable   [News Ltd.]

Later during that trip she went on to win the British Title, the Wimbledon of Squash, for the first time. Ever since her feats have been breathtaking, and obviously, to players such as England's Karen Gardner who was bundled out of the 1976 British Title 9-0, 9-0, 9-0 in a sparse nine minutes, humiliating.

Others to feel the icy breeze of Mrs. McKay's racquet include Clair Richards ousted in 12 minutes in 1974, Irene Rowe in 11 minutes in 1972, and Mary Rust in 12 minutes in 1975.

By this stage Mrs. McKay, who lived in Canberra and ran eight courts with her husband in the suburb of Dickson, could beat all 700 men who played the game in the National Capital.

KEN HISCOE . . . never knew when to give in

[Slazenger]

KEN HISCOE. GEOFF HUNT, DICK CARTER, CAM NANCARROW ... household names

Even to this day she practices mainly with men to get decent opposition.

"It's because the competition is better and the men are fitter" she says.

"I always get a better game playing against a man and there's really not much point in practising with people I can beat."

Almost every morning she would go for two-mile jogs in the streets near her home with her husband to supplement her keep fit programme.

Even the most blase sports followers began to sit up and take notice when in 1971 Mrs. McKay defeated fellow Australian Jennie Irving 9-0, 9-3, 9-1 in 25 minutes to win her tenth British Open Championship on the trot.

The victory brought her level with the record most Britons thought their Janet Shardlow would hold forever.

"I'll be back next year", Mrs. McKay told anxious British newsmen before boarding her homeward bound jet.

Indeed she was and with a 9-1, 9-1, 9-2 win over South African Katy Malan a quite outstanding record was hers.

Work and plan as they liked, rivals simply had no answer to the on-court brilliance of the quietly spoken Australian.

"She's like a snooker player—always thinking one shot ahead", one frustrated opponent said of Mrs. McKay.

Her 12th British Open Championship came in 1973 when she ruthlessly disposed of New Zealand champion Cecilie Fleming 9-1, 9-0, 9-1 in just 16 minutes.

No. 13 didn't present any superstitions with Mrs. McKay crushing 22-year-old London physiotherapist Sue Cogswell 9-2, 9-1, 9-2 in 23 minutes. But Mrs. McKay needed half an hour to defeat compatriot Marion Jackman 9-3, 9-1, 9-5 to win the 1975 decider.

The following year fellow Australian Sue Newman pushed Mrs. McKay to 39 minutes in the final before bowing out 2-9, 4-9, 2-9.

Fresh from her 16th British Open win Mrs. McKay made a rare appearance in Australia and defeated Miss Newman 9-5, 9-7, 9-1, in the final of the NSW Open on April 26, 1977.

Rare, because she is now fully occupied with the running of a 17 court complex with her husband in Toronto. Following the win, Mrs McKay for the very first time hinted she may not return to England in 1978 to seek another British Open. "I want to get out while I'm on top. I never want to be beaten again", she said.

It's doubtful even a partisan British crowd would enjoy seeing that.

It's probably been a bit unfortunate for Australia that so many topline men players were on the scene more or less at the same time.

Hiscoe, Carter, Hunt and Nancarrow are all household names and players who contributed to each other's careers on the court.

Ken Hiscoe, rated as Australia's greatest exponent of the squash racquet, could always be found at Bondi Beach if he wasn't carving someone up on court.

An active member of the Bondi surf club, Hiscoe went on to represent NSW in the R and R teams which won Australian Championships at North Steyne and Perth.

During the winter months Hiscoe was a promising Rugby League lock in Eastern Suburb's President's Cup team.

But it was on the squash court that Hiscoe etched his name in to the sporting record books.

Aged 24, Hiscoe in 1963 became the first Australian to win the British amateur championship when he defeated Egypt's Tawfi Shafik 9-3, 9-7, 5-9, 9-7 at London's Lansdowne Club.

It was Australia's first real attempt for an overseas title and proved our boys were right up with the best in the world.

So hard did Hiscoe hit the ball in those days British officials were thinking of laying on a special reserve of balls after he burst two balls in three matches.

He was a man who would play, and win, with injuries which would have stopped most others from even taking the court.

A major turning point in Hiscoe's career came in 1963 when top Egyptian professional Mohammed Dardir was persuaded to come to Australia.

Dardir, one of the best players ever to pick up a racquet was responsible for vastly improving Hiscoe's as well as other leading Australian's games.

Although major overseas tournaments continued to escape Hiscoe he became almost unbeatable in his home country.

He and Geoff Hunt turned professional

[News Ltd.]

KEVIN SHAWCROSS . . . exciting newcomer

together following a Test match between Australia and South Africa in Sydney in 1971.

As an amateur Hiscoe had won six Australian, seven NSW amateur titles and six NSW open titles as well as the British amateur and South African championships.

Since turning professional Hiscoe has toured and coached right around the world.

Melbourne-born Geoff Hunt was another squash player who at his peak was hailed as the best in the world. Introduced to the game by his health-conscious father, Hunt went on to win every major title around the globe.

At age 17, in 1965, he first went to England and reached the final of the amateur championship, in the process beginning what became legendary battles with Britain's No. 1 Jonah Barrington.

Hunt took out the first of four British titles in 1969 when he beat fellow-countryman Cam Nancarrow in straight sets.

The title also came his way in 1974, 1976 and 1977.

Hunt turned professional in 1971 and has a considerable interest, along with his father, in a 15-court complex at Fitzroy.

In between a long list of tournament wins, including nine in his home State, Hunt has experienced some low spots in the game.

In 1975 eighth seeded Qamar Zaman beat him in the British open quarter finals, a painful lesson for the world champion who later admitted he had not done his homework and underestimated his Pakistan opponent.

Revenge came not so long afterwards when Hunt defeated Zaman in a five-setter to win an Irish Dunlop open which took 100 minutes to finalise.

In March 1976 Hunt became the undisputed King of squash when he won the first combined world and British Open title.

In a 130-minute cliff-hanger Hunt emerged victorious over Pakistan's Mohibullah Khan (7-9, 9-4, 8-10, 9-2, 9-2) at Wembley.

Hunt came off the court practically out on his feet and said "It was one of the hardest matches I have ever played, I was very tired towards the end".

The amazing stamina of both players was tested even in the first game which took 36 minutes to complete.

A couple of months later Mohibullah got square with a 1-9, 9-7, 9-4, 2-9, 9-6 win over Hunt in the final of the British Grand Prix tournament in London.

It was the Australian's first defeat in a three-month tour of England.

There was a sensation when the pair clashed in the final of the Australian open title in Sydney in June, 1976.

On the final point of a tense second game Hunt's racquet opened a cut under Khan's left eye. The referee, Greg Robberds, ruled Khan had hampered Hunt's shot and awarded the game-winning point to the Australian.

With blood streaming down his face, Khan appealed to the umpire who stood by his decision.

Visibly upset and shaken, Khan made a thumbs-down gesture as he followed Hunt from the court for the break.

More determined than ever Khan came out and took the third game 9-7 but Hunt eventually triumphed 3-9, 9-7, 7-9, 9-0, 9-2 in 90 minutes. Hunt completed his dream of winning every major title in the world when he took out the Pakistani Masters at Karachi in December 1976.

"It has been one of my main ambitions to beat the Pakistanis in Pakistan before their own crowds and it was most satisfying to do so," he said afterwards.

That year Hunt won 19 of the 24 tournaments he contested and since he had turned professional five years earlier had lost just 18 of his first 424 matches.

Hunt attributed his astonishing run of success to being fitter than ever before, a major factor on the way to winning the second World Open title with a 9-7, 10-8, 1-9, 0-9, 9-4 victory over Qamar Zaman at Adelaide in October 1977.

Prior to leaving on one of his trips to Britain, Hunt underwent a series of tests at the Repco Fitness Centre at Cranbourne, near Dandenong, Victoria.

The tests revealed that Hunt had an oxygen intake of 94, which compared more than favourably with Olympic gold medallist Kip Keino's reading of 86 and the average VFL footballer's middle to low 60's.

Dick Carter, along with Hiscoe and Hunt, was a member of Australia's exclusive "top three club" for more than a decade.

Carter, who turned professional in 1974 after his first loss in 75 matches for NSW, was able to more than hold his own in any company right around the world.

A back injury in 1972 put a check on Carter's career and cost him the chance of adding to his 41 Tests for Australia.

With his bags packed in February for a tour of America with an Australian team Carter sustained a serious injury during a practice game.

He collided with a far bigger opponent and two days later realised the seriousness of the accident.

One of his legs shrunk five-eighths of an inch and he was forced in to a strenuous programme of exercises to build himself up again.

That he managed to pull through is typical of the whole attitude of the mild mannered champion.

Carter was a blood, sweat and tears player, agile and durable, a fact which he attributes to his regular five mile beach runs at dawn

GEOFF HUNT . . . world champion playing Mohibullah Khan

from Ramsgate to Brighton and back. He reached the prestigious British amateur championship final on two occasions but left English shores both times without the trophy.

Egyptian Aftab Jawaid won the 1966 final while Carter also went down the following year in a gruelling five-setter to Jonah Barrington.

"Now I know how Ron Clarke feels about all those consolation medals", he said after the second defeat.

In other countries things weren't quite so bad as Carter today can proudly display trophies for having won the New Zealand and South African championships. In reaching the 1966 British final Carter defeated Geoff Hunt, then aged 18, in a tough five set match, 6-9, 9-6, 9-2, 8-10, 9-5 which took 100 minutes to complete. In 1967 Carter gained revenge from the previous year by defeating titleholder Jawaid in straight sets in a semi-final.

It was a tough school in those days but Carter defeated Hunt the first five times they met and wasn't beaten by Cam Nancarrow until 1969. "They used to say that when Ken Hiscoe was finished at the top I would take his place. Trouble is, I've grown old with him", Carter once said.

He turned professional immediately after Queenslander Mike Donnelly ended his 74 match winning sequence for NSW in 1974.

Cameron John Nancarrow would never rue the day he finally set aside his golf clubs and, with his left hand, gripped a squash racquet which took him right to the top.

Nancarrow has come a long way since the day his father won a racquet and a set of shoes in a raffle at the newly opened Rockdale squash centre. The courts were just a few doors up from the Nancarrow home and the temptation to try out his newly won prize was far too great for the lad.

Having whittled his handicap down to 12, Nancarrow for a couple of years mixed golf with squash. But by the time he had turned 16 Nancarrow knew in which directions his ambition lay. He and his close friend, Billy Reedman, began logging up hours at the squash centre in a search which at that stage had little more purpose than a dog chasing its tail.

[News Ltd.]

CAM NANCARROW ... set aside golf clubs for squash racquet

"Bill de Corsie owned the courts and he allowed Billy and me to play there almost every day for two years, virtually for nothing," Nancarrow recalls.

By that stage there was nothing uncertain about what Nancarrow was chasing.

Local tournaments began coming Nancarrow's way through his vigorous stroke play.

Twice he reached the final of the world amateur championship — in Melbourne in 1967 and in New Zealand four years later.

Both times fellow countryman Geoff Hunt stopped Nancarrow's search for the ultimate.

Once Hunt and Hiscoe had turned professional Nancarrow had some big shoes to fill for Australia.

Nancarrow's luck was better in South Africa where he won that country's title in 1966 and 1973.

Billy Reedman, Nancarrow's sparring partner from years gone by went on to be twice runner up in the British amateur.

After another near miss, runner up in the 1969 British open, Nancarrow finally landed a big one.

In September he defeated Britain's Bryan Patterson 9-2, 9-5, 9-1 in the world championship final at Durban.

The victory came in 32 minutes but it took Nancarrow less time to decide to turn professional almost immediately afterwards.

Thus ended a magnificent amateur career which had seen Nancarrow win the Australian, British and Canadian championships the previous year.

Because of the sheer playing strength of the game in Australia (almost 800,000 throughout the country) squash officials are confident a new golden era is just around the corner.

Where John Cheadle in the 1950s, Owen Parmenter in the early 1960s and more recently, Kevin Shawcross, came through the ranks so too is emerging an exciting new crop.

Players like Mike and Frank Donnelly and Terry Cheetham from Queensland, Victorians Mark Tomasini and Kim Richards, Dean Williams from Western Australia and Sydney's Ian Yeates.

With the sort of dedication Geoff Hunt talks about these men could soon have their names engraved on the world's major trophies.

GRAHAM CORNES . . . flying high for South Australia against Western Australia, Football Park, Adelaide, 1977

7 AUSTRALIAN RULES

By MIKE SHEAHAN

MIKE SHEAHAN, 30, is a general sports reporter on "The Age" newspaper in Melbourne and a prominent football writer. He has covered football in Perth, Adelaide and Hobart and won the Victorian Football League's award for the best feature story in 1976.

The unlikely trio of an extrovert, a conservative and an academic, has dominated football in the past decade.

Ron Barassi, Tom Hafey and John Kennedy have made the spoils of football their private little contest in Victoria, which remains Australia's premier football State.

Nine premierships in 10 years—and a Barassi influence in the other—reflects a power struggle unparalleled in the VFL's 80-year history.

Teams coached by these men have occupied 14 of a possible 20 grand final slots in the period.

For the record, Hafey leads with four premierships at Richmond from five grand finals. Barassi has won three flags—with Carlton and North Melbourne—from six attempts, and Kennedy has taken Hawthorn to two premierships in three attempts.

Barassi, outspoken, flamboyant and ruthless, remains the biggest football name in the land. The former champion Melbourne player revived Carlton, and carried North to the impossible dream.

Quiet little Hafey, the non-smoking, tea-sipping, football addict, moulded the most successful team since Melbourne's historic run in the fifties. He led Richmond to its first flag for 24 years and followed up with three more in seven years.

Former schoolmaster Kennedy has coached Hawthorn to its three premierships—1961, 1971 and 1975.

Despite their contrasting personalities and differing styles, the three men have been obsessed with the same aim and all have been eminently successful.

While the power struggle raged in Victoria, South Australia's inimitable Jack Oatey had it all his own way. He steered Sturt to five successive premierships—from 1966 to 1970.

In Perth, the rewards have been more evenly spread with five of the eight clubs sharing the past 10 flags.

In Tasmania's fragmented football set-up, the rich Hobart-based Sandy Bay has been the trendsetter. Significantly, Sandy Bay's run was engineered by Kennedy pupil, Rod Olsson, who returned to Victoria in 1976 as coach of Geelong.

To select the champion team of the era is to provoke arguments, but it is difficult to dispute Richmond's claim to the title. Four VFL premierships and three Australian titles backs the argument.

Just to prove the point, Richmond thrashed Sturt in two of the national premiers' championship matches.

The Tigers reaped the benefits of its class of '67, the year they assembled a bunch of kids later to become legendary names.

From Tasmania came Royce Hart; the Victorian towns of Nathalia and Kyabram provided Francis Bourke and Dick Clay; while Kevin Sheedy and Kevin Bartlett came through the ranks. They were to form the backbone of all-conquering Richmond for the next eight years.

Hafey, a Richmond player of little note and a fitness disciple, was just the man to mould the youthful talent.

Armed with a rare passion for the game and the revolutionary ideas of the late Len Smith, Hafey went to work—and Richmond went to the top.

The Tigers tailored a team for the wide-open Melbourne Cricket Ground—the finals venue. He remodelled the all-important centreline with height and strength, and backed the skill of his men against all opposition.

The theory failed only once—1972—and Carlton had to kick a record grand final score of 28.9 (177) to do it.

Richmond still kicked 22.18 to fail by only 27 points—a score higher than any previous winning total in a grand final.

The man behind the Carlton triumph was captain-coach, John Nicholls, arguably the greatest ruckman in football history.

Nicholls inherited a ready-made premiership combination from the retired Ron Barassi and played a major role with his tactics off the ground—and his six goals during the match.

When Nicholls was forced into retirement by the Carlton hierarchy less than two years later, he had played a then-record 331 VFL games.

He joined Carlton from country club Maryborough in 1957, won the best and fairest award five times, captained the Blues to three premierships—and represented Victoria a record 31 times.

He quit the Blues after 19 years on the eve of the 1976 season, but returned to football in 1977 as coach of South Australian club, Glenelg.

Like Nicholls, Barassi's retirement lasted just one season. The VFL Cinderella club, North Melbourne, lured him back to football with the greatest challenge of his career, plus a healthy contract.

He took only two years to vindicate their judgement, lifting North Melbourne into a grand final only two years after they had finished last.

The following year—1975—North's 50-year dream turned to reality when Barassi won the club its first VFL flag. It was probably the most expensive flag in Australian football history.

In a recruiting splurge estimated to have cost $1 million, North gave Barassi the most select group of recruits ever assembled.

North bought top Victorian trio Barry Davis, Doug Wade and John Rantall; and recalled champion WA rover, Barry Cable.

To this group was added WA Sandover Medallist Graham Melrose, South Australia's Magarey Medallist, Mal Blight, and wooed Carlton's controversial star, Brent Crosswell.

PETER KNIGHTS . . . Victoria and Hawthorne's centre half-back

[S.A.N.F.L.]
BARRIE ROBRAN . . . triple Magarey Medal winner

On September 27, 1975, before 110,551 partisan spectators, North crushed Hawthorn for a 55-point win to end the longest wait of any VFL club for a premiership.

While Barassi and the men who engineered the triumph wept for joy, Hawthorn's Kennedy was already planning revenge for that final Saturday in September 12 months later.

And what a revenge it was . . . Not only did Hawthorn win the '76 premiership, its victim was North Melbourne.

Kennedy's second premiership in five years and his third in 16 years, signalled the exit of one of the best, and certainly the most respected, of modern coaches when he slipped into retirement.

Hawthorn was one of the few Victorian clubs to build its premiership hopes on local talent.

While Richmond, Carlton and especially North, achieved the ultimate aim with extensive nationwide recruiting programmes, all of them helped widen the gap between Victoria and the other football States.

The Victorian clubs, armed with cheque

JOHN KENNEDY ... coached Hawthorn to three premierships

books, continued to plunder the youthful talent from WA, SA and Tasmania, and even extended their operations into the developing States—Queensland, NSW and ACT.

The irreparable damage was reflected in Hobart in June 1977, when a second-string Victorian team humiliated a Tasmanian team by 109 points. The previous Saturday the 12 VFL senior teams included 16 Tasmanian-born players.

The damage in Tasmania nearly proved fatal.

The island State's major competition, the Tasmanian Football League in Hobart, was ailing under financial strain brought about by rapidly falling attendances.

Local observers blamed the Victorian pilfering of the most exciting of Tasmania's players. They said they only got fringe players and "has beens" in return.

Champion full-forward, Peter Hudson, gave weight to the argument when he played two seasons with Glenorchy in 1975-76, preparing for his comeback at Hawthorn.

Hudson took the club into successive grand finals and more importantly, bought people back to football with his goalkicking genius.

Tasmania's decline was reflected early in the 1976 season of the ill-fated National Football League. While South Australia had eight club sides participating in the knock-out competition and Western Australia six sides, Tasmania was restricted to a representative team from its three major competitions—and was eliminated in the first round by WA club South Fremantle.

In 1976, the NFL looked certain to be the salvation of Australian football. With VFL representation and the prospect of total national participation, the game's long-term future looked assured.

After a promising first year, the VFL selfishly withdrew and started its own night series at VFL Park in direct opposition—with the obvious aim of taking over the NFL role.

The national series had the real benefits of interstate competition at club level, and the exposure of the stars of each State to an Australia-wide television audience.

While the competition reinforced Victoria's superiority, it also gave VFL clubs the opportunity to see potential recruits under testing competition.

Triple Magarey Medallist, Russell Ebert, Port Adelaide's 28-year-old centreman, proved

TOM HAFEY ... VFL's leading coach

himself probably the best footballer never to play in the VFL.

Ebert, who won the medal in 1971, 1974 and 1976, destroyed Footscray in one game and was the individual star of the inaugural series.

Ebert joined Barrie Robran, Lindsay Head, Len Fitzgerald, Dan Moriarty and Tom McKenzie as a three-times winner of SA's top individual award. The Port Adelaide skipper has resisted numerous rich offers to move to Melbourne. Ebert and Robran have won the medal six times in the past decade.

Robran, 30, North Adelaide's star centre half-forward, won the medal in 1968 and 1970 — and in North's premiership year of 1972.

Yet even the great Robran can't match Ebert's incredible effort of 1976 when he polled 42 medal votes to win by 17.

Ebert's 1971 medal win was followed by the success of Woodville's first Magarey winner, Malcolm Blight, who was to become one of Victoria's most talented and highly-paid, players with North Melbourne.

Blight, 27, all-Australian in 1972, moved to Victoria in 1974, missed the grand final that

RON BARRASSI . . . outspoken, flamboyant, ruthless

year with glandular fever, but was part of the history-making premiership team of the following year.

The blond ruck-rover, with the springs in his heels, rapidly earned himself a place in that select group of match-winners.

Another star of the decade was Glenelg's goalkicking phenomenon, Fred Phillis.

Phillis led the goalkicking five times in eight years from 1969 and "topped the Ton" three times. In 1969, when he kicked 137 goals, his magnificent performance earned him the Magarey Medal, making him one of a select group of key forwards to win top awards.

Over in Western Australia, it was sharp-shooting, Austin Robertson jnr., who was dominating the goal square. Robertson, who joined Subiaco in 1962, led the goalkicking table in his first season and another seven times.

When he retired in 1974, his goals' total at Subiaco was 1,278. He topped the century six times including a mammoth 162 in 1969. He also booted 60 goals for South Melbourne, his father's old club, in 1966.

Western Australia's remarkable production of top players continued in recent years. Graham Farmer, Barry Cable and Graham Moss, all WA imports to Victoria, proved themselves three of the best ever.

COLLINGWOOD v. CARLTON

RUSSELL EBERT . . . incredible effort [S.A.N.F.L.]

Farmer became legend as a ruckman and handball exponent, Cable perfected the roving art, Moss the first Sandgroper to win Victoria's Brownlow Medal.

Moss's triumph came in 1976 with Essendon, but Victoria wasn't to see him play as the reigning champion. He returned to Claremont as captain and coach at the end of that year.

Yet it is Farmer and Cable who share the mantle as Western Australia's greatest football sons.

They won five Sandover Medals, as Western Australia's best player, from 1956 to 1973, two Tassie Medals as the best in interstate competition, and have played nearly 750 games between them in two States.

Perhaps the greatest achievement in a career dotted with honours, was Farmer's starring role in Geelong's 1963 premiership win. In addition to the premiership, Farmer won the club's best and fairest award and was runner-up in the Brownlow Medal.

He returned to Perth in 1968 to captain-coach West Perth to two premierships in three years before Geelong brought him east again as coach.

Between 1954 and 1971 he amassed 392 games — 36 State games, 101 for Geelong and 255 for East Perth and West Perth.

Geelong bought him for $3000 in 1962 in what was the bargain buy of football history. Cable didn't come as cheaply, but he was just as valuable.

Like Farmer, Cable made a late start in the top level of Australian football. He never had any doubts he would succeed, and he made all the sceptics eat their words with a brilliant first season in 1970.

He won the club's best and fairest award, to add to the eight he won at Perth, yet the real seal on his brilliance came when he returned to North in 1974 at the age of 30 on a three-year contract that was to be extended for another two years after the 1976 grand final.

The little left-footer, with a lifelong passion for the game, reached the 350-game mark midway through the 1977 season and immediately set his sights on 400.

FITZROY v. NORTH MELBOURNE

HAWTHORN v FOOTSCRAY action

Only one man has played that number of games at senior level—Fitzroy's champion utility player, Kevin Murray, played 424 games from 1955 to 1974 in Victoria and Western Australia. His total of 333 with the Lions is a VFL record; a mark he set at 36 despite a chronic back injury that forced him to wear a brace for several years.

In 1969, at the age of 31, he became the oldest, and probably the most popular, Brownlow Medallist after several near-misses.

Murray took the games' record from John Nicholls, who held the honour for less than a month. "Big Nick" was retired by Carlton soon after breaking Ted Whitten's record of 321 games.

Of the group of contemporary veterans, only Cable survives. While Farmer, Whitten, Nicholls and Murray have left the scene in the past decade, so too have two of the most celebrated players in history.

Triple Brownlow Medallists, Ian Stewart and Bobby Skilton have retired to move to coaching jobs with new clubs. Skilton, the former South Melbourne champion rover, is finding personal success far more elusive at Melbourne, while Stewart's charmed run continues at South Melbourne.

Stewart, the most recent player to win three Brownlows, and the only man to do it at two clubs, could be joined by North Melbourne's captain and dual winner, Keith Greig.

Every decade has its highlights, but the period from 1967 to 1976 will occupy an unusually large part of the game's history.

It marked the introduction of "cheque book" football, a near full-time involvement for players, changing styles, and the marketing of the game.

All were inevitable in the march of time.

While the period has been dotted with progress and highlights, it also produced two tragedies.

In April 1975, Footscray's $50,000 purchase from North Adelaide, Neil Sachse, became a quadraplegic in a sickening collision with Fitzroy's Kevin O'Keeffe.

Sachse had his neck broken in only his second VFL game and was carried off the ground on a stretcher, never to walk again.

Less than two years later the football world mourned the loss of Hawthorn's cheerful and popular captain, Peter Crimmins.

Crimmins was struck down by cancer in his late twenties and died after a gallant fight against the disease. His death came only days after he listened on radio to Hawthorn's 1976 premiership win.

His popularity was reflected when the VFL sanctioned a testimonial game at VFL Park a few weeks later. VFL Park, only a pipe dream when Crimmins started his career, hosted 45,000 people in a moving tribute to one of the game's most popular men.

Hawthorn renamed its best and fairest award to commemorate the Crimmins name in a period which will be remembered for many varied reasons. Sport provides many emotional moments and the Peter Crimmins story is one of them.

VFL president, Allen Aylett, who took office early in 1977, forecast regular and spectacular changes on the way to the League's centenary.

The new emphasis on technology, marketing and public relations gives Dr. Aylett a better than even-money chance of being right in his ambitious forecast.

Listening time at three-quarter time

8 RUGBY LEAGUE
By BILL MORDEY

BILL MORDEY is chief Rugby League writer for the Sydney "Daily Mirror" and the new "Sunday". He's written and commented on Rugby League for more than 20 years to establish himself as an expert authority on the game. For the past 10 years Mordey has travelled the world with Australian teams and has seen every major League game played.

The ending of an unequalled era of football dominance a decade ago spun Rugby League onto a speeding roller coaster racing towards the twenty first century.

For 11 seasons St. George had ruled roughshod against all comers to set a world record-winning sequence in first grade football.

The effort by the famous Sydney club of total domination is touched only by the "First Lady of Squash", Heather Mackay.

From 1956 until 1966 it was a case of St. George winning the premiership and a fight among the other clubs to line up and accept a Grand Final hammering.

Rivals of Saints were driven to the brink of despair and frustration in their efforts to topple the champions who mercilessly annihilated all challengers.

Arch rival Western Suburbs tried to buy the coveted crown held so proudly by St. George only to be driven back to the ranks in three fateful deciders of the early 1960s.

The Saints were the scourge of the premiership to all but their own club followers who enjoyed a "Roman Holiday" for those record 11 victories.

But all good things must end and the year of 1967 opened with a buzz of excitement as Rugby League decided that change was necessary to a game which had stood the test of time since formation back in 1908.

Under pressure, senior officials of the game decided to introduce a limited-tackle system which was being accepted in England.

At the same time two fledgling clubs, Penrith and Cronulla-Sutherland won promotion to first division to extend the Sydney competition to 12 clubs.

For several years the Rugby League had resisted the challenge from Second Division to provide two additional competitors in top grade, so their doors at Phillip St. were bombarded.

Wentworthville, Ryde-Eastwood, Penrith and Cronulla all had strong claims, but eventually it was the latter two clubs who won through.

First off came club insignias—Sharks for Cronulla, Panthers for Penrith to join with the already established Tigers, (Balmain) Bears (North Sydney), Magpies (Wests), Blues (Newtown, later to be renamed Jets), Dragons (St. George), Berries (Canterbury, later to be renamed Bull Dogs), Eels (Parramatta), Rabbitoh's (South Sydney), Roosters (Easts) and Sea Gulls (Manly later to be called Sea Eagles).

Then there had to be acceptance of the new four-tackle rule which was baffling players who had grown up on unlimited football.

All were equal—players and coaches alike —as experiment after experiment was tried. The field goal shot took prominence with players like Eric Simms virtually worth their weight in gold after team mates took the ball down field to a kicking position.

Simms rewrote the record book with his kicking and was aided greatly by the dropped goal where he was so adept.

Later the value of this type of score was to be reduced to only a point to keep snap attempts to a minimum, and these days it is used only rarely, mostly to break a tied situation between teams.

The public seemed enthralled by the new fast and unpredictable game of League and in the second year of four-tackle football crowds for the season peaked to a record. But after the high there came a down and the rule was changed to six-tackles which still exists today.

Throughout the past decade controversy has raged among players, officials, coaches and spectators about the relative merits of limited and unlimited football.

Billy Smith, one of the all-time greats and the last survivor, until recently, of the great St. George era, believes the game was best when unlimited tackles were allowed.

"You got much more football with the unlimited tackle," Smith said. "The four and then six tackles took something of sustained interest away from the spectator. And I believe the scrapping of the old third grade competition for a new-look under 23 series also deprived players of a great learning ground.

"In third grade there were always a couple of hard-heads running about, either slipping in form or coming back from injury. Young blokes on the way up could learn from their experience. Maybe they weren't as quick, but the knowledge of their years of playing was there to be captured by the young.

"These days, with the age limit, there aren't any of the old smarties to teach the up-and-coming kids who have to mark time in their learning until reaching reserves or firsts," Smith added.

ARTHUR BEETSON . . . pies to premiership

By comparison, the young breed of newcomers, such as the International utility star Allan McMahon, have never played unlimited football.

"I like six tackles, but then I've never tried the old game," McMahon said.

In modern times officialdom has attempted to keep pace, and the former stubbornness against change has been replaced with an attitude of keeping abreast with the calendar. The League tried to introduce a ceiling-payment to players which would have cut costs to clubs, but there was no solidarity among its ranks.

In 1974 a home-and-away system was introduced and in 1975 a restriction of 13 imports to each club was passed as a law of the game. For 1977 the International Board decided, at Australia's instigation, that traffic of players between Australia and Great Britain must cease.

The English clubs had been plundered by rich Sydney rivals and denuded of playing strength to where Australian victory in Inter-

[Rugby League Week]

BOB FULTON . . . international wizard

[Rugby League Week]

nationals was mere formality. The world scene since 1968 has been dominated almost constantly by Australia, although Great Britain hit back in 1972 in a world series played in France.

Even that victory was undecided as Australia and Great Britain drew the game, played extra-time and were still locked on the scoreboard before the Englishmen were declared winners on a count back.

Prior to that Great Britain had won an Ashes series in 1970 by two Tests to one. But since then its been Australia first and the world fighting out second place as most of the top overseas players were lured from their homelands by the might of the Sydney dollar.

This pause in International trafficking of League talent has been designed to allow France, New Zealand and Great Britain to rebuild. The stars unearthed and then polished to top class will represent their countries as the world League scene reverts to the old system of tours.

Kevin Humphreys, Chairman of the Australian Rugby League, has been the strongest of supporters for a temporary pause in overseas transfers.

"Local clubs will develop their junior talent and I'm certain the game will benefit," Mr. Humphreys said. "With the end of poaching, overseas players will bring other world countries back stronger than ever," he added.

His point is valid. Attendances reached an all-time low for the recent NSW v Great Britain clash played at the SCG, and attracting only 7,000 fans.

Clashes between Australia and the Poms, have historically been the backbone of League. Its obvious the time has arrived for definite action to rekindle competition.

Three Test series over a longer period of time is what the paying public wants, and the wishes of France and New Zealand for World Championship clashes have been shelved. These two weaker countries claim involvement against only the big two—Australia and Great Britain—will update their own standards.

But the hand of help had to be recalled in a state of emergency to bring League back to a system which has packed grounds both here and abroad for 70 years.

Off the field Rugby League in the past 10 years has survived scandal among its playing representatives with some escapades being labelled infamous. Players have been fined, had papers marked "never to tour again" and threatened with dismissal on tour. But as professionalism takes over the once semi-amateur game, so too do attitudes change.

In recent away trips the trouble makers have been culled out and a new look of pride has taken over Australian touring sides. With huge sponsorships coming into Rugby League, top officials insist the image of the game be updated accordingly.

"No major business house wants to be associated with a bunch of larrikins or louts," explained League Promotion Committee chairman Bob Abbott.

"Sponsors are pouring fortunes into the game, and it speaks volumes for Rugby League that they want to be associated with the code. It is only fair they be represented by people they can be justly proud of. The League is aware of past problems, and we've acted accordingly to ensure teams don't bring discredit to the game, or the country they represent," Mr. Abbott said.

With sponsorship, yet another era is dawning in football and the days of full-time professionals isn't any longer a pipedream. Most of the major clubs have sponsorship, or are on the verge of completing deals worth hundreds of thousands of dollars, and there are some cases of individual sponsorship of players.

Cronulla recently had a sponsor supporting English skipper Roger Millward for a season while Easts' Arthur Beetson is also involved in a similar deal.

Since the end of Saints' dominance of the premiership scene, six clubs have shared the competition honours with Souths winning four titles.

Manly took their first title in 1972 since joining the League in 1947, prior to winning two more crowns to emerge as a dominant force of the 1970s. Easts won the premiership twice in 1974 and 1975 while Balmain was victorious in perhaps the upset of the decade against Souths back in 1969.

Stories of courage and physical endurance unfold from these Grand final days as players hammer each other to achieve a life-time goal.

GRAEME LANGLANDS . . . a gallant Dragon

[Rugby League Week]

EASTERN SUBURBS . . . 1975 premiers prior to preliminary final success over Manly-Warringah 28-13. From left: (Back row) John Peard, Elwyn Walters, Ian Schubert, Arthur Beetson (captain), Bunny Reilly, Reg Clough, Jack Gibson (coach). (Front row) Bill Mullins, Johnny Mayes, Mark Harris, Bruce Pickett, Kevin Stevens, John Brass, Ian Mackay.

South Sydney was first to take over the crown left vacant by St. George who still have fans claiming the rule change was introduced to loosen their grip on the pennant. Souths, in the year of 1967, was full of youth and enthusiasm blended with tough men who were to emerge as the backbone of Australia's football dominance. Johnny Sattler, Bob McCarthy, Ron Coote, John O'Neill, Jimmy Lisle, Mike Cleary and Elwyn Walters were all to win Test honours from that 1967 premiership-winning side coached by Clive Churchill.

The youth and speed of Souths was pitted against the seasoned toughness of Canterbury-Bankstown led by undisputed ironman Kevin Ryan. And the match developed into a clash of brute strength won eventually by Souths 12-10 after the two teams had been locked 10-all in the second half.

The following year it was the bridesmaid of League, Manly to challenge Souths for the title. Future Internationals in the form of Eric

Simms, Jim Morgan, Bob Honan and Dennis Pittard were in the team of defending champions who threw back Manly's bid. That match finished with a try to either side and it was the goal kicking of Eric Simms that won the day for Souths.

The brilliant full-back booted five tremendous pressure goals to pave the way for a 13-9 victory and set Souths on the path to a hat-trick of titles. 1969 shaped up as a formality for Souths as their young brigade of the previous two years had developed into the most dangerous side in the premiership.

Souths, led by Sattler and O'Neill, were rough and tough, but backed up aggression with all the skills of the game, plus plenty of speed.

It was Balmain to emerge as Souths' challengers after the Tigers scored a slender one point 15-14 victory over Manly in the final. In the semis Souths had looked convincing, beating Balmain 14-13 scoring two tries to one, and only great goal kicking by South African Len Killeen kept his side in the match.

Peter Provan, brother of Saints' famous son Norm Provan, was to lead Balmain into the Grand final, assisted by the wily veteran of English football Dave Bolton. Balmain went out with a plan not to allow the South Sydney machine to function smoothly, and they hindered the champions at every opportunity. Souths supporters still claim the pennant went to a team "sitting on the ground" as Balmain stalled their way through.

At one stage in the game Sattler protested to referee Keith Page of the number of stoppages in play as Balmain's weary 13 went to ground seeking ambulance attention. Even at half time, with Souths behind 6-nil, the giant club wasn't perturbed, and the team reappeared confident of running away in the second half. But Souths that afternoon just couldn't get into the rampaging stride for which they were famous. The Balmain defence smothered every move.

Bolton was the mid-field genius who drove the nail into Souths' coffin when he swooped on a loose ball in the second half which led to Syd Williams scoring the only try of the game.

At full time Balmain had won 11-2 with Killeen kicking two goals and Bolton two snapped field shots. Souths left the SCG arena smarting at the loss, vowing to return the following season to make amends.

True to their declaration the Rabbitoh's were back in 1970 to clash with Manly and the 80 minutes were to provide one of League's greatest efforts of courage.

The give-and-take-everything Sattler was felled early in the match by a high tackle from a rival Manly forward, and needed treatment before continuing on. It was only after Souths had won 23-12 that it was learned Sattler had half a dozen teeth snapped at the gums and his jaw broken in the early incident.

Unable to talk after the game Sattler was imploring his club officials not to say anything of his injury so he could win selection with the Australian touring team. His effort in staying on the field that day, let alone playing a dominating role in the thick of scrums and rucks, must rate brave enough to be crazy.

The huge crowd had no idea of the pain Sattler endured for most of the 80 minutes as he guided his team to a three try to nil win.

Next season in 1971 Souths were again victorious this time at the expense of St. George who had fought tooth and nail throughout the season. But they didn't take the title without plenty of anxious moments. After leading 11-0 Souths found themselves hanging on the ropes with a point lead at 11-10 during the second half.

Manly-Warringah celebrated a first grade history of 25 years in first grade in 1972 and the club desperately wanted to cap the quarter century with a premiership victory.

Behind the scenes officials had bought wisely to build a competition-winning team. And while Manly were to achieve the club goal of taking the pennant, the 19-14 grand final win over Eastern Suburbs was charged with confusion.

Referee Keith Page caused the storm of the

MICK CRONIN . . . goalkicking genius
[Rugby League Week]

decade when the game ended in controversy with Easts claiming they were robbed. Twice at vital stages Easts had tries disallowed and their followers claimed two tries awarded to Manly shouldn't have been awarded.

Easts charged that Ray Branighan, formerly with South Sydney, had scored off a forward pass and that hooker Fred Jones hadn't grounded the ball when his try was awarded. In their own defence Easts claimed John Armstrong had scored about 10 minutes before half time when the side were clinging grimly to a 4-2 lead.

Page ruled a double movement in this case.

Fifteen minutes into the second half Ron Coote dived across Manly's line, but Page ruled the rangy lock dropped the ball before grounding. At that stage Easts were down 4-8 and the likely conversion would have shot them to the lead and recharged the tired limbs of players.

Manly enjoyed the tag of "champions" and entered 1973 determined to successfully defend the crown.

This year brought yet another change to the laws of the game with a five-team series of semi finalists being devised. It also heralded a chance for Cronulla to take a championship after only six short years in top division football.

Manly went on to win 10-7, but the match provided 80 minutes of anxiety and could have swung either way. The International wizard, Bob Fulton, sparked his side with two dazzling tries and it was almost a single-handed effort to win.

Cronulla had their chance late in the game, storming home after being down 8-2 with only 10 minutes play remaining. At a time when scoring could decently be expected to have finished, both teams were adding points— Cronulla with a converted try, and Manly from a penalty.

Then came Cronulla's lost chance.

The Sharks put on a move close to Manly's line in a desperate bid to score near the posts with England's Tommy Bishop calling the play. Bishop weaved and there was a gap for his runner Ken Maddison, but the Kangaroo forward took the wrong side and Cronulla's hope faded into nothing.

The next two years, 1974 and 1975, were to bring to light the genius of coach Jack Gibson with Easts and also introduce the American connection to Sydney. Gibson is the keenest student of the game and will go to any lengths to learn, and improve on, methods of whipping a team to success.

His basics are defence to keep intact his own team's line, not conceding penalties and generally a safety-first approach. But he also introduced an attacking flare which excites with his runners in full flight.

In the first of Easts back-to-back victories it was Canterbury who were kept scoreless and hammered into submission by 19-4. Easts defence in the Grand final was impregnable, with every man covering as if his very life depended on the making of a successfull tackle. And in reply Easts scored three tries.

However, the second of Easts' triumphs was easily the best as they romped away to a mammoth 38-nil win over St. George. It was 5-0 at half time, but the second session provided a landslide for the rampaging Easts who finished with eight tries.

Manly came back in the winners circle in 1976, this time at the expense of Parramatta, another of the clubs never to have won a title. But Parramatta did leave the SCG scoring two tries to one, but down 13-10 in the match.

Parramatta made Manly work for every moment of the game and several times held a handy lead, only to see it whittled away. It was also another performance of courage from their skipper Ray Higgs who played for 60 minutes with a fractured cheek bone, but still remained in the thick of the fray and the bridesmaid tag again belonged to Parramatta after a spine-tingling 9-all draw and 20 minutes extra time, only to return the following week for a replay showdown with a magnificent St. George—back in the winning vein 22-0 under former club giant Harry Bath.

But I doubt if the cycle has done the full turn to again see a long St. George reign.

Under the current system and laws the gap has lessened between the top teams. Nevertheless the Saints are always hard to beat, especially when they get their noses in front—and that's where they stand in 1977.

9 RUGBY UNION

By NORM TASKER

NORMAN TASKER is Rugby writer for the "Sydney Sun", who has toured extensively with Australian Rugby teams. His coverage of international Rugby has taken him to South Africa, New Zealand, the British Isles, France, Canada and America and he has accompanied every touring team in Australia in the past decade. Tasker recently retired as a grade referee in the Sydney competition to become head coach of leading Sydney club Gordon.

The odds were liberally quoted at 100 to one about Australia winning a Test of the 1971 series against France. Winning both was a 200 to one bet. When Frenchmen gather a pride about their national Rugby team, they express it without inhibition or restraint.

More than a few of Greg Davis's Wallabies of 1971 gratefully snapped up a piece of the action, and whether or not such hefty financial interest was their prime motivation, the subsequent 13-10 victory in Toulouse that November probably was the best moment in the last decade of Australian Rugby.

The journey from the Toulouse dressing room to the team bus was no more than 50 metres. As the players wearily wended their way along the narrow path they had to carve that day through hordes of disappointed Frenchmen, many of whom vented their distress by spitting upon the victors, there was no doubt they had won a considerable victory for the Australian game.

Such magic moments, alas, have been all too fleeting.

The years 1968 to 1977 were not vintage years for Australian Rugby. Australia is peculiarly placed on the world Rugby scene, so fragmented is our national football interest. Overseas Rugby nations who command vast public support marvel at the manner in which Australia competes on the world Rugby stage when the massive influences of Australian football in the south and professional Rugby League in the northern States are taken into account.

Success, however, has been an all too infrequent visitor. Of 42 Tests in the 10-year period, Australia have won 12, lost 28 and drawn two. Of the 12 they have won, seven have been against minor nations Fiji, Japan, Tonga and the United States. It has not been the grandest of Australia's international Rugby periods, despite impressive strides made domestically in the expansion of the game's playing numbers and popular appeal.

Perhaps such meagre pickings tend to make the magic moments more memorable, but studded through the 42 internationals that Australia played between 1968 and 1977 are some performances of heroic quality, and some team efforts that will stand with any in the world.

Who, for instance, could forget the tenacity of the Australian side as Peter Johnson's men beat France 11-10 in 1968? As the brilliant French centre Jo Maso spun web after web of attacking intrigue, Australians kept throwing themselves into defence with the sort of persistence King Canute might have liked in his unhappy duel with the tide.

The dynamic performance of Greg Davis's team in whipping Scotland 23-3 at the Sydney Cricket Ground in 1970 was a high-point for any decade to envy. And the genuine admiration of the New Zealand coach J. J. Stewart as he stood in the Australian's dressing room after a 16-16 draw of inordinate skill with the 1974 All Blacks at Ballymore and said simply, "bloody well done", was magic in itself.

Ballymore saw plenty of those moments through the late sixties and early seventies. Not least was the fantastic performance in 1968 by a young and inexperienced Australian side, confronted with perhaps the most successful All Black team of all time under Brian Lochore, who were beaten by a single point.

They saw what would have been one of Australia's more historic victories snatched from their very grasp by a penalty try, somewhat hastily awarded, in the final moments of play.

In latter days, two defeats of England in 1975, and a succesful tour of the British Isles

STUART GREGORY . . . international lineup champion

brought an end to a slump which, through 1972 and 1973, had seen such ignominious performance as a 38-3 defeat by the All Blacks and, oh such woe, defeat by Tonga in a "Test".

The 1975-76 Wallabies in fact probably began a new era of success in the Australian game, or at least gave rise to great hope of it. They romped through their provincial programme as no Australian team before them and were unlucky not to have gathered better international success than the one triumph against Ireland.

In terms of the absolute best in the last 10 years of Australian teams, the side built between 1974 and 1976 would go close to taking the prize. It developed brilliant new forwards like the long-haired Sydney flanker Ray Price and the dynamic Brisbane lock Mark Loane, surely one of the most powerful athletes to have donned an Australian jumper.

They also gathered a measure of technical expertise, through the great advances made in Australian coaching through the mid-seventies, that allowed them to better compete in the most basic areas of the game—notably the scrum.

But it is difficult to get away from that 1971 team, and their Herculean performance against France at Toulouse, when the word "best" is being bandied around, and comparisons made.

Good teams take a long time to work up. By the time the Wallabies reached France in

1971 they had been honed through four years of pretty solid international effort, starting with the New Zealand All Blacks of 1968. Des Connor, the former Australian and New Zealand half-back of vast international experience, had taken charge as coach at that time, and he brought a team together, and largely maintained it, through a series against the All Blacks —and two major series against South Africa.

It was a time of change for Australian Rugby.

The great era of John Thornett's Wallabies, who had commanded the world stage with astonishing success through the early sixties, had come to an end. Connor had at his disposal a handy residue, however.

Ken Catchpole, arguably the finest Rugby player Australia has produced, was still there to dictate matters at half-back. The ubiquitous breakaway of Thornett's 1963 march through South Africa, Greg Davis, was still very much on deck, and the longest-serving of all Australian hookers, Peter Johnson, gave the tight forwards stable leadership.

To these bulwarks were added a host of newcomers who stayed on for some years, and through the early seventies gave Australia a team that always promised much, without— save for those few golden moments—ever fully realising their potential.

If the best performance of those years was the Toulouse effort of 1971, and that team the best of its period, it was only the culmination of much that had gone before. The new men had their blooding against New Zealand in 1968.

Phillip Smith and John Brass, the centre pairing from the Randwick Club in Sydney who had toured Britain in 1966-67, came into their own. John Cole was a new and pugnacious young winger, Arthur McGill a dependable, if unspectacular, young full-back.

Stuart Gregory slotted in for a long term as a second-rower, and perhaps the most significant development of all was the emergence of the Newcastle pocket dynamo John Hipwell as Test half-back.

Hipwell had been a member of the 1966-67 Wallabies to Britain as an 18-year-old under-

PETER JOHNSON . . . Australian record holder

83

study to Catchpole. As a protege of Cyril Burke, the champion Australian half-back of the forties and early fifties, Hipwell's development was well-chronicled, and there was never any real doubt he eventually would fit into the line of great scrum-base men with whom Australia had been blessed seemingly for generations.

His tour of Britain had done nothing to dispel that faith. It was not an easy job to shadow a master like Catchpole, but Hipwell did it as a youth with distinction. In fact, he played a good part of the tour with a broken fibula—a broken leg in laymen's terms—and won a reputation for toughness and durability to complement his skills.

Hipwell made the number one spot in Australian Rugby in unfortunate circumstances. Catchpole's Australians were hardly given a chance when they took on Lochore's All Blacks at the Sydney Cricket Ground in June, 1968. Yet this young and vibrant team gave a good account of itself before going down 27-11.

In the process one of the great international careers was brought to an end. In trying to haul him from a pile of players on the ground, the great New Zealand second-row forward Colin Meads tugged on the leg of Catchpole who was comprehensively trapped. The force of the resultant "tug of war" did horrendous damage to the muscles in his upper leg.

Much debate raged afterwards as to the circumstances of the injury, but as Catchpole hobbled about that night it quickly became clear a great era had come to an end.

In fact he was unable to play any Rugby at all for more than 18 months, and it was a reflection of his enormous courage and personal discipline that he fought back to play a couple more club seasons, albeit well below his old standard, but still well enough to set him a class above other Sydney half-backs.

Catchpole had been greatness itself.

It was a tough act for Hipwell to follow, but from the moment he darted over for a try in the early stages of the second international in Brisbane the following week, there was little doubt he would make it. In time, he turned out

RAY PRICE . . . a footballing genius [News Ltd.]

KEN CATCHPOLE . . . the world's greatest half back

to be one of the best, by a long chalk, of the past 10 years, topping his career by leading Australia to two Test wins against England in 1975, and on their successful tour of Britain the following summer. His entry to the Test scene was one of Australian Rugby's more spectacular triumphs, even though it ended in defeat. Ballymore Park in Brisbane is an arena which almost demands fervour above and beyond the ordinary.

Anybody who has been there for a match between NSW and Queensland, when the populace has been exhorted to come along and "Boo a blue at Ballymore", will testify to that. The fervour abounded that sunny afternoon in 1968 as the Australians, minus Catchpole and with Johnson their new captain, took the mighty All Blacks to the absolute brink.

It is worth noting here that Lochore's All Blacks, under the iron hand of coach Fred Allen, had passed undefeated through Britain the previous summer, and had set a standard of free-running Rugby which led many to assess

them as the best All Black team of all time. Such comparisons are probably odious, but the 1968 New Zealand team certainly was a very good one.

Australia got up to all manner of tricks in that second Test. Connor had played for years under Allen as half-back for Auckland through a successful run as New Zealand's Ranfurley Shield champions. He knew the All Black game backwards.

Conceding the fact his forwards could not command against such giants as Meads and Strachan, Tremain and Muller, he contrived a spoiling game of intriguing proportions.

The Wallabies played two-man and three-man lineouts, stood up in blanket defence to smother anything the All Blacks had, and simply wore them down by the most destructive defensive game an Australian team has ever mounted. Committed to a style that called for the backs to run, the All Blacks were totally flummoxed.

With a minute to go they trailed 14-18,

thanks largely to their own frustration and a flood of penalties against them which were duly goaled.

Then came a moment which history surely will never let go. The New Zealand centre Bill Davis stab kicked ahead with time running out. As he did so the Australian winger Alan Cardy impeded the progress of his rival Grahame Thorne, and almost simultaneously the Australian centre Barry Honan dived at the legs of the troublesome Davis.

The ball ran into in-goal and then dead, with the replacement Australian centre Alex Pope in hot pursuit.

Nobody really knew what was happening as the Brisbane referee Kevin Crowe ran to the posts and awarded New Zealand the penalty try, simply goaled, which gave the All Blacks victory by 19-18.

Meads was heard to mutter something like "the silly bastard's given them a penalty try", or so the legend goes, and the rampant Ballymore crowd was overcome by a deathly hush.

Crowe said later the try had been awarded against Honan's tackle on Davis. Subsequent film evidence proved the tackle quite legal, made while the ball was still with him. Pope probably would have got to the ball before anybody else anyway, or certainly the ball would have gone dead before any All Black got there.

KEN WRIGHT . . . mercurial   [News Ltd.]

From all angles, subsequent agreement was duly reached that the referee had erred. But 19-18 remained the score. Nevertheless, it was a turning point for Australia, and a good base on which the subsequent seasons could be attacked.

Through South Africa in 1969, under Davis, the team gathered new strengths.

Owen Butler, a Canberra second-rower who had played top level basketball and carried those leaping skills into his lineout play, was a definite acquisition.

And Roy Prosser developed solidly here too as a prop. Prosser had first won a chance with the Wallabies to New Zealand in 1962, but after several years in limbo he returned in 1966 and finally claimed a place of permanence in the Test side of 1968.

The South African tour introduced to international Rugby the bulky Kiama centre Geoff Shaw, a 20-year-old who went on to play a significant part in the development of Australia's image through the seventies. He finished up captain of Australia for much of the 1975-76 tour through Britain after the injury to Hipwell, and played a key role in almost every intervening series.

The Wallabies did not win a Test in South Africa in 1969. They might have won two but for elementary mistakes, the most chronic of Australia's international Rugby problems, and a lack of necessary bulk and expertise to compete in the heavyweight forward areas, particularly the scrum.

With these deficiencies in mind selectors maintained that team *in toto* for a Test against Scotland the following season. The Scots were a disappointing lot on tour, finding the shortness of their tour and the violent change in weather and ground conditions difficult to accommodate.

Their failings, though, could not detract from an Australian performance which blitzed them 23-3 at Sydney Cricket Ground. It had maturity about it, as was wont to be the case after the major tour of the year before.

Butler and Alan Skinner were dominant at the lineout, the centres Shaw and Stephen Knight were brutal in defence, crippling any attack the Scots thought they could muster.

[News Ltd.]
JOHN HIPWELL . . . tough act to follow Catchpole

ROY PROSSER ... sound tradesman [Sydney Sun]

In the end victory was total. "A team to match the great ones of the early sixties", reflected Johnson, whose return to the Test side at hooker had played no small part in the win.

The turnover in Wallaby teams is more extensive than most. By 1971 new strengths had arrived, but the hard road of the previous winters at least had provided a core better schooled in the tough ways of international forward play.

A troubled tour by a South African team led by Hannes Marais developed newcomers like Peter Sullivan, a rangy breakaway forward from the Gordon Club in Sydney, and Jeff McLean, whose great pace and goal-kicking skills proved useful for several years.

McLean continued a family Rugby lineage. His grandfather and three uncles had played for Australia, and subsequently his younger brother Paul did too, claiming distinction in Britain in 1975-76 as one of Australia's best post-war full-backs.

The South African side of that winter was one of their best. Frik du Preez, a giant second-rower who leapt like a gazelle at the lineout and ran like a cheetah in the open, was on his last tour. They had rock-hard strength in the forwards and pace and flair in the backs, and they overcame the troubles of a tour sadly afflicted by political demonstrations to score three Test wins.

By the French tour of the following November the Wallabies had gathered one exciting new ingredient. The previous winter Sydney selectors had plucked a flaxen-haired schoolboy from the ranks of Matraville High School and Randwick Club and played him full-back against Scotland. Two years later Russell Fairfax had made such an impact on the Rugby scene he took his place as a Wallaby at 19 and gave the team in France the spark they needed to turn their now-experienced forward base to profit.

Everything came right that day in Toulouse. For a while it seemed the French might live up to pre-match indications. They ran in a couple of quick tries, led 11-0 in seemingly no time, and ran with such dexterous imagination the Wallabies had trouble working out which way they were going, let alone keeping up.

But the centres Shaw and David L'Estrange turned the match with a couple of tackles. Their crashing defence was so sound in fact, particularly from Shaw, the Frenchmen ended up chucking the ball over their heads or running in circles rather than take the punishment.

L'Estrange picked up a gift intercept try just before half-time, and in the middle stages of the second half Cole swept in from the blind wing at a tight-head scrum heel, carved a gaping hole in the French defences to send L'Estrange across for his second try. The Wallabies trailed 10-11 when McLean took a long kick at penalty towards the end, piloting it over from a wide angle to the ecstatic delight of the Australians.

It was, in terms of the courage of its execution and the relative records of the two teams, a classic win.

Australia had at last developed forward power. Butler and Gregory gave good ball at the lineout, Prosser, Johnson and David Dunworth stood the pressure in the front-row and returned it. Fairfax played with subtle flair at five-eighth. Davis, Sullivan and Bob McLean were tireless in the back-row. McGill at full-back wore extensive pressure well, particularly in the dying moments.

It was the best peak Australia had achieved, probably since their triumphs against Wales and England on the Wallaby tour of 1966-67. The French did not like it.

Davis's nose was spread all over his face in one unseemly incident, and much foul play ruined the tone of the match. In the end the French captain Benoit Dauga refused to shake hands with Davis when the Australian captain offered commiserations leaving the field. Their pique could not alter the score.

In listing the best players through the 10-year period, Fairfax would probably beat McGill and Paul McLean for the full-back spot, the position he played in Britain in 1973. He had a touch of magic, a brilliant nose for attack, which covered occasional defensive and positional lapses.

John Cole and Laurie Monaghan would get my wing spots. Cole was in a class of his own through most of those 10 years. Others came and went. McLean did well, Rod Batterham was a class performer restricted by injury, Terry Forman a flyer on his day. But Monaghan had a stability and a flair something akin to Fairfax at times, and by 1976 he stood above his contemporaries.

The old pairing of Phil Smith and John Brass would get the centre votes. They had all the qualities, pace, imagination, defence and understanding and the shame is they did not have many more years together.

At five-eighth, the most electric of the period was the latest, Ken Wright, whose devastating play against England in 1975 brought a new dimension to Australian five-eighth play. He should have seen more action in Britain. John Ballesty was another outstanding five-eighth performer, without Wright's attacking brilliance.

Catchpole only fringed the area in question, so Hipwell takes the half-back spot.

Greg Davis would slot into one back-row place, though his poor handling skills would leave something of a question mark over him in the modern game. Ray Price, the dynamic flanker of Tests against the All Blacks in 1974 and England in 1975 would not be disputed for another flank role.

There were plenty of good ones. Barry McDonald, in flashes, Peter Sullivan, who went on to captain Australia, were extremely good. But Price captured the twin qualities of skill and toughness, and an enormous determination to win, that put him in a class of his own.

At No. 8 the latest of them, Mark Loane,

MARK LOANE . . . on verge of greatness

stands supreme. His strength and power in running, the raw aggressiveness of his game, established him as world-class through 1975 and 1976. Even the great Mervyn Davies conceded that.

Owen Butler and Stuart Gregory get my vote as the second row pair for their better performances, rather than an average of them all. France underlined their capabilities in 1971. They might not have always played to them, but as a pair they were more commanding than later campaigners, Reg Smith and Garrick Fay.

The pity of the decade, perhaps, is that a giant like Ross Teitzel, potentially the best second-rower of the period, could not see his way clear to continue playing, or that selectors prematurely discarded the talents of Peter Crittle, who played through the middle sixties.

By 1975 the science of scrummaging had been so expertly analysed that modern props would have to command an advantage against former props.

Tight head props offer a good selection. Roy Prosser was a sound tradesman, possessed

of mauling skills somewhat ahead of his time, Ron Graham of 1975 vintage a resolute performer.

But the pick of them, for sheer scrummaging strength and technique, was John Howard. His game overall perhaps did not match the skill of some others, but his scrummaging was without peer, and on the basis that the scrum dominates the modern game, he gets the vote.

Loose head has not been an Australian strong point.

Jim Roxburgh was a tireless worker, but far too light. Stuart Macdougall could be similarly described, for he lacked the real strength to survive. Perhaps the advantage of better skills in latter days give Victoria's John Meadows an advantage. He stands with the rest, anyway, with Peter Johnson commanding at hooker.

It has been a fluctuating period, beset with exalting peaks and depressing troughs. But through it all Australia has managed to hold its head reasonably high against some pretty hot opposition. Progress has been hard won.

GREG DAVIS . . . dynamic performer

[News Ltd.]

10 SOCCER

By TOM ANDERSON

TOM ANDERSON—Australia's leading Soccer writer writes for the "Sydney Daily Mirror", and played for Queens Park Rangers and Leyton Orient. He also represented Scotland as a youth and schoolboy and played in the first schoolboy international at Wembley against England. Migrated to Australia in 1962 and has since covered two Socceroo World Cup campaigns. He is also a wellknown TV Soccer commentator.

Over the last 10 years, Soccer has come-of-age in Australia and is now well on its way to becoming the country's leading winter sport.

In the past, it was usually scorned upon, regarded as the game played just by the migrants who flocked to these shores. But the game was plagued by bad administration and constant squabbles, making it a bit of a joke in the eyes of the sporting fraternity.

Not even the modern immortal dreamers among Soccermen could have imagined that the game could ever have reached the standard and popularity it enjoys today.

The man most responsible for changing the image and face of Soccer was the present President of the Australian Soccer Federation Sir Arthur George.

When he was appointed President in 1970, Sir Arthur set about the mammoth task of putting Soccer on the map with great distinction and dignity, not only in Australia, but in the eyes of the world. And this is exactly, what happened. The game has taken on a completely new image to become big business.

Under his leadership, sponsorship has been won, and through sponsorship, success has come. Now Soccer is a household word and indeed there are more youngsters playing the game in Australia than any other sport.

Of course, this has been helped by the fact that Soccer is the World Sport and the most skilful game of all. Over the past 10 years, two things have brought Soccer into prominence in the eyes of the sporting public.

The first was the Socceroos, as the national team, qualifying and playing in the 1974 World Cup finals in West Germany—the other the formation of the Philips National Soccer League of Australia in 1977.

Australia's first tilt to qualify for the World Cup finals started in 1965, when the national team met North Korea in Cambodia to determine who should go forward to represent Asia in the 1966 finals in England.

Two games had to be played in the sweltering heat of Phnom-Penh, against the then "mystery" team of North Korea.

The result was a near disaster and Australia, under coach Tiko Jelisavcic, went down 6-1 in the first game and lost 3-1 in the second, to give the North Koreans the honour of going to the finals with a 9-2 aggregate.

But Australia were not too dismayed. In 1969, they once again tried to win their way through to the World Cup finals in Mexico—this time in 1970. But problems arose when Australia was drawn in a sub-group for the preliminary rounds with South Korea, Japan and Rhodesia.

The preliminary games were to be staged in Seoul, Korea, and went ahead without Rhodesia, as the South Koreans would not allow the Rhodesians into the country. The Aussies won the series against South Korea and Japan, and had to travel to Lourenco Marques in Mozambique for a play-off against Rhodesia where they were successful.

Israel was the last hurdle in the final elimination battles scheduled for Tel Aviv. The Aussies lost 1-0 against the Israelis and in the return game in Sydney drew 1-1 for the Israelis to get through to Mexico. Once again the World Cup finals had eluded Australia!

Fortunes changed in 1973, when it came time to qualify for the 1974 World Cup finals in West Germany.

Under the leadership of coach Rale Rasic, the Socceroos went into this sortie more confident than ever before. ASF President Sir Arthur George acquired sponsorship for the World Cup venture, firmly propped up by $250,000.

ADRIAN ALSTON . . . winning goal to reach World Cup finals

[Anton Cermak]

The team worked diligently as never before and there was an air of confidence ringing round the Soccer halls of Australia. The national team also acquired a new name—The Socceroos, a name that was later to be heard all round the world.

In the first World Cup preliminary games the Socceroos accounted for New Zealand, Indonesia, Iraq and Iran and won their way through to the final elimination round against South Korea. Would it be third time lucky for the Aussies or would it be failure once again?

This final series was played on a home-and-away basis with the winner going through to Germany the following year.

In the first game at the Sydney Sports Ground, the Socceroos disappointed, slumping to a 0-0 draw. It was an unhappy party that left for Seoul for the return clash, obviously with the 1965 and 1969 failures firmly entrenched in their minds. However, after being two goals down in Seoul, the Socceroos fought back magnificently to force a 2-2 draw to earn a replay in Hong Kong three days later.

The date of the replay—November 13, 1973—was a night that will always be remembered by every Australian who was fortunate to be present in that Stadium in the Crown Colony.

This was the night when the Socceroos put it all together to turn in a performance that made every Australian in every part of the world proud of his Soccer team. And the big moment for the Socceroos came in the 60th minute of the game, when midfielder Ray Richards hit a free kick into the South Korean defence.

The ball reached wee Jimmy Rooney who carefully side-footed onto Jim Mackay who blasted it into the South Korean goal from 25 metres out.

At long last, Australia was through to a World Cup final series after eight, long years of failure and disappointment. That night Soccer did come-of-age in Australia. At long last the public realised we had players who could play the game.

However, there were still the doubters when the Socceroos left in all their glory for the finals in West Germany. The cynics predicted Australia would get her bottom well and truly spanked by the "big guns" from Europe and South America.

The Socceroos were drawn in Group 1 along with West Germany, East Germany and Chile.

The Australian party that left for the West Germany finals, by way of matches in Indonesia,

92

Israel and Switzerland was indeed a proud one:

Goalkeepers; Jack Reilly, Allan Maher, Jim Milisavljevic, Defenders; Doug Utjesenovic, Peter Wilson, Manfred Schaefer, Col Curran, Harry Williams, Ivo Rudic, John Watkiss, Midfielders; Ray Richards, Jim Mackay, Jimmy Rooney, John Warren, Dave Harding, Strikers; Atti Abonyi, Adrian Alston, Peter Ollerton, Maxie Tolson, Ernie Campbell, Branko Buljevic, Gary Manuel.

The official ASF delegation was Sir Arthur George (President), Tom Grimson (delegate), Brian Le Fevre (secretary), John Barclay (manager), Rale Rasic (coach), Les Scheinflug (assistant coach), Eric Worthington (technical adviser), Dr Brian Corrigan (team doctor) and Peter Van Rijn (physiotherapist).

The Press Corps — Tom Anderson (News Limited), Bill Allan (AAP), Martin Royal (ABC), Brian Mossop (Sydney Morning Herald) and David Jack (Sydney Sun).

The Socceroos first game was against East Germany at the Volksparkstadion in Hamburg on June 14. Naturally the side was a little nervous on their debut into the big-time, but performed in fine fashion to prove to the world they had something to offer International football.

The East Germans won 2-0, but the Aussies had gained respect with their display.

The second game was West Germany, who went on to become World Champions. The Socceroos again lost — this time 3-0. But again their performance was a good one and they came out of the clash covered in glory.

Let's face it, to go down 3-0 to the World Champions in their own backyard was not a bad effort from the lads from Down Under!

The third and last game of the series was against Chile at the Berlin Olympic Stadium. This time, the Socceroos drew 0-0 and with a bit of luck could easily have won the game.

So there it was — two respectable defeats and a worthy draw in the greatest sporting event in the world. Australian Soccer was on the way to big and better things.

Another first for Australian Soccer in this World Cup series, was the selection of referee Tony Boskovic to officiate. Boskovic became the first Australian referee to do so.

Sadly for Australian Soccer a poor overall display saw the Socceroos bundled unceremon-

[Anton Cermak]

PETER WILSON . . . Australian skipper for 1974 World Cup clash with West Germany

iously out of the 1978 World Cup, despite sound showings in the Inter-Continental tournament in July 1977 with Arsenal, Celtic and Red Star Belgrade.

On the club scene, 1977 will be remembered as the year of the Philips Soccer League of Australia and the time when Soccer was the first sport to go "national" in Australia. An Australia-

WORLD CUP . . . West Germany in control against Australia

wide Soccer competition had been the dream of many go-ahead club administrators for many years, but little or no action had been taken to get the project off the ground.

In stepped Sir Arthur George with the backing of Philips Industries — and the competition was underway.

Fourteen teams were chosen — St George, Eastern Suburbs Hakoah, Western Suburbs, Sydney Olympic and Marconi from Sydney, South Melbourne, Footscray, Fitzroy and Mooroolbark from Melbourne, Brisbane Lions and Brisbane City from Brisbane, Canberra City from the ACT and Adelaide City and West Adelaide from Adelaide.

The new venture caught the imagination of the sporting public and it pumped new life into the flagging spectacle of Australian club Soccer. Attendances spiralled and the standard of play improved beyond all expectations.

Coaches and players realised Soccer in Australia had at long last become big business and a complete professional attitude was need-

ed to compete successfully with the ambitious clubs in the new competition.

The coming of the PSL, as the competition was named, also brought star guest players to Australia during the European off-season — England and Arsenal's star Malcolm "Supermac" Macdonald with South Melbourne, Derby County's Charlie George to St George, Bologna's Roberto Vieri to Marconi, Tottenham Hotspur's Ian Moores to Western Suburbs, and Dundee's Billy Pirie to Sydney Olympic.

These guest players helped to add glamour to the game and attract more fans.

The PSL also gave many young junior players something to aim at with a target for the future. In the not-too-distant future, many PSL clubs intend going full-time professional on the same basis as the top professional clubs in Europe and South America. Another pleasing factor and a winning one at that is that the PSL eliminated much of the controversy that went hand-in-hand with Soccer administration in the past. Petty squabbles between PSL admin-

RALE RASIC . . . matchwinning coach against Indonesia 1973

[Anton Cermak]

[Anton Cermak]

PETER OLLERTON . . . a header against Red Star Belgrade 1977

istrators do not hit the headlines of the sporting pages as was the blight of Soccer not so many years ago.

The PSL, in fact, has been the saviour of club Soccer in Australia and it should continue to be successful for years to come. During the last 10 years, there have been some very talented and fine players come into prominence in Australia—stars within their own right who do credit to the game, and have done much to spread its popularity.

Present Australian team captain Peter Wilson is without doubt the greatest captain the country has ever had. Wilson captained the team in West Germany with the big defender believing in the theory one must lead by example.

Former Australian captain John Warren is another player whose name is synonymous with all that is good in the game. Warren was awarded an M.B.E. for his services to Soccer and is the perfect example of the local boy making good.

Warren reached the top through dedication and hard work and is currently applying the same principles in his new coaching career with PSL club Canberra City.

Talent is something that can't be hidden and when Socceroo midfielder Jimmy Rooney plays it's "talent unlimited". Rooney is a player who knows nothing less than giving 100 percent and has a heart as big as his body!

When top grade players are mentioned, the name Adrian Alston must not be omitted,

[Anton Cermak]

ATTI ABONYI . . . contests for possession in Australia-Iran World Cup qualifying round

PETER OLLERTON . . . in action for Australia against Iran

[Anton Cermak]

as Alston was one of the big successes in the 1974 World Cup finals. After West Germany, Alston was transferred to Luton Town in England, from his Australian club Safeway United. Now he is starring in America with the Tampa Bay Rowdies and is a young man who has made his profession pay.

They are just four of the many fine players who have been seen in action in Australia over the past 10 years—players who have blazed the trail for the young stars of the future.

To select the best Australian team over the past 10 years would be difficult, as Soccer has improved so much during the last 12 months alone. Despite that, here is my selection of the best team of the decade.

In goals three players came into the reckoning, South Melbourne's 1974 Socceroo Jack Reilly, Ron Corry who played in the 1969 World Cup elimination series and present national team goalkeeper Allan Maher.

I would have to plump for Reilly. The big fellow was brilliant at his peak and had all the attributes that it takes to make a top class custodian.

In defence, two players are automatic choices—Peter Wilson and John Watkiss in the central stopper positions. Both are giants of men and at their peak would be immovable and impassable barriers.

There are a number of contenders for the fullback positions such as George Harris, Harry Williams, Stan Ackerley, Col Curran, George Keith and Doug Utjesenovic. All are fine players with proud records.

I would go for Curran and Williams. They have proved to be two of the fastest and best attacking fullbacks Australia has ever produced.

Midfield is another department where Australia has enjoyed a wealth of talent over the years, with such great performers as John Warren, Jim Mackay, Jimmy Rooney, Ray Richards, Manfred Schaefer to name a few. After due consideration I rate the combination of Jimmy Rooney, Ray Richards and Jim Mackay the best.

When it comes to strikers, players of the calibre of Ray Baartz, Tommy McColl, Adrian Alston, John Kosmina, Atti Abonyi, Peter Ollerton and Branko Buljevic have to be considered. In this department where speed, shoot-

[Anton Cermak]

JOHN KOSMINA . . . in action for Australia against South Korea during 1977 World Cup qualifying rounds

[Anton Cermak]

JOHN KOSMINA . . . heading towards goal in Philips League clash between West Adelaide and Canberra City

ing power and goals count, I go for Alston, Baartz and Kosmina.

So my Australian all-Star team over the past 10 years would be (in 4-3-3 formation)— Goalkeeper; Jack Reilly; Defence; Col Curran, Peter Wilson, John Watkiss, Harry Williams; Midfield; Jimmy Rooney, Ray Richards, Jim Mackay and Strikers; Adrian Alston, Ray Baartz and John Kosmina.

There have been a number of top class coaches in action who have proved their worth in the only manner a fine coach can – by producing results.

On the national level, Jim Shoulder, Rale Rasic, Joe Venglos, and Joe Vlasits are all men with great ability. Although their basic coaching fundamentals are the same, each individual has his own methods of getting the message across to his players.

Rasic did a magnificent job in winning a berth to West Germany in 1974 when the odds seemed stacked against him.

Shoulder used an entirely different approach but his failure to reach the World Cup finals led to his resignation.

One of the biggest drawbacks in Soccer in Australia over the past decade has been the lack of coaches to coach juniors and youth sides.

But once again the ASF have solved the problem and progress has been made since Englishman Eric Worthington was appointed National Director of Coaching for Australia in 1973.

Worthington has installed full-time regional Directors of Coaching in every State throughout the Commonwealth. These State Directors now produce coaches qualified to look after the needs of the thousands of kids thirsty for knowledge of the finer points of the game.

If Soccer is to progress as quickly in the coming 10 years as it has in the last, then coaching will play a big part in this development.

All in all it has been a great period for Soccer in Australia, especially with the International breakthrough. However there is still a long way to go and much hard work to be done to reach the pinnacle of success.

There will be pitfalls in the road ahead, but with clear thinking and commonsense these pitfalls can be overcome. Soccer is THE world game and that is why it will eventually become Australia's major sport — it's as simple as that!

11 ATHLETICS

By JIM WEBSTER

JIM WEBSTER has regularly covered Olympic and Commonwealth Games for the "Sydney Morning Herald" as well as being the paper's top Golf and Rugby Union writer for many years.

Winning at the Olympic Games is the only way success is judged in track and field.

That's not to say it is entirely fair, but the Olympics is the only occasion when all the best athletes of the world are together and competing under identical circumstances; none has an advantage over any other in any shape or form.

This is the occasion when the pressure is greatest, the competition fiercest—and the reward the greatest.

To be an Olympic champion is everything. To be a world record-breaker, but unable to win at the Olympics, is not nearly the same.

Therefore, my list of Australia's best track and field competitors over the past decade must begin with our two gold medal winners of that period, Maureen Caird and Ralph Doubell. Each won their medals at the 1968 games in Mexico City. Maureen Caird, who could forget her? She had that gay, carefree, happy-go-lucky way where nothing seemed to bother her. Life was to be enjoyed. She loved riding her pony and playing her guitar.

Athletics never seemed to consume Maureen like other champions. She had a great natural talent and what she achieved was a manifestation of this emerging talent, rather than that which comes from long work.

Maureen went to Mexico City, only as Australia's second hurdle to Pam Kilborn, but at a pre-Games meeting there she skipped over the 80 metres hurdles in 10.4 sec. only 0.1 sec. outside the world record—and 0.2 sec. faster than she had ever run before.

Suddenly Maureen was a chance, a big chance for the gold medal. Came the fateful day and Maureen showed under that happy disposition of hers beat the heart of a champion, for she won the final from Miss Kilborn and Taiwanese Chi Chen and equalled the world record at 10.3 sec.

At 17 years and just a few weeks, she became the youngest track and field champion in Olympic history.

It was the first time she had ever beaten Miss Kilborn, who at 29, had suddenly seen her final chance of Olympic glory blown away.

Some time later Miss Kilborn was credited with some criticism of Miss Caird's ability, but the youngster, wise beyond her years, made the most pertinent of comments—"I don't care what she says about my ability, she couldn't beat me the day it really mattered".

Doubell's victory in the 800 metres final was greeted at home with incredulity. Few people had ever heard of him. He was much better known in the United States where he had a highly successful stint at the indoor meetings leading up to the games, winning six times as many starts.

In the final Doubell was a good seven metres behind at the 400-metre mark, but staged an extraordinary finish to outrun Kenyan Wilson Kiprugut over the final 80 metres.

He had planned to be a long way back, and then finish strongly.

It had to do with a physiological theory that a runner does not incur an oxygen debt by starting slowly at Mexico City's 7,000-feet altitude. Here was proof of its truth.

To add to the splendour of the moment, Doubell's time of 1 min. 44.3 sec. equalled the world record set by New Zealander, Peter Snell, in 1962 and, as a matter of interest, was 26.7 sec. faster than that of the last Aussie to win this event, Edwin Flack, in 1896.

So Doubell, 23, an employment officer from Melbourne, who worked at the time for the same company as Herb Elliott, suddenly went from being a nobody in Australia to a somebody, all in the space of just over 100 seconds. The pity was more was not seen of Doubell afterwards.

So Caird and Doubell were the best, make no mistake about that, for they were the only ones to produce the goods at the Olympics. Yet they were not nearly as well known as another couple, Ron Clarke and Raelene Boyle.

Neither Clarke nor Miss Boyle were champions in the sense they succeeded at the Olympics, but each had great qualities.

Clarke was a great runner, Miss Boyle a great competitor.

Indeed Clarke's only equals in the 100-year history of organised distance running are probably Paave Nurmi, Emil Zatopek and Vladimir Kuts.

He set 18 world records, from two miles to 20,000 metres—more than any athlete.

The magnitude of Clarke's running tends to be obscured by his non-success at the most important times, but his strength of purpose,

RALPH DOUBELL . . . defeating Wilson Kiprugut to win the 800 metres gold medal at the Mexico Olympics
[News Ltd.]

[News Ltd.]
RON CLARKE . . . renowned world record breaker, no gold

his humility, his courage, the amount he trained and the absolute ruthlessness of his running set him aside from all other athletes in the four years from the end of 1963, when he was at his very zenith.

So many of his great times were executed in lonely majestic splendour, with Clarke against the clock and no mortal to be seen.

His greatest world record?

The great six miles/10,000 metres double in Oslo in July, 1965 when he ran 26 min. 47 sec. and 27 min 39.4 sec. in the same race stands as a beacon in distance running.

Also, let it not be forgotten, that Clarke, for all his defeats in major championships, can boast a very impressive record of victories against his most serious rivals.

Clarke beat Kip Keino in 10 of the 19 occasions on which they met over eight years, and also held marked superiority over Olympic champions, Mohammed Gamoudi (7-5), Billy Mills (6-1), Gaston Roelants (10-0) and Naftali Temu (9-3). Only Michel Jazy and Jean Wadoux, of France, and Bob Schul and George Young, of the United States, reversed the trend.

The pity of Clarke is that the greatest race he ever ran was one in which he came sixth — the 10,000 metres final at the same Olympics where Doubell and Miss Caird won.

Clarke went to Mexico City having reshaped the world's long distance records, but having failed to win an Olympic or even a Commonwealth Games gold medal.

This was his last Olympics and he had prepared for it with the dedication of a person in a religious order. He was a pinnacle of fitness.

But, we asked, would there be enough oxygen up there in that city in the clouds to drag into his lungs? Enough to keep his legs pounding, instead of reeling?

His main rivals were all "high livers". They came from an altitude similar to that of Mexico City. Clarke knew he would be conceding them yards start because of their altitude familiarity.

The afternoon proved tragic.

Clarke was right up with them, with two of the torturous 25 laps remaining, but suddenly began fading fast. They swept by him.

The race was won by Naftali Temu, the long legged Kisli tribesman from the high country of Kenya. He beat Ethiopian, Mamo Wolde — who was to win the 1972 Olympic marathon — after the two of them had staged the most unbelievable fight over the last lap.

Third was Mohammed Gamoudi, of Tunisia, a silver medallist ahead of Clarke in the same event in Tokyo. Just as had been predicted, the men from the mountains had triumphed.

Clarke came in sixth — distressed, ashenfaced and tottering. He fell flat on his stomach on the grassed centre area just a moment after dragging himself over the line.

Clarke whiffed 60 litres of oxygen in the 10 minutes before he came to. "He just ran beyond his capabilities", Australian team medical officer, Dr. Brian Corrigan, explained later.

"The idea was for him to run at a steady rate early and then cover the last four laps much quicker. But in the last two laps he was in trouble. He got a sense of tiredness and weakness.

"In the last lap he found severe difficulties. His vision was affected and his concentration

RAELENE BOYLE . . . the 200 metres gold at Christchurch with Denise Robertson taking the silver   [News Ltd.]

Pole vaulting . . . split second timing essential

wandered. Anybody else would have given up, but he kept going.

"And because he kept going he had a circulatory collapse. When I reached him he was ashen-faced and completely unconscious. His heart was beating irregularly. There was just not enough oxygen for him at this level. He ran past the limits of endurance".

Ironically, in his greatest race, he wasn't beaten by other mortals. His place of birth had dealt him the most savage blow of all.

Raelene Boyle, like Clarke, was never an Olympic champion, but she went nearer, more often, to being one than probably any sports competitor at the Olympics.

Raelene was a 17-year-old schoolgirl at Mexico City, and not very well-known. In the 100 metre final, with 20 metres left, Miss Boyle was in third place, but was mowed down in the last few metres and beaten for the bronze medal by a whisker.

She was officially told she was third and, soon after, told she had, in fact, finished only fourth.

That made her ever so determined to win a medal in the 200 metres —and she did. The final was won by Poland's great Irena Szewinska, in a world record of 22.5 sec. with Miss Boyle second and another Australian, Jenny Lamy, third.

That was the start of Raelene's marvellously promising career. It seemed she would

be at the very peak of it in four years time at the Munich Olympics and there would be no way of stopping her winning at least one, and most likely both sprint finals.

In between time were the 1970 Commonwealth Games in Edinburgh, and predictably Raelene won both sprints there. So Munich, more so than ever, looked to be waiting for Raelene.

When those Olympics did come round, she was 21-years-of-age, bouncing fit and with a continuous pattern of fast times leading up to the Games. But one thing she never counted on was Renate Stecher, of East Germany.

A gentle person by nature, Miss Stecher nevertheless had a build that would not be misplaced among a gang of waterside workers. She beat Miss Boyle in both finals.

Of the many times I have seen the Australian girl run, they were her two best races. She had never run better. Up on her toes, beautifully balanced as always, her blonde hair streaming out behind her, she was really motoring. It didn't happen very often during her long career at the top, but on that day, that one vital never-to-return day, there was someone faster.

And, I say unequivocally, if Misses Stecher and Boyle ran against each other on 100 occasions, when each was able to produce her supreme effort, the East German would win every time. She was just slightly better than Miss Boyle ever was.

Raelene had an extended career for a sprinter, for she continued on to win the sprint double again at the Christchurch Commonwealth Games in 1974 and then went to her third Olympics at Montreal in 1976.

That was disastrous.

Raelene's best was behind her, but with three Olympic silver medals it was worth one final chance for a gold. When Raelene ran fourth in the 100 metres final, the writing was on the wall.

She could not have won the 200 metres— always her best event—unless she did better than she had in the shorter race.

Yet she never did make that 200 metres final.

Raelene had a break ruled against her in a semifinal because of movement of her shoulders and then, quite inexplicably, ran out of the

Baton changing . . . can win or lose medals

blocks too soon at the next attempt at a start and was automatically disqualified.

Why she would go out too soon the second time is unfathomable. She was fast enough to give the others a start, and catch them.

The answer lies buried somewhere in Raelene's subconscious. She doesn't rightly know.

She says she was flustered after getting the first break. Flustered? After all those years of top competition?

I have always felt that subconsciously Raelene knew she was not going to win the final and here, after one break, was the opportunity on a platter to avoid the pending defeat.

I stress I do not feel Raelene consciously broke the second time, rather her subconscious had taken over.

Raelene was never the number one choice of Australian officials on the popularity chart. Why? I don't know, other than the fact she was a tomboy by nature. But I do not know of any particular incident which deserved their ire.

But come the Pacific Conference Games in 1977 and Raelene was left out of the Australian team after being beaten into third place in the trials over 100 m — and not contesting the 200. She should not have been omitted from the big time . . . there has never been a greater competitor in Australian track and field.

Three Australian world record-holders who never received the national recognition of Miss Boyle, who had never held a world record, were steeplechaser Kerry O'Brien, marathon runner Derek Clayton, and hurdler, Pam Kilborn.

The great pity about both men was that, like Clarke, they were unable to win a gold medal in an Olympic or Commonwealth Games.

O'Brien only just missed a medal at the 1968 Mexico City Olympics. He was an arm's length from one — being that far behind American, George Young, who was third.

With 150 metres left, Young and O'Brien were leading the race, but O'Brien made a "botch" of the last water jump.

The "kick" of the Kenyan pair, Amos Biwott and Benjamin Kogo, took them past O'Brien and then Young, too, could not match their stamina.

KERRY O'BRIEN . . . missed the gold [News Ltd.]

O'Brien was so upset at missing a medal that he ran full pelt from the stadium, three miles back to the Olympic village.

O'Brien was still to reach his peak. In July 1970 in Berlin he ran a world record of 8 min. 22 sec. It was a good world record too, for it lasted till Anders Garderud, of Sweden, ran 8 min. 20.8 sec. in Helsinki, a little over two years later.

At the Commonwealth Games in Edinburgh, shortly afterwards, O'Brien, as the new world record-breaker, was hot favourite to win.

It was his monumental chance for a. gold medal — if only at the Commonwealth level.

Alas, it was not to be, for O'Brien fell in the very last stages of the race and the event was won by his countryman, Tony Manning — a quiet, smiling postal worker who never had O'Brien's skill but, nevertheless, had the heart of a lion.

He always ran on legs of determination and that afternoon, when O'Brien came a cropper, nobody had the speed to catch him.

There is no official world record for the marathon, because each course, though over the standard 26 miles and 385 yards, varies in its composition.

But in May 1969 in Antwerp, Clayton ran an unofficial world record for this hardest of all events when he clocked 2 hr. 8 min. 33.6 sec. Here again was a case of the best unfortunately not being able to win when the best were against him — and the world was watching.

At the 1968 Mexico City Olympics, Clayton was never too far behind but came in seventh — exhausted. In that same race John Farrington, although racked by stomach cramp after the first 15 of the 42 kilometres, completed the torture in 43rd place.

The Munich Olympics four years later was worse for Clayton. He finished 13th, wobbling like a drunk. He had no excuses.

"I'm glad it's over," he said, "I'll give it away now. There are other things in life — I think I'll play golf".

I made mention of Miss Kilborn earlier in dealing with Miss Caird. She was a wonderfully-talented athlete, for not only did she once hold the world record for the 80 metres hurdles, but also the 200 metres hurdles.

And she was a long jumper, a pentathlon competitor and a sprinter of exceptional class. At varying times she represented Australia in each of these disciplines.

Because of her versatility, Miss Kilborn won many national and international honours, but the Olympic gold medal, to which she had great claims, eluded her on the day.

Those I have discussed to this point have been the best of the Australians over the past decade, but that is by no means the end of the Australians who made the world's all-time list.

Australia has always been short of men who could skip over 100 metres in fairly quick time, but we have had an outstanding 200 metres runner in recent years in Peter Norman.

Norman had a peculiarity in his running I don't think I've ever seen before. For about 120 metres he ran without any great speed at all; inevitably he was still somewhere in the middle of the field.

Then . . . whoosh! away he'd go.

Suddenly he developed a turn of speed for those last 80 metres, the likes of which I've never seen before.

I clearly remember warning American, John Carlos, one of the big tips for the 200 metres at the 1968 Mexico City Olympics, about the way Norman unwound at the end of a race. The advice fell on deaf ears.

In the final, the great American runner, Tommie Smith, reduced his own world record to a phenomenal 19.8 sec. Carlos was watching Smith finishing ahead of him when Norman, in a flash, appeared from nowhere on the other side of Carlos to snatch second place in 20 sec.

That made him the world's fastest white man.

Peter Fitzgerald was a more recent sprinter of some class. Australia has continued to turn out good 1,500-metre runners since Herb Elliott; for the last few years there have been Chris Fisher, Graham Crouch and Ken Hall.

Besides Clarke, the best of our other distance runners, Tony Benson, Dave Fitzsimons, Chris Wardlaw, Bill Scott, David Chettle, Farrington and Clayton have all been highly-respected throughout the world.

Only recently have we had some good 110-metre hurdlers in Warren Parr, Max Binnington, the unhappy soul who thought he heard the recall gun in his heat at the Montreal Olympics and stopped running, and Vin Plant.

In the 400 metres hurdles, Gary Knoke's 49.3 sec. put him in the first 25 in the world.

High jump has been a strong point with Australia for sometime and Peter Boyce, Tony Sneazwell and Lawrie Peckham, all jumping higher than 7 ft. 2 in.

Don Baird in the pole vault and Peter Farmer in the hammer-throw have both made their marks in the United States, where they are living. Allen Crawley and Murray Tolbert were outstanding long jumpers, and Tolbert's omission from the team for Munich after jumping 26 ft 9½ in. with five jumps over 26 feet, cannot be explained.

Phil May was a consistently-outstanding triple jumper and might have gone to the very top, but for a serious foot injury. He always had a great rival in national domestic competitions in Nick McGrath, undoubtedly the smallest competitor of world class in the time he was competing.

[News Ltd.]
DEREK CLAYTON . . . leading the 1969 British marathon

The Montreal Olympics in 1976 saw the emergence of an exciting young runner in Rick Mitchell, who improved with each race at the Games till he made the 400 metres final. On him rest great hopes for the future.

Australia's women athletes have always been far stronger than the men by world standards. Sprinting has been their great forte, with Miss Boyle, Dianne Burge, Jenny Lamy, who picked up the bronze medal behind Miss Boyle in the 200 metres final in Mexico City, and Denise Robertson. All were world ranked.

A remarkable feature about Miss Boyle is the length of time she has remained at the top, for she won her first Olympic silver medal in 1968 at 17 and now, nearly 10 years later, is still among the fastest women in the world.

Middle distance running among the girls has also been a strong point over the period in review.

Judy Pollock, unkindly dubbed the "gal-

[News Ltd.]

PETER NORMAN . . . the silver medal in the 1968 Olympic 200 metres

PETER FARMER . . . local competition lacking

loping grandma", was a gentle person, but a quite determined competitor who ran more on will-power than God-given speed.

She won an Olympic bronze medal behind Betty Cuthbert in the 400 metres at Tokyo in 1964, set world records for 440 yards (52.4 sec.) in Perth in 1965 and 880 yards (2 min. 2 sec.) in Stockholm in 1967, and with two children and at 36 years of age ended her career at the 1976 Montreal Olympics.

Charlene Rendina was also a magnificent middle distance runner. Though she never went to an Olympics, the most gifted of our field

games competitors was javelin thrower, Petra Rivers, who had more ability than many who have been awarded that honour.

The advent of the KB Games should enhance performances over the next 10 years. The brewing company is to be congratulated for their foresight through the individual efforts of former champion hurdler, Ken Elphick who put the concept together. Sponsorship such as KB's gives athletes world class competition in their own season as vital preparation for Olympic and Commonwealth Games.

12 SWIMMING
By DICK TUCKER

DICK TUCKER is one of Sydney's leading sports writers who has specialised in swimming, football and cricket in 20 years of covering international events at home and overseas for the "Sydney Daily Mirror".

The demise of Australian swimming at Montreal was as predictable as it was shattering. It had been tottering for the last 10 years, but finally the buoys that have kept it afloat for so long collapsed.

In other words there was no one at Montreal that could match the epic deeds of their immediate predecessors—Michael Wenden, Shane Gould, Karen Moras, Lyn McClements, Beverley Whitfield and Gail Neal.

Steve Holland and Jenny Turrall were the main hopes, but Holland couldn't outstay the Americans and Jenny lost the battle with her weight. The net result was that Holland's third in the 1500 m freestyle was the only medal gained by our 28 swimmers—the worst result for Australia this century at an Olympic Games.

It was a sad and humiliating occasion for those who remembered vividly the wonderful successes of the middle 50s and the early 60s.

Champions like Murray Rose, Jon Henricks, John Devitt, Lorraine Crapp, Dawn Fraser, David Thiele, the Konrads, John and Ilsa, Kevin Berry and Bob Windle who carried us through to 1964.

By 1967 new stars were emerging notably Wenden, a young man of tremendous dedication and single mindedness who had his first taste of international competition in the 1966 Commonwealth Games, at Kingston, Jamaica.

He promptly gave notice of his marvellous potential by capturing the freestyle sprint, a title he retained at Edinburgh in 1970 and again at Christchurch in 1974 before he finally retired.

With him at Kingston were a number of world record holders including Kathy Wainwright, a super distance swimmer who like Karen Moras a few years later was unfortunate to reach her peak during a Commonwealth Games year rather than the Olympics.

Also there was Peter Reynolds, a class backstroker and in world class in freestyle too; Olympic breaststroke champion Ian O'Brien, sprinter Dave Dickson and Olympic 1500 m champion Bob Windle, all of whom like Wainwright were on the way out.

So it was left to Wenden to become the key man as Australia prepared for Mexico City, hoping rather than expecting we might be fortunate to match the 1964 efforts in Tokyo of four golds won by Fraser, Berry, O'Brien and Windle—one less than Rome in 1960 with Devitt, Rose, Konrads, Thiele and Fraser. The peak was at Melbourne in 1956 when Fraser, Henricks, Rose, Theile, Crapp and the two relay teams grabbed eight golds between them.

But no one, except Wenden himself, expected to pull off the sprint double at Mexico against the crack American team.

"I set my heart on winning gold in the 100 and 200 only two weeks before the events," recalls Wenden, now one of the bright young men in the marketing division of the Commonwealth Bank in Sydney. "I always adopted the same approach about my swimming.

"At the outset I would be content to make the final. As I became better in training I would think I would be pleased to win a bronze. Then as was the case at Mexico I suddenly knew I could win."

Wenden is totally realistic about Australia's swimming debacle.

"For years it has been bound to happen," he said. "But until Montreal we've always been fortunate to have a couple of swimmers to rise to the occasion so that the overall picture looked far healthier than it really was. It all created an entirely false impression that made last year's failure all the more dramatic.

"Simply, our complacency was finally blasted wide open."

MIKE WENDEN . . . captured gold in the men's 100 metres at the 1970 Commonwealth Games at Edinburgh

Despite his Mexico City triumphs, Wenden ranks his third in the 100 m freestyle at the first world championships in Belgrade in 1973 as the high point of his career.

"I had something to prove then," he said. "Officials here, even an Australian selector, had told me two years before that I should give it away and let some younger swimmer have a go.

"It was a tremendously tough period. I was finishing my last year at University for my economics degree and my wife Narelle had just had our second daughter. I trained myself, but it made it all so much more difficult and I never really did enough. There just wasn't time."

Yet in the light of future performances it took the ultimate in super swimmers to beat Wenden. He was American Jim Montgomery who at Montreal became the fastest man in the world in the water by smashing the 50-sec barrier for the sprint.

Five years earlier at Mexico it was Wenden who had had the last laugh.

To win the 100 m he powered his way past the joint world record holders Zac Zorn and Ken Walsh and over the 200 m he literally knocked all the stuffing out of cocky Don Schollander, hot favourite for the event.

For a long time afterwards the American lay gasping for breath on the floor of the dressing room completely exhausted by Wenden's scorching pace in the rarefied conditions.

Australia's only other swimming gold medal at Mexico went to Lyn McClements in the 100 m butterfly. And as Wenden puts it, it was a "real con job."

He and manager Stuart Alldritt were only some of those who convinced the tall West Australian lass she could win.

Australia also picked up silver medals with Greg Rogers, Graham White, Windle and Wenden in the four by 200 m freestyle relay and in the women's four by 100 m medley relay with Lynne Watson, Judy Playfair, Judy Steinbeck and McClements. Three bronze came with Moras in the 400 m freestyle; Greg Brough, 1500 m and the men's four by 100 m relay with Rogers, Robert Cusack, Windle and Wenden.

By the time he had finished his career at Christchurch, Wenden had amassed two gold, a silver and a bronze at the Olympics and nine golds, two silver and a bronze at Commonwealth Games.

Ironically, on the couple of occasions he was eclipsed internationally, other Australians produced superb performances — Shane Gould, Beverley Whitfield and Gail Neal at Munich in 1972 and Holland in Belgrade a year later.

Shane was magnificent, grabbing three gold medals in the 200 m and 400 m freestyle and the 200 m medley, as well as a silver in the 800 m freestyle and a bronze in the 100 m freestyle — to complete the most dominant one-woman performance in the history of Olympic swimming.

"For a combination of endurance, application and adaptability Shane was amazing," was the tribute of Wenden who finished fourth and fifth defending his two titles.

Of Holland he said: "He was quite incredible. In a series of swims he slashed nearly three-quarters of a minute off the 1500 m world record just when experts thought no one would ever break the 16-minute barrier".

Shane first gave notice of her wonderful

ability in 1968. I remember it well as I was in Brisbane covering the Australian team settling in at their Scarborough camp for training for Mexico.

She clocked a 62-plus for the 100 m freestyle—the fastest ever by an Australian 12-year-old. By 1970 the rave notices were coming thick and fast. No sooner had Karen Moras captured the freestyle treble at the Edinburgh Commonwealth Games than Shane, who was then being trained in Sydney by Forbes Carlile, was being hailed as her successor.

She rewrote the Australian record book.

Not for 50 years, in the days of Fanny Durack, had one person emerged so supreme.

It was an indication of things to come later in the year at Munich where she set herself a Herculean task of capturing five individual gold medals—plus the relays. It involved 12 swims in nine days, a colossal impost for a 16-year-old girl, but she breezed through her gruelling itinerary even though she was beaten in a couple of events.

Arguably, for sheer sustained power, her 400 m swim was the best. And as a pointer to the future her 200 m medley victory was intriguing.

KAREN MORAS ... reached peak for Commonwealth Games

SHANE GOULD . . . powers her way to another title

Finishing close behind her on an outside lane was a young East German lass called Kornelia Ender who was to succeed her as swim queen, four years later at Montreal.

Without detracting from Shane's stunning efforts, the triumphs of Beverley Whitfield in the 200 m breaststroke and Gail Neal in the 400 m medley had more appeal because they were so unexpected. Beverley was rated some chance on times, but Gail wasn't really considered.

Australia's sixth swimming gold medal in the 400 m freestyle, was achieved by default when Brad Cooper was belatedly awarded it after America's Rick Demont was found to have been taking a banned drug for asthma. It was a sour way to win a gold medal even though Cooper was a great swimmer who never quite reached the dizzy heights expected of him.

The other medalists were Graham Windeatt (silver, 1500 m) and Bev Whitfield (bronze, 100 m breaststroke).

The following year at Belgrade in the world titles Cooper sacrificed his own winning chances to become the pacemaker for Holland in his phenomenal 1500 m success—perhaps the most extraordinary international swimming event of all time.

Holland came onto the scene like a whirl-wind, chopping great hunks off the 1500 m mark every time he set himself. Just before he left for Belgrade he lowered the standard by an astonishing 14.8 secs.

He was only 15 and competing in his first major international meet. Against him was Demont, a seasoned campaigner and a superb judge of pace who earlier in the championships had become the first to ever shatter the four minute barrier for 400 m. The luckless Cooper was second, also ducking under four minutes.

The 1500 m was a thriller right from the start with the Australians outfoxing Demont in much the same way as the Americans were to do to "Superfish" at Montreal.

At the 200 m mark Demont didn't know whom to trail, pacesetter Cooper, whom he knew, or the unknown Holland. He chose Cooper and it was to prove his undoing.

Holland moved to the lead at the 500 m and thereafter opened the gap on Cooper and Demont by a second a 100 m. Holland went through the 800 m in a world record 8 min 16.27 secs.

At one stage he was nearly 5 sec in front of the American. Although Demont surged back, he couldn't catch the Brisbane schoolboy who sprinted to the finish.

To everyone's amazement Holland tum-

STEVE HOLLAND . . . an unassuming champion

bled and spurted off again with Demont in hot pursuit. Amid the roar of the crowd they raced another two laps before they finally pulled up. The rivals explained later that they were so engrossed in their personal tussle they failed to hear the signal for 100 m to go.

Holland's time was a world record 15 min 31.85 sec with Cooper third in a personal best 15 min 45.04 sec—better than the winning time in Munich.

One of the most fascinating features of the incredible race was that Holland's laps were so evenly timed that any eight consecutive 100 m would have constituted a world record for the 800 m. The next Australian to take the swimming world by storm was Sydney schoolgirl Jenny Turrall who became our lone gold medalist at the second world championships in Cali, Columbia in 1975.

Like Holland, she was 15 and had to contend with vastly experienced Americans Heather Greenwood and Shirley Babashoff in the 800 m event. Greenwood tried to steal the race with a fast early pace, but it proved to be perfect

BRAD COOPER . . . a gold medal in the men's 400 metres freestyle at the Munich Olympics

for Jenny who was near the rear of the field for the first 200 m.

At the 400 m mark Greenwood was still three seconds ahead of the Australian, but by 600 m Jenny had hit the front and there was no stopping her even though her time of 8 min 44.75 sec failed by 1.27 sec to break her own world mark established in London earlier in the year. Her 100 m times were remarkably consistent, averaging 65.6 sec with a variation of only 0.2 sec.

Afterwards, in paying high tribute to his star pupil, Forbes Carlile sounded an ominous warning.

"I've never seen a more evenly swum distance event," he said. "There is no doubt if she had been pressed she would have broken her world record. But this can wait, although a lot depends now on Jenny's motivation and continued enthusiasm, and most important whether she can control her eating and maintain her streamlined shape.

"What happens out of the water around the family meal table will be very important to Jenny and her prospects at Montreal."

Unfortunately Carlile's worst fears became a reality and Jenny finished a most disappointing eighth in the 800 m final at the Olympics. She was only one however, of a host of failures in Canada, yet manager Joe King in his report wasn't as critical as he should have been, perhaps because he and coach Terry Gathercole must accept much of the blame for our flop — though they all really were victims of the antiquated swimming structure of this country.

The significant part of King's report read: "The results of the Australian team were disappointing, but 18 members (64.29 p.c.) did improve on their selection times in one or more event. Much has been made of the overweight girl swimmers. Without brushing aside lightly this lack of self discipline and dedication, the fact is that with few exceptions both men and women were outclassed by the sheer power and class of the opposition. The high standard of the opposition is highlighted by the fact that on six occasions, when best of Australian records were broken, we did not qualify for either the semi final or final.

"We would have needed fantastic improvement on Sydney selection times to have won our usual quota of medals."

FORBES CARLILE ... moulder of champions

No sooner was the report tabled than veteran swimming official Syd Grange, who is also vice president of F.I.N.A. the world controlling body, put forward ideas on how the position could be remedied.

He pointed out major areas where we lagged far behind the other top swimming nations:

- Lack of facilities, particularly 25 metre indoor pools.
- Failure of government authorities to give the same status to sport in the school system as educational subjects and the lack of competition and effective coaching at this level.
- Lack of international competition because of costs and any substantial government financial support and, to a lessor extent, from the private sector.
- Inadequate scientific and sports medical backup services.

All these are commonsense suggestions, but implementing them is another thing, particularly when the recent white paper prepared by the Confederation of Australian Sport showed that during the 1976-77 financial year only a miserable pittance of $5,280 found its way to sporting associations from the $356,000 allocated to recreation and sport.

So the future looks grim, perhaps more hopeless than most realise and the general public care — Olympics are very much a two week wonder every four years in most people's eyes.

But knowing Australian swimming someone, despite the odds, will bob up again and stir the prospects of success in Commonwealth and Olympic Games. This time though to strike gold, he or she will have to be a super, super-fish to combat not only the East Germans, Americans and Canadians in the water, but the archaic swimming here.

Here is a list of Australia's individual gold medalists in international competition since 1967:

1968 Olympic Games, Mexico City, Mexico
- Michael Wenden: 100 and 200 m freestyle
- Lyn McClements: 100 m butterfly

1970 Commonwealth Games, Edinburgh, Scotland
- Michael Wenden: 100 and 200 m freestyle
- Graham White: 400 m freestyle
- Graham Windeatt: 1500 m freestyle
- Karen Moras: 200, 400 and 800 m freestyle
- Denise Langford: 200 and 400 m individual medley
- Lynne Watson: 100 and 200 m backstroke
- Beverley Whitfield: 100 and 200 m breaststroke
- Maree Robinson: 200 m butterfly

1972 Olympic Games, Munich, Germany
- Shane Gould: 200 and 400 m freestyle; 200 m individual medley
- Beverley Whitfield: 200 m breaststroke
- Gail Neal: 400 m individual medley
- Brad Cooper: 400 m freestyle

1973 First World Championships, Belgrade, Yugoslavia.
- Steve Holland: 1500 m freestyle

1974 Commonwealth Games, Christchurch, New Zealand
- Michael Wenden: 100 m freestyle
- Stephen Badger: 200 m freestyle
- John Kulasulu: 400 m freestyle
- Stephen Holland: 1500 m freestyle
- Brad Cooper: 200 m backstroke
- Neil Rogers: 100 m butterfly
- Mark Tonelli: 100 m backstroke
- Sonia Gray: 100 and 200 m freestyle
- Jenny Turrall: 400 m freestyle
- Sandra Yost: 200 m butterfly

1975 Second World Championships, Cali, Colombia
- Jenny Turrall: 800 m freestyle

1976 Olympic Games, Montreal, Canada
- None

JENNY TURRALL . . . (foreground) with arch-rival Sally Lockyer

HONDO GRATTAN . . . captured the imagination

13 TROTTING

By IAN CRAIG

IAN CRAIG commenced his broadcasting career at Richmond greyhounds in 1962. In 1965 he was appointed to the full time staff of Radio 2UE, where he stayed until 1968 when he moved across to Radio 2KY, as major race and trotting commentator. He has been associated with Rex Mossop's Sports Action programme on Channel 7 since 1966, chairing the Punters' Post Mortem panel.

When one sits down to write on the last decade of trotting the mind boggles. Where do I start? The excitement and enjoyment experienced through the deeds of horse and driver has been immense.

Without much doubt the most popular light harness racer, over the last ten years, was Hondo Grattan. Affectionately known as "The Bathurst Bulldog" because of his great tenacity, reared and trained at "The Lagoon" just outside Bathurst in Western NSW, Hondo Grattan captured the imagination of the trotting fraternity whenever he raced.

In my experience, I have never known a horse to receive ovations like those afforded Hondo whenever he stepped out to race—or after a win. He excelled in an era of many great horses. He won 26 races at Harold Park, a record that still stands, was judged NSW Harness Horse of the Year on two occasions, became the only horse to win two successive Inter Dominion Grand Finals—Harold Park in 1973 and Gloucester park in Perth in 1974.

He won the NSW Harness Horse of the Year award in successive periods, 1973 and 1973/74, the Miracle Mile in 1974, two Lord Mayor's Cup victories, plus a host of other fine performances. Hondo Grattan was eulogised in song—and given a civic reception in his home town of Bathurst. He amassed $215,402 in prize-money, winning 58 races, 17 seconds and 18 thirds from 120 starts—and was the first pacer to earn $200,000 in stakes on Australasia's racetracks.

When he won the 1973 Inter Dominion in Sydney, Hondo Grattan joined an elite group of pacers that have gone through an Inter Dominion series undefeated.

The 1976-77 season brought to a close the race driving career of Perc Hall, having reached the compulsory retiring age of 65.

Acclaimed by trotting experts the world over, Perc in his final season achieved the magnificent feat of driving his 500th winner at Harold Park. At the meeting on February 11, 1977, Hall drove the former New Zealand mare Ronrobin, owned by his close friend, Frank McKuttrick, to success to notch the magical 500.

Emotional scenes followed at the trackside presentation ceremony to the veteran reinsman, who at one stage was overcome, demonstrating clearly just how important driving is to him and how much he adores the sport of trotting to which he has devoted most of his life.

One of the most courageous horses of the decade was the Tasmanian Halwes.

A recurring hoof problem created a setback of major proportions to this hardy standardbred. It caused his last-minute withdrawal from the 1968 Inter Dominion Grand final in Auckland, New Zealand, a race for which he was a raging pre-post favourite.

I was one of his most ardent admirers and to this day I will not forget the urgent message flashed to my broadcast box at Alexandra Park that night. It started "please relay to your Australian listeners the late scratching of Halwes on veterinary advice". To most, following brilliant heat performances, it seemed only a matter of him going around to win the Grand final.

As history tells, all was not lost to Australia that night at First Lee, driven by Kevin Robinson, became the first Aussie pacer to win an Inter Dominion Grand Final on New Zealand soil.

Leading Sydney trainer-driver Kevin Newman was associated with Halwes for the greater part of his career, and he likened driving the horse to that of a powerful limousine. He ran 1.57 and 3/10s in a time trial at Harold

Park, was voted NSW Harness Horse of the Year in 1968 and won a Lord Mayor's Cup from 36 yards behind.

The fastest horse I have seen over the last few years was undoubtedly the West Australian, Mount Eden. Who will ever forget the Miracle Mile of 1971? Mount Eden, a big pacer, refused to move away properly in the run up for the rich event, and caused a fake start.

The starter risked criticism the second time when he let the field race with Mount Eden trailing out a long last. Before a crowd of 24,492, Mount Eden was six lengths last after half a furlong.

Not to be denied, driver Jack Miles decided to make his run three furlongs from home, and Mount Eden went around his rivals as though they were standing still. He won as he liked by 15 yards in 1.58 and 4/5 for the mile, which was only 1/5 of a second outside the record, despite losing so much ground at the start.

Following the 1971 Inter Dominion Grand final fixture at Addington Raceway, Christchurch, New Zealand, Mount Eden ran a mile time trial in 1.56 and 3/5 on a dead track. He clocked 1.56 and 7/10 in a time-trial at Harold Park, establishing an Australian record.

PERC HALL ... magnificent feat

[News Ltd.]

HALWES ... courageous

He became the first horse to better two minutes on the Melbourne Showground's course, clocking 1.59 and 4/5, a world record for a three-furlong track.

The most sensational Inter Dominion held in the last 10 years was the 1971 final at Addington in Christchurch, New Zealand.

The Western Australian combination of Junior's Image and driver Phil Coulson narrowly defeated the favourite, Stella Frost, with Manaroa a close third.

Coulson fearlessly pushed out of a pocket with two furlongs to go, with his main rival Stella Frost inconvenienced for a clear run at that stage. Coulson's tactics at the time obviously proved winning tactics.

Drama was to follow. It was found Junior's Image had returned a positive swab, and at the subsequent inquiry Coulson was disqualified for seven years and fined $1,000 for having administered a drug to the horse before the Grand final.

The New Zealand Trotting Conference judicial tribunal spent four days hearing the case, and the amended placings became Stella Frost first, Manaroa second and Last Flood third.

Whilst on the subject of New Zealand Inter Dominion Grand finals, one of the most impressive big race wins was recorded by Young Quinn at Auckland in 1975.

Driven by the youthful John Langdon, substituting for the injured trainer and regular

MOUNT EDEN . . . memories of Miracle Mile 1971

driver Charlie Hunter, Young Quinn produced a devastating finish to win in New Zealand record time.

The memory of that night will always remain with Langdon. He made history by also winning the Trotters' Grand final with Castleton's Pride, like Young Quinn trained by Charlie Hunter.

Shortly after his Inter Dominion triumph, Young Quinn was flown to Australia to compete in the rich, prestige Miracle Mile at Harold Park.

Most critics wiped him off as the likely winner as he drew barrier six, the outside of the front line from behind the mobile barrier. No horse has won a Miracle Mile from that alley and Young Quinn only arrived in Sydney less than 24 hours prior to the big event.

As history shows, Young Quinn overcame all obstacles to run effortlessly, this time driven by Hunter. Young Quinn has subsequently proved himself a grand campaigner in the United States.

One of the finest performers over recent seasons has been Paleface Adios. Aptly named, he is a striking chestnut with a huge white blaze extending down his face and over the left eye. Despite his good looks and dashing per-

formances, he did tend to be overshadowed by Hondo Grattan when the pair clashed.

Paleface defeated Hondo on many an occasion, however the crowds seemed to be on Hondo Grattan's side most of the time. Paleface Adios really came into his own following the retirement of his arch rival, especially in Queensland where he is absolutely idolised.

When he won the 1977 Clive UHR Championship at Albion Park, not only did the win earn him Australia's first Grand Circuit award, but took the earnings to almost $360,000, making him the second highest stakewinner in Australasia, with the New Zealand galloper, Battle Heights totalling $386,885.

Paleface Adios has the wonderful average of one win in every two starts. He became the first three-year-old in Australia or New Zealand to break the two-minute barrier. He ran 1.59, taking out the Simpson Sprint at Harold Park in 1973, and was voted 1974/75 NSW Harness Horse of the Year.

Lucky Creed proved a great favourite with light harness followers. Little was known about the Queenslander until he was brought to Sydney in 1969 to compete in the rich provincial series "The Carousel".

Lucky Creed won the final in dashing fashion, and this was to be the forerunner of bigger things to come.

He strung together success after success and won 23 straight races following victory in a mobile free for all at Harold Park in January 1970. The following day he made it 24 in a row with a win in a free for all at Kembla Grange.

LUCKY CREED . . . 23 straight victories

However, Lucky Creed's long succession of wins ended when narrowly beaten by Cocky Raider in the Australia Day Cup at Harold Park on January 30, 1970.

His mighty effort of 24 successive wins still stands as a record in Australia, as does his 23 wins in NSW during the 1969-70 season, including 11 at Harold Park. Lucky Creed won the 1970 Miracle Mile beating the 1970 Inter Dominion winner, Bold David.

Whilst on the subject of Queenslanders, a driver to emerge as one of the top in Australia is Kevin Thomas. A relative newcomer to the industry, his short career has captured the imagination of the trotting world, especially in his home State.

Thomas established a record performance in the 1975-76 season, driving 161 winners.

Another Queensland reinsman, Keith Addison, helped keep Australian trotting under worldwide notice when he won the 1975 World Driving Championship.

Queensland is the newest State as far as major pacing is concerned. Albion Park commenced racing in September 1968, and already has successfully conducted two Inter Dominion carnivals.

Trotting in Melbourne and Adelaide took a step forward with the transfer of meetings to new courses.

The regular Melbourne track was the Showgrounds, and in Adelaide the Wayville Showground. Both tracks were tiny, and authorities in both States realised the shortcomings of both.

The main Melbourne course is now Moonee Valley, which is sited inside the galloping track, the Showground's circuit is only used if a galloping meeting is held in the afternoon at Moonee Valley. The new Globe Derby course in Adelaide has proved a winner, and was the scene of the 1976 Inter Dominion championship.

The Miracle Mile, instituted in 1967 at Harold Park, has proved the most prestigious event in the last decade. The emphasis is on

PALEFACE ADIOS ... a striking chestnut

speed, with various prizemoney incentives. Only six starters compete by invitation, and the cream of Australasia's pacing talent compete.

The greatest shot in the arm to NSW trotting in recent times has been the introduction of Trifecta betting. Punters utilising this form of wagering must correctly forecast the place-getters in finishing order—first, second and third.

Off course turnover particularly, was tending to fall, but with the advent of Trifecta wagering turnover has skyrocketed and should continue, with such lucrative dividends in the offing.

Ace driver, Kevin Newman, has created a record that is likely to take some beating in NSW. Newman has now won the Harold Park drivers' premiership eight times. He handled a record 52 winners at the Park in the 1973-74 season, and in April 1977 drove his 1,000th winner.

A hoodoo seems to hang over Newman in Inter Dominion finals. He has had no luck in some of these events, and was to have driven Halwes, who as mentioned earlier, was a late scratching from the 1968 final.

One of the unfortunate aspects of recent times in NSW has been the demise of the square trotter.

This type of racing has proved colourful and exciting, but to prepare a trotter as compared to a pacer is a more demanding task for trainers. Most leading mentors have discarded thoughts of preparing a square-gaiter now. Race clubs endeavoured to conduct and promote this form of racing with little luck.

Victoria, however, is still strongly involved in the square trotting ranks.

Rip Van Winkle, a magnificently-actioned young performer has proved a star performer recently. By and large his efforts in his age group have made him vastly superior to his rivals. His NSW and Queensland Derby wins were made to look easy although he had little luck in the Victoria Derby. In the latter half of 1977 he won the Spring Cup at Harold Park and the National Pacing Championship in Adelaide.

Rip Van Winkle is a son of Thor Hanover, whose stock have made a remarkable impact on the Australian scene in latter years, but "Rip" is on the threshold of becoming one of the greatest Australian standardbreds.

KEVIN THOMAS . . . 161 winners

One of the grand campaigners over the last 10 years has been the Western Australian, Binshaw. He won the 1967 Inter Dominion final at Perth's Gloucester Park.

Binshaw had much of his racing career interrupted by a leg injury, however he was still able to race successfully until the age of 13.

Cocky Raider, a little pacer with a big heart, earned the admiration of trotting folk in the late sixties and early seventies. On many occasions he came from seemingly hopeless positions to get up and win.

In 1969 he was judged NSW Harness Horse of the Year. Cocky Raider won 18 races at Harold Park, including a Spring Cup, Summer Cup and Australia Day Cup. Originally trained in the west of NSW at Goolagong, he was only one of many star pacers trained in the country areas of the State.

Rocket Glenfern was yet another pacer to win the hearts of the public. "The Rocket" lived up to his name when on numerous occasions he would come with scintillating bursts of speed over the last two furlongs. Rocket Glenfern was plagued with suspensory ligament trouble throughout his career.

KEVIN NEWMAN . . . ace driver [News Ltd.]

An untimely death after only a short time at stud could have prevented Rocket Glenfern from establishing himself as a top sire.

The New Zealander, Manaroa, made himself a household name amongst Australasia's trotting fraternity. Dubbed the "Ugly Duckling" because of his awkward conformation including a roach back and rat tail. He cost himself many wins through being unreliable at the barrier, however his pace and toughness were never questioned.

Manaroa won a Lord Mayor's Cup and paced 1.59 and 3/5 against time, both at Harold Park.

Live telecasting of trotting events, particularly in NSW and Victoria, has done much to further popularise the sport. The ABC in NSW directly telecasts the last three races at Harold Park, which includes the Daily Double and Trifecta events, and all other races are replayed following the final event.

With the advent of colour television, and the new track lighting at Harold Park, it blends to make ideal viewing. Channel 7 in Melbourne has been telecasting Showground and Moonee Valley fixtures for many years.

Radio and press have played their part in the growth of the light harness industry. Administrators in recent years have placed the accent on young racing.

Many of the older brigade of better-performed horses have found their way to America, however their loss has been compensated by a number of vintage crop juvenile pacers.

The introduction of TAB betting has proved the life-blood of most race clubs who were facing financial ruin until the off course system came into existence. The handouts to clubs in the early stages of TAB betting quickly grew, however distribution has levelled off in recent times.

Many people from time to time ask me to name the best horse I have seen during my career.

It is impossible to compare horses of different eras. Outside the last decade, Cardigan Bay was my pin up pacer, but dealing with the last 10 years Halwes, Hondo Grattan and Young Quinn appeal to me.

The trio has been discussed earlier, but all possessed pace, power and toughness and were able to offset setbacks of varying degrees.

Trotting will continue to prosper. It is the only form of racing—trots, dogs, gallops—where a man can be the sole person associated with his horse. He can own, train and drive it himself, offsetting costs considerably, and if his horse makes the grade, a great deal of personal satisfaction.

COCKY RAIDER . . . 1969 'Harness Horse of the Year'

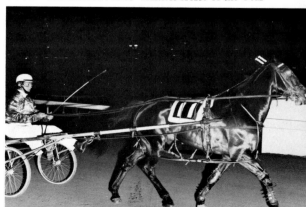

The mobile barrier has proved popular with patrons. Some trainer drivers are against this style of racing and its use is limited in NSW. However in our newest major trotting city Brisbane, the mobile gate is extensively used at Albion Park.

Statistics taken on mobile races at Harold Park show that the number four alley is the most successful, closely followed by gate three.

Decentralisation of trotting has become reality in Sydney over recent times. Tracks such as Bankstown, Fairfield and a little further west, Penrith, have built up large followings as all three are situated in heavy growth areas.

Trotting fans residing in the metropolitan area of Sydney are certainly well-catered for with the variety of tracks available within a radius of 40 miles from the city. In addition to those already mentioned, paceways like Hawkesbury, Richmond and Menangle are proving popular. Bookmakers have helped add glamour to Australian meetings, and I for one have found it strange overseas as all tote fixtures seem to lack atmosphere.

The last decade of trotting has proved exciting and enthralling and if the next 10 years are as good as the past, trotting followers will certainly be in for a treat.

RIP VAN WINKLE . . . vastly superior to rivals

ASCAPELLA MISS . . . a dour stayer

14 GREYHOUNDS
By JEFF COLLERSON

JEFF COLLERSON is the greyhound racing writer and tipster for the Sydney "Daily Mirror" and the "Sunday". Collerson, 32, joined the "Mirror" in August, 1968, after two years at the "Daily Telegraph". He has had two books published on the sport—the "Greyhound Year Book" and "The Greyhound In Australia". Collerson is well travelled and won the NSW N.C.A. Tipster of the Year contest in 1974 and has bred, owned and trained winners.

The past decade has produced the two greatest boom periods in the 50-year history of mechanical lure-dog racing in this country.

The mid and late sixties saw the "poor man's racehorse", as the greyhound is universally known, become almost as popular a betting medium as the galloper in some parts of Australia, and certainly as big as harness racing in most areas.

After the initial burst of prosperity the sport experienced a levelling off in the early 70s, even a slight slump, but it took off with a bang again in 1977.

Three words explain greyhound racing's elevation above the "cloth cap image" the sport had in the 1950s — Zoom Top and Trifecta.

Zoom Top, who won the NCA Greyhound of The Year award in 1968 and for an unequalled second time the following year, is to dog racing what Tulloch was to thoroughbred racing.

It is impossible to compare champions of different eras, but it is generally conceded Zoom Top is the greatest bitch of all time in this part of the world. Many still consider Chief Havoc, a male greyhound, who won 26 of 35 races in the late 40s, to be her superior.

Zoom Top, a fawn bitch by the great stud dog Black Top from Busy Beaver, was owned and trained by retired builder Hec Watt, and raced from October, 1968, until April, 1970. In that short time "Sweetie", as Zoom Top was known to the Watt family, contested an amazing 136 races.

She won 68 and ran 39 placings, including 15 record-equalling or breaking runs. Most of the time, her only real opponent was her litter sister Busy's Charm, also raced by Watt, who ran 113 times for 50 wins and 37 placings.

But Zoom Top was the more versatile of the two, and this, as well as her consistency, cemented her position as the all-time favourite of race-watchers. She was equally at home in races from 300 to 800 yards and it's doubtful if there will ever be a champion to match her record.

The reason for this is few trainers would undertake a campaign for their greyhounds to compare with the one Watt set for his champion. He readily admits he "broke every rule in the training book" with Zoom Top.

Watt repeatedly mixed Zoom Top's distances — a definite "no-no" — and trial track regulars often related stories of Watt galloping Zoom Top 300 yards on a Sunday morning, just a few hours after an arduous 800 yards race, to ensure there was nothing amiss with the bitch for another 800 yards engagement perhaps only 48 or 72 hours away.

Watt always knew Zoom Top, Busy's Charm and their litter brother Top Bomber, who was a classy sprinter, would be special. He was so rapt in them as pups, by Black Top from Busy Beaver, that he gave away greyhound training for two years to concentrate on rearing them. It was probably the smartest decision Watt ever made.

Zoom Top earned $59,000 in prizemoney, her best wins being the 1968 Harold Park Summer Cup, 1968 Wentworth Park Sydney Cup, 1968 and 1969 Wentworth Park Gold Cups, 1968 Wentworth Park St Leger — and 1968 and 1969 Harold Park Association Cups.

When she won the latter race in 1968 she was competing in her sixth race in 19 days — testimony to her durability. And her popularity was evidenced when she won the Sydney Cup later that year — racegoers began applauding and cheering their idol 100 yards before the winning post — a rare tribute at the greyhound races. Zoom Top was so tough she refused to rest when kennelled for long periods

ZOOM TOP . . . greatest bitch of all time

so she virtually rejected any suggestion of a spell.

Such was Zoom Top's domination of the Sydney greyhound scene that in July, 1969, Harold Park officials were planning to construct a special handicap starting box for the mighty galloper. Zoom Top was running out of opponents—trainers of her contemporaries were refusing to race against her in the usual scratch races—and Harold Park directors were keen to ensure that her retirement was not brought on prematurely.

Fortunately the officials' fears were without foundation because new aspirants to Zoom Top's title of Australia's best all-distance greyhound continually emerged.

Zoom Top's spectacular career was not without controversy. In November, 1969, trainer Watt was invited to run her in an invitation race at Goulburn, in the NSW southern highlands. Rain was the order of the day and the greyhounds and their handlers were supplied with rain-rugs and coats.

Punters who sent Zoom Top out an even-money favourite stood in stunned horror as Zoom Top came out of the starting boxes still wearing her plastic rug, which prevented her stretching out properly. Her old rival Bunyip Bint won the race easily.

Watt, who had been suffering ill-health, had a mental blackout and simply forgot to remove Zoom Top's "raincoat"! As a result, he was banned for some time from being allowed to again lead his greyhounds to the starting boxes.

But that one unpleasant memory of Zoom Top's racing life is obliterated by the highlights.

Such as:

- When private clockers timed her to break the world's 800 yards record at Harold Park on May 26, 1969;
- When she became the first greyhound outside the US or Britain to attain more than $50,000 in earnings;
- She was accorded the biggest ovation

ever given a greyhound at Harold Park when she beat Australia's best sprinters in a special invitation event on April 5, 1969;

- Women racegoers daubed her with lipstick in unprecedented scenes of adoration after she won the Queensland Cup at Beenleigh.

Zoom Top was retired in top condition. In November, 1973, she whelped a litter of four dog and two bitch puppies to leading stud dog Thunder Lane.

Unfortunately none of Zoom Top's progeny has measured up to anywhere near their mother's racetrack class, although ironically, Busy's Charm, the litter sister who lived in Zoom Top's shadow as a racer, has produced the goods at stud. To Benjamin John she whelped a fawn dog called Busy's Chief, who became a fine all-distance performer to take out the 1974 NSW St Leger.

If Zoom Top was the four-legged answer to greyhound racing's new-found prosperity in the 60s, it was an abstract thing called the Trifecta—or "Big T"—which resurrected greyhound racing in the mid 70s.

The sport was in the doldrums at the time the Trifecta—America's favourite way of gambling on greyhound racing—was introduced to Melbourne and Sydney dog tracks. But it took off like no other form of betting has before, soon outstripping the popular Daily Doubles as the most solidly supported betting medium, and accounting for up to 60 per cent of totalisator betting pools.

Although greyhound racing, with its eight-runners maximum per race, lent itself perfectly to Trifecta betting, the other forms of racing—thoroughbreds and trotting—were soon clamouring for its introduction too.

Trifecta betting—which involves punters trying to select first, second and third place-getters in correct finishing order—was soon paying dividends of up to $20,000 for a one dollar investment and the old lure of "a lot for a little" had ex-punters rushing back to the dogs, trots and races, and hooked thousands of new devotees.

Greyhound racing encountered its worst scandal since the notorious days of the "ring-ins" in the 30s when the Special Invitation Stake, won by Zoom Top at Harold Park on April 5, 1969, was declared "a gigantic conspiracy to defraud the public."

Mr Jim Carr, at the time Chief Stipendiary Steward at Harold Park, made this statement after the race in which Zoom Top, 6/4 favourite, beat Gala's Dream, 20/1, by a long neck. Sammie Sparrow, 5/2, was four lengths back, third while the other starter Rokoko, was a distant last. Rokoko was the 7/4 second favourite.

Mr Carr was suspicious at the betting trend of the race and immediately called in CIB Detectives to interview trainers. He also ordered drug tests to be done on Sammie Sparrow and Rokoko, and also on Amerigo Lady, another favourite who performed badly at the same race meeting.

Bookmakers' ledgers were impounded for examination, and four days later, Norm Smith, then Harold Park racing manager, said: "A certain few bookmakers held abnormally high amounts on the Special Invitation and also on Amerigo Lady's race." The club even went to the extent of collecting discarded betting tickets to see if they tallied with entries made on betting sheets by bookmakers' clerks.

The Australian Jockey Club's analyst then reported that urine samples taken from Sammie Sparrow and Amerigo Lady had contained the drug theobromine, but that blood samples proved negative. Urine and blood samples taken from Rokoko failed to trace any drug, the analyst's report added.

But a veterinary surgeon's report on Rokoko stated the morning after the April 5 race the dog was "depressed and lethargic" and despite the result of the drug test, Rokoko's trainer Bill Plowright was adamant his champion had been nobbled.

Three weeks later the Harold Park club veterinarian Reg Hoskins's surgery was ransacked, and detectives believed the intruders were out to destroy records pertaining to the April 5 race meeting at Harold Park.

The facts of the case pointed to a doping gang being in possession of a drug which could not be traced in the usual testing methods, and the whole affair to this day is still shrouded in mystery. Disqualifications were handed out to two trainers, on the grounds they were negligent in allowing their dogs to be "got at" by dopers, and to bookmakers on charges relating to improper betting transactions.

But most people in the greyhound world feel the real culprits were never caught.

Not since the mercurial Black Top, who raced in the early 1960s, has a greyhound been such a force on the racetracks, and later at stud, as Benjamin John. A contemporary of Zoom Top, Benjamin John first attracted the attention of the experts when he won a sprint in near record time at Dapto, on the NSW south coast, early in September, 1968.

Trained by the famous Stan Cleverley, who has prepared thousands of winners all over Australia since 1928, Benjamin John was a white and fawn dog whelped in November, 1966, by Take A Bow from Rebel Wayne.

Victorian-owned and bred, Benjamin John's best win was the 1969 Australian Cup at Melbourne's Olympic Park. But he beat Zoom Top in a 555 yds race at Dapto, and was slightly unlucky when third to that bitch in the 1968 NSW St Leger final at Wentworth Park.

Benjamin John was one of the most travelled champions of his era, winning the 1969 Hobart Thousand in race record time, setting a 540 yards track record of 28.9 sec there and once ripping $25,000 from bookmakers in a hit-and-run visit for a minor race at Olympic Park.

His career was interrupted when he fractured a bone in his leg in July, 1969, after winning 28 of his 48 races in top company. But he proved himself a true champion by bouncing back to emerge top pointscorer in the National Sprint Championship series only two months later.

Benjamin John clinched that honour with a semi-final win on the tight Wentworth Park track, but after the race trainer Cleverley commented: "I wish the big one was at Wenty, not Harold Park." Cleverley, who always rated Benjamin John lengths better on small tracks than on roomy ones like Harold Park, was referring to the championship final.

BENJAMIN JOHN . . . most travelled champion

RED ZERO . . . Benjamin John's arch rival

Sure enough, Benjamin John's arch-rival in the sprinting department, Red Zero, was sent out a 7/4 on favourite for the final on September 20 and overcame a slow start to win by eight lengths from Busy's Charm and Pied Rebel.

Red Zero's trainer Len Tonks, had picked up his know-how in what he termed "the toughest school of them all." That school was fox terrier racing, which apparently thrived in Newcastle in the middle thirties.

"I raced foxies long before I had a greyhound," Tonks said after Red Zero's win. "They were furious little chasers and we used to race them after a rabbit skin on a piece of wire. Of course the sport was illegal, but it was very popular with the miners and big wagering took place before the police broke the sport up and forced me into greyhound training."

As Red Zero earned $13,000 prizemoney before a leg injury forced his retirement in November, 1969, it's unlikely Tonks had much to complain about the police action.

Benjamin John was retired to stud not long after, in February, 1970, after being one of three greyhounds who combined to earn $51,925 prizemoney for Cleverley the previous year. The other two were Milimsimbi and Bunyip Bint. At Stud Benjamin John proved a phenomenal success, his stock including Benny McGrath, Little John, Koombar, Fantasy Lady, Woolley Wilson, Classy Benjamin, Alpha Brava, The Wee Lassie, Ungwilla Lad, Camden Glider and the brilliant Queenslander Ben Hamilton.

By virtue of the fact practically everyone who attends greyhound race meetings can afford to be an owner, trainer or breeder himself, the sport has produced more "rags-to-riches" stories than any other form of racing.

The greatest of the past decade is probably Paul Cauchi, one of Australia's most famous trainers. Born in Malta in 1936, Cauchi had never set foot on a racecourse, let alone trained greyhounds, when he came to Australia in 1952. But the 16-year-old with a passion for fast motor cycles became interested in greyhounds through attending race meetings with friends.

Finally he took two dogs on lease, one he was told, with "a little ability", and the other, "a dud, but good to learn with." The better of the pair died of hepatitis but Cauchi, training by trial and error and a good serving of common-sense, won eight races with the no-hoper, a dog called Roy's Ace.

In 1966 he bought 27 acres at Kellyville, not far from the Richmond and Penrith NSW TAB tracks. This site became the showplace of Australian trialling set-ups. As well as running a thriving stud farm and controlling the trial track, Cauchi has still found time to put the polish on some pretty handy racers.

He won the 1975 and 1976 National Sprint Championships with Queenslander Coorparoo Flyer and Clover Duke respectively, the 1972 Wentworth Park Gold Cup and 1972 Association Cup with Ragsie and dozens of big sprint races with Miami Moss and Pied Rebel.

Pied Rebel, along with Top Simbi, ranks as

PIED REBEL . . . Queensland's finest dog

the finest dog to come from Queensland in the past 10 years. Pied Rebel was desperately unlucky in big race finals, and when he was beaten by Victoria's Regal Hermes in the National Sprint Championship final in 1970 at Olympic Park, Pied Rebel tasted defeat for the sixth time in 12 months in such races.

Trainer Cauchi lodged a match race challenge against Regal Hermes immediately after the Championship final, but the club committee refused to sanction the challenge.

Pied Rebel broke a toe and was retired in March, 1971, as the winner of $24,000 prize-money from 37 wins, 17 seconds and 11 thirds in 81 races.

In 1969 he reached the finals of the National Championship, Harold Park Classic, NSW St Leger, Melbourne Cup and Christmas Gift, while the following year he was again a National Championship finalist and a semi-finalist in the National Derby, Melbourne Cup and Australian Cup.

He reached the semi-finals of the latter

race again in 1971, just before breaking down. Pied Rebel's career was interrupted by frequent injuries and a spell of inactivity caused by water diabetes. Former Queensland police inspector Paddy Rynne bred the dog, and owned him throughout his career.

But while Pied Rebel did most of his racing in NSW, where he was trained, Top Simbi was a real home-grown product as far as Banana-landers were concerned.

Now standing at stud in Queensland, Top Simbi won 17 of his first 20 starts in his home State and shattered Victorian-owned champion Ragsie's 558 m record at the 'Gabba, Brisbane track with a run of 32.48 sec. At time of writing this record still stands—it was set in mid-1973 —even though most of the top NSW and Victorian greyhounds "have had a crack at it" since. Top Simbi is one greyhound who gave the lie to the myth about greyhounds being savage, or having to lead a spartan training existence to win races. He never slept anywhere but on a mattress in trainer Bert Kennedy's bedroom

TOP SIMBI . . . slept on mattress

and was adept at unlocking doors when he felt like taking himself for a stroll.

In fact Top Simbi's proficiency at this almost cost him a start in a big race, which he won. Letting himself out for his "morning constitutional", Top Simbi came off second best in a scrape with a German Shepherd dog and was slightly injured, having to be patched up to get to the post on race night.

Top Simbi was probably one of Australia's most naturally great gallopers of the past 10 years, because throughout his tremendous career the dog received no help from his trainer — and that's according to the man himself, Bert Kennedy.

Kennedy often told his great friend Ern Mobbs, who raced Top Simbi's sire Milimsimbi, "Ern, I'm a mug at this greyhound training game, but this dog can just train himself. All credit should go to the dog."

Milimsimbi was a product of two of the all-time greats of Australian greyhound breeding. Black Top, the country's best-ever sire was his father, and his dam was Tamerine, who can lay claim to being the finest brood bitch since the War.

Little wonder he was a champion. He was owned by former professional athlete Ern Mobbs and his wife Elsie, who co-owned Tamerine with Cleverley's wife Beryl.

Trained early in his career by the "old master" Cleverley, Milimsimbi chalked up the Melbourne Cup at Sandown Park and the Vic Peters Memorial Classic at Harold Park among his numerous victories.

Returned to Mobbs for training, Milimsimbi continued in his winning vein, taking out the Anniversary Cup, also at Harold Park, and beating Silent Retreat in a memorable 500 yards match race at the same venue.

"He ran 26.4 on every occasion I put him down at Harold Park, and that's an amazing performance on winter tracks," Mobbs says. "And the only reason he was retired was that he ran out of opponents.

"I just couldn't get a draw with him. I'm not taking anything away from great sprinters like Ungwilla Lad and Smooth Keith who have won nine and ten races in a row at Harold Park, but official thinking is different nowadays.

"When Boots (Milimsimbi) was racing, officials wouldn't give you a run if they thought your dog was so good he would stifle betting. But now they build a field around a champion, even if the dog is going to be 5/1 on.

"They figure that the public wants to see a champion in action as much as possible and I agree wholeheartedly with this approach. A man can wait a lifetime to get that elusive champion and it's pretty frustrating to be forced to leave him sitting at home in his kennel on race night.

"But they didn't always have that attitude, certainly not when 'Boots' was racing."

Like most superior racing dogs Milimsimbi was described by Mobbs as being the most placid and docile greyhound he has had. "He walked casually to the starting boxes, never pulled on the lead, and he never barked", was Mobbs's summing up of the black flash.

Harold Park is acknowledged as the finest greyhound track in Australia, and some say the world.

Like other Australian courses its facilities lag behind the plush American circuits, and even some palatial English tracks like Walthamstow, but its shape and size make overseas greyhound owners and trainers drool with envy.

Harold Park is a true speedster's track—its 457 m (formerly 500 yards) start has one long straight run, then a long gradual sweeping bend, and a lengthy homestraight to the winning post. The best Harold Park dogs of the past 10 years reads like a who's who of greyhound racing, but I doubt if there has been a finer performer on its soil than El Gazelle.

Owned, trained and bred by Zell and Tom O'Connell at Point Clare, a tiny township near Gosford, NSW, El Gazelle, known as Laddie to his owners, is by The Smoother from their bitch Zell's Babe. El Gazelle was never tried on the tight Wentworth Park track because he suffered constantly with toe injuries, and the giant Harold Park layout put less pressure on his "dickey" appendages.

But on the huge Glebe track he won 14 races in 12 months before one of his "bad" three front toes "collapsed" completely. Zell O'Connell has never been a believer, like some trainers, in having dogs' dislocated or broken toes amputated, but she regrets to this day she did not try this tactic with El Gazelle.

El Gazelle is one of the most clever greyhounds I have seen.

He rarely won his races by big margins, because I have no doubt he KNEW he was in a race. This isn't to say he was not a keen chaser—he was tenacious—but by the same token he would only go as hard as his rivals forced him.

O'Connell takes up the story: "From his puppy days he had a lot of brains and I always knew he was going to be good.

"He usually won at Harold Park around the 26.4 mark, but one night he did run 26.19, and that was because a pretty fast dog called Dusty Trail pushed him to the limit.

"He nearly always led by four lengths on the home bend and then ran off the track. Many a dog caught him there, but he always came again in the straight to beat them." Undoubtedly racing was a game to "Laddie" and his running off to let his nearest rivals catch him was all part of the fun.

Mrs O'Connell rates El Gazelle's best win the night he won the consolation final of the Dave Alexander Memorial, once again at Harold Park, his favourite track.

"He came out a dozen lengths behind the field, but was in front by the time they hit the first corner," she says with pride. "It was as if he had grown wings."

South Australia is, along with Queensland and Western Australia, one of the fledgling

States of Australian greyhound racing. And just as Top Simbi and Mister Toewyte have put Queensland and the West respectively on this country's dog racing map, Ascapella Miss has done the same for South Australia.

A February, 1972 whelping of the fine NSW performers Chariot Charm and Fullock, Ascapella Miss was trained throughout her career by the incomparable Doug Payne, the Bart Cummings of Adelaide dog racing.

Payne also trained Bristol Sue, the only greyhound to rival Ascapella Miss in South Australia's relatively short tin-hare racing history, but Ascapella Miss is the more famous nationally.

A dour stayer, Ascapella Miss raced 44 times for 24 wins, 10 seconds and four thirds in the process earning $24,200 prizemoney and another $1,000 worth of trophies.

Her best wins were the 1974 Harold Park Association Cup, 'Gabba (Brisbane) All Star Classic—in which she set the 704 m record of 41.61 sec—South Australian Champion Puppy Stake, SA St Leger and the Coca-Cola Cup at Gawler.

She remains, at time of writing, the Gawler 750 m record holder, and at one stage won six successive long distance races at Harold Park, equalling Zoom Top's record-winning sequence.

The greatest difficulty in supplying the greyhound section to this book is selecting those dogs that made the past 10 years special. Obviously more great greyhounds will be left out for space reasons than any other athlete—human or animal. Reason for this is that a greyhound's racing life lasts only on average, 18 months, and so new champions are emerging constantly. In fact when Zoom Top retired in April, 1970, Lizrene was born. And Lizrene was to Victorian fans what Zoom Top was to counterparts in NSW.

In spite of inflated prizemoney Lizrene remains Australia's greatest greyhound money-earner, amassing $61,229 by winning 59 of her 98 races. She was only out of the money eight times.

LIZRENE . . . top money winner

EL GAZELLE . . . Harold Park specialist

And she was never beaten from her favourite box position, number eight, winning from the outside trap eight times from as many attempts. But Peter McGuinness, who trained Lizrene, is quick to point out she drew the dreaded box five on 26 occasions, yet still managed to win from there all but once.

"A champion can win from any box," is McGuinness' firm contention, and Lizrene bears testimony to his theory. McGuinness acquired Lizrene for nothing. A breeder mated his bitch Joanne Lu, with McGuinness' stud dog Prince Kua, and asked McGuinness if he would agree to take 50 per cent of the litter of pups in lieu of the service fee.

McGuinness agreed, but when Joanne Lu had 11 young ones McGuinness took only three. They were Baron Power, a fine sprinter who now stands at stud, a pup who later broke a shoulder, and Lizrene.

Lizrene was an instant success, winning 10 of her 15 sprint races before being switched to the more gruelling long-distance stuff. At that she really excelled although surprisingly McGuinness rates her greatest moments as wins on out-of-town tracks.

"Her best win was when she beat Miss High Lo, the then NSW champion, and several other topliners in the All Star Challenge at Wangaratta, while to me her most exciting victory was her success in the Golden Diamond Trophy at Newcastle," says McGuinness.

Lizrene's best track was Sandown Park, where she won 23 times, while she contested 22 race finals and won 19 of them. Now at stud, Lizrene has had three litters with her best so far being the promising sprinter Forcardos.

While Lizrene is Victoria's most famous stayer of the past two decades, two greyhounds battle for the title on an Australia-wide basis.

They are Half Your Luck and New Mariner.

Half Your Luck won 45 races and more than $50,000 prizemoney including 12 straight wins on his home state city tracks.

His best wins were the 1973 Australian Cup at Olympic Park, Challenge Stake, NCAM Centenary Cup, Olympic Park Sprint Championship, Lord Mayor's Cup and 1972 Warragul Cup in which he gave rival finalists 2 m start and won by three lengths.

The white and black son of Worthing-Mini Note, whelped in December, 1970, ran record time at Sandown Park and once beat arch rival New Mariner four lengths in a match race. An immediate success at stud, Half Your Luck is already third on the Victorian sires' table.

New Mariner, a giant fawn dog whelped in March, 1971, was by Black Top from Cursorial and won the 1973 Melbourne Cup at Sandown Park and Courage and Challenge Cups at Olympic Park in the same year. He raced for only 11 months, having 35 starts for 17 wins and 13 placings.

But it was in NSW, particularly on the huge Harold Park track, which so suited the big dog's long-striding galloping fashion, that he really made his mark.

New Mariner wasn't beaten in five NSW races, winning both semi-finals of the 1973 National Sprint Championship and beating Half Your Luck four lengths in the sizzling time of 26.28 sec (457 m) in the final.

Unquestionably he was one of the fastest dogs ever to race at Harold Park—in my mind the ultimate test—and had his trainer Ray Jennings prepared him in NSW, New Mariner could have become the most dynamic Harold Park sprinter of all time.

Speaking of Harold Park, while that spectacular circuit regularly produces its own breed of champion sprinters, dogs who are supreme there over all others, while not being

so on other smaller layouts, it does not quite have the same effect with stayers.

Usually long-distance greyhounds handle all tracks alike, but one notable exception in the past decade has been Travel Rev.

A flop at Wentworth Park—Sydney's other metropolitan course—Travel Rev is considered by many experts as the best Harold Park stayer of them all—Zoom Top and world record holder Bunyip Bint included.

Raced by a shy unassuming lad from the Sydney suburb of Malabar named Alf Hayes, on lease from his breeder Freddie Smith, Travel Rev's best wins were the 1971 Harold Park Association Cup—in race record time—and the 1970 Harold Park Summer Cup—also in record breaking figures.

Travel Rev stood head and shoulders above his contemporaries so much at the course that back in August, 1970, after only three races there, rival trainers were refusing to enter their dogs against him.

Admittedly Travel Rev had won his three events by a staggering total of 33 lengths, so it was little wonder Harold Park officials at the time had to virtually beg trainers to nominate for top grade distance races there.

Smith and Hayes once refused a $20,000 US offer for their champion, who fractured a wrist midway through his career, but came back to break Zoom Top's race record in the Association Cup, after which he was retired.

Like all sports, greyhound racing contains its share of hard luck stories.

There can be no argument about the unluckiest dog of the past 10 years—Alpha Brava. As if it was not bad enough he was a slow beginner, sickness and injury robbed him of important races on which he looked to have a mortgage.

He came down with a coughing virus on the eve of the 1975 Young Star Classic, then a skirmish with a domestic dog saw him lame on the day of the final of the 1975 NSW St Leger.

A slow start cost him his chance in the 1975 Silver Chief Puppy Classic final in Melbourne, but in spite of his tardiness at the boxes he managed to come from midfield at the halfway mark of the 457 m Vic Peters Memorial Classic final at Harold Park on November 1, 1975, to smash the then 25-year-old race record.

A dog who could handle any type of track,

Alpha Brava may have been a sensational stayer, but injuries prevented his stamina being tested. Certainly though he is the classic example of the greyhound who could have been anything had he been a fast box dog.

For sheer strength, ability and will-to-win, he deserves a mention in "the best of the last 10 years" category.

Rod Deakin, of Keysborough, Victoria, is arguably Australia's most outstanding breeder of fine greyhounds. Certainly he IS the top breeder of great stayers.

No volume on "the best of the last 10 years" of greyhound racing would be complete without reference to Deakin's performers.

He has reared, raced or bred no fewer than 37 track record-holders and winners of 63 features.

His record-holders over the past decade have been: Corcoran (Shepparton, Vic.; Gawler, SA; Angle Park, SA; and Olympic Park, Vic.); Allocate (Shepparton, Vic.); Plunderola ('Gabba, Q'ld); Ima Take (Traralgon, Vic.); Landena (Sandown Park, Vic.; and race record breaker, Wentworth Park, NSW); Yannaview (Warragul, Vic.); Redwood View (Gawler, SA); Binding (Gawler, SA); Coping (Wangaratta, Vic.); Rich Benefit (Angle Park, SA); Stardust Lady (Whyalla, SA); Varley (Angle Park, SA); Yanoble (Angle Park, SA); Chadford (Cessnock, NSW); Vermeer (Darwin, NT); Tracemond (Bolivar, SA); Geeta (Strathalbyn, SA); Scout Mistress (Lithgow, NSW).

In the last 10 years Deakin's big race winners have been: Plunder Road (Vic. Silver Chief Stake, Hobart Thousand, Vic. St. Leger, Interstate Challenge); Corcoran (National Distance Championship and Sandown Cup); Allocate (Vic. Puppy Championship, HP Summer Cup, HP Xmas Gift final); Ramille (Maiden Thousand, Hobart, and Vic. Oaks); Sargood (National Distance Championship and Tasmanian Distance Championship); Plunderola (HP Association Cup); Westmore (HP Xmas Gift final); Wonalda (Vic. Oaks); Retreat (Vic. Oaks); Starkie (Vic. Derby); Rellething (Vic. Derby); One By One (Vic. Derby); Tinkering (Vic. Derby); Slim Design (Vic. Derby); Crete (Vic. Laurels); Titus (SA Distance Championship); Wonoka (Sandown Cup); Westward Ho (Aust. Marathon Championship); Alveray (Olympic Park Distance Championship); Damerest (SA Spring Cup); Titus (Olympic Park Lucky Dog Trophy heat & final); Magneto (Davidson Memorial, Sale, Vic.); Bolta's Gift (National Distance Championship, McKenna Memorial, Sandown); Chadford (Cessnock Derby).

ALPHA BRAVA . . . injuries prevented stamina

15 SNOW SKI-ING

By DAVID McCAMEY

Presently the leading Rugby League writer with "The Australian". After starting his journalistic career as a racing writer with the same paper he has progressed through almost every major sport in the country to his present position. A keen skier, 26-year-old McCamey has many contacts in the sport and considers it one of his favourite relaxations.

Officials baulk when you ask the question: What have Australians done during the last ten years? "In skiing it isn't the past which concerns us, the future is more important," they say.

But what has Australia—a land with more snow than Switzerland—achieved in the sport in the last decade? We have produced a champion and have a crop of young enthusiasts waiting in the wings to show their wares.

The champion was, of course, Malcolm Milne, a 28-year-old Victorian farmer of hops and tobacco. He, more than any other person, put Australia on the skiing map and forced the skiing world to recognise its potential.

And he did it despite the Australian snow-fields, not because of them, for our snow is either inaccessible or of a poor quality unsuited to skiing.

Milne, who as a 15-year-old learnt of his brother Ross's death, while training for the 1964 Winter Olympics in Innsbruck, became the first Australian to win an internationally-recognised downhill event and the first to gain a medal in the world championships.

And in the manner most Australians appreciate he achieved his initial success, in the downhill at Val d'Isere (France) in December 1969 as the underdog.

"I knew I was going fast at the half-way mark when the people started roaring and screaming and I realised I had made a good time," he said after the race. "Everyone was so happy—that's what made it so good. I think everyone wanted me to win."

Even so the win shocked the skiing press and prompted "The Times" correspondent to write: "It is still hard to accept the fact that a solitary Australian could take on the collective might of all the Alpine countries and the North Americans and beat them fair and square."

Still another remarked it was like France beating Australia at Australian Rules football.

But Milne had proved Australians could be successful in skiing and was to go on even further as a professional in North America after 1972, but not before he had received his share of notoriety.

Before the 1972 Winter Olympics in Sapporo, Japan, Milne was one of 10 international skiers threatened with expulsion by the then president of the International Olympic Committee, Mr Avery Brundage. Milne was accused of receiving payments, in kind, for using a manufacturer's equipment.

This fuss was over a nation only just recognised in the sport and over a skier who was more than fortunate to have even competed in an international downhill event.

A year after Ross Milne was killed the French ski coach, Honnore Bonnet, visited Australia and was so impressed with Mal's skiing he invited him to France to train.

But the 16-year-old needed his mother's permission and she gave it only on the condition that he did not try the downhill. There had also been lobbying in Europe that, because of the lack of downhill events "Down Under", all Australians be banned from downhill racing.

Happily that lobby found little support, and after four years Bonnet succeeded in getting Milne permission from his mother to try the downhill.

From such a beginning Australia's first truly international skiing champion was made. Since Milne there have been few others to really earn that title, but the current crop of Australian skiers are determined to succeed.

Among them is David Griff, a young skier who managed a very creditable eighth in the World Cup in March this year. Griff is a Sydney

Speed . . . exhilaration . . . expectancy

ROSS MILNE . . . a champion

lad who, like all the talented Australians, must travel overseas at every opportunity to gain experience and knowledge.

"It isn't that the coaches in Australia aren't good—we've got 40 overseas coaches in Australia this year—but in Europe and America the competition is so fierce you have to keep proving consistently good," Griff said.

"I've seen the tremendous growth of the sport in Australia, especially at Thredbo, during the last 10 years and we are only just scratching the surface. Ten years ago there were only two lifts at Thredbo, now there are eight."

Griff, the recipient of a Leyland sporting scholarship this year, will be off overseas again this year and will almost certainly have his closest Australian rival, Robbie McIntyre, with him. Griff is rated at 22.41 on the international FIS scale this season, the lower the score the better for downhill, and McIntyre at 25.29. It is interesting to note that while Australia has no great height in its snowfields, Australian skiers seem to have developed a passion for the downhill, probably due to Milne's earlier successes.

Other top flight youngsters in Australia are Anthony Guss (36.23 in downhill), Kim Clifford (52.93) and Joanne Henke (52.27).

ROSS MARTIN . . . close to world standards

Milne, Griff and company have received most of the skiing accolades in Australia, but an Australian-at-heart is almost forgotten.

He is Manfred Grabler. An Austrian by birth who tried unsuccessfully to become naturalised as an Australian to allow him to compete for this country in the Olympic Games. Grabler was beaten by a Catch 22.

He was told to serve a 12-month residency period in Australia to qualify for his citizenship, but such an admission of loyalty to this country could have set his skiing back years.

Still, he was recognised by the Australian Ski Federation and received financial assistance from that body in his rise to the top. While representing under the Australian flag in Europe, Grabler rose to the elite in downhill events and was rated sixth in the world in the early seventies.

But these are past and present people and the ASF, in its bid to increase the number of top flight Australian skiers in future years, has earmarked over $100,000 for development during the year beginning September 1—without Federal Government support.

Part of the programme will be to assist at least 40 young skiers to Europe and America for the 1977-78 season. And this is only for the Alpine section of Australian skiing. The Nordic side, probably the fastest growing facet of the sport in Australia, will get almost $30,000.

The Nordic officials have similarly embarked on a program of junior encouragement and development, but they face a harder task than their Alpine compatriots. Australia has never produced a really top flight Nordic or cross country skier.

Nearest to world standards, naturally dominated by Scandinavian countries, would be Ross Martin and Laurie Jortikka.

Martin represented Australia overseas every year, except 1971, between 1966 and 1975, including the 1968 Winter Olympics in Grenoble and the world championships in 1970.

He has an excellent array of Australian wins to his credit, but Australians are well and truly hampered in their quest for higher honours by the relatively late start the sport received here.

Until the early 1960s, with the introduction of the Paddy Palin Classic—a 30 kilometre cross country race from Perisher to Charlotte's Pass

AUSTRALIAN OLYMPIC TEAM ... Innsbruck 1976 (from left) Geoff Henke (manager), David Griff, Sally Rodd, Kim Clifford, Joanne Henke, Robbie McIntyre, Martin Kersher (coach)

and return—Nordic skiing in Australia was virtually unknown.

Even the first Paddy Palin in 1965 drew less than 10 competitors, a far cry from the 200 or so contestants who regularly compete now. The Paddy Palin proved more popular than inaugurators Palin and John Morgan envisaged and encouraged skiers to rediscover older endurance cross country events such as the Kiandra to Kosciusko (50 km) and the Bogong to Hotham (80 km).

The former was first mooted in 1927 and won by Sir Herman Slink in just over two days. The record now stands at eight hours 11 minutes and is held by Robbie Kilpinen. The race, used as a test of both competitive skills and endurance, became tragic in 1965 when Charlie Derek died in his attempt to lower Kilpinen's record, set the year before.

Races such as these, the KAC Martini and the Volvo Nordic Tour have helped create a competitive spirit among cross country skiers in Australia. It has also firmly entrenched the need for instructive coaching in technique and involvement and to this end the ASF Nordic Committee has brought to Australia a number of top European and American coaches in recent years.

The first of these visits was in 1967 when leading Norwegian coach Mike Brady made the first of his three tours. He was accompanied by Mikkel Dobloug, Marcus Svendsen and Dag Jensvoll.

Together this quartet showed up the lack of technical expertise in Australian cross country skiing and ultimately led to the emergence of Kilpinen and Kore Grunnsund.

Grunnsund showed a remarkable adaptability in his training methods and soon had an eager Ross Martin under his wing learning and developing his skills. The coach was quick to instil into his pupil the necessity of overseas training and competition.

This one vital point, stressed by both Kilpinen and Grunnsund, has led to the remarkable improvement in Australian Nordic skiing over the last 10 years. But there is still a long way to go. The average Australian skier has a tremendous overall strength, but lack of finesse holds him back from all but a toehold on international recognition and success.

The lack of Australian success in international Nordic events led the Australian Olympic Federation to reject their pleas for inclusion in the five-man skiing team for the 1976 Olympics.

The AOF ratified five Alpine skiers for the Games, but because our Nordic skiers weren't expected to do well they were dropped from the team and four years of training and competition were wasted.

Ross Martin, in a letter to AOF president Sir Edgar Tanner, described the decision "as the greatest single unjust blow that could have been dealt to one of the fastest growing sports in this country."

MALCOLM MILNE . . . Australia's first international winner

16 YACHTING
By BOB ROSS

BOB ROSS—Internationally recognised as a top authority in yachting and sailing, is the "Sydney Morning Herald" correspondent covering America and Admiral's Cup series, Sydney—Hobart and national class titles, and is editor—publisher of the popular "Australian Sailing" magazine.

Australian yachting, in the past 10 years, has been a burgeoning recreation as well as a sport, with an annual growth rate in the sale of stock yachts—many of which may never race.

A census conducted by the Australian Yachting Federation—organising body for the racing side of the sport—showed nearly 120,000 yachtsmen sailing with affiliated clubs in 1976.

But Australian yachtsmen have learned in the past decade that growth in numbers does not necessarily mean higher competitive standards. They have had to work hard in the racing segment of the sport to maintain the international respect earned over 10 years ago.

Like many other Australian sports, yachting broke dramatically into international competition in the late 1950s and early 1960s.

Rolly Tasker, the Perth sailmaker, won a world championship in the International Flying Dutchman Class—now the Olympic two-man dinghy—in 1958.

Gretel, designed by Alan Payne for a syndicate headed by the late Sir Frank Packer, scared the daylights out of the US yachting establishment by taking a race in the America's Cup challenge of 1962 and going close to winning two other races.

Bryan Price and Chris Hough of Adelaide won the 1963 world 505 dinghy class world championship at Larchmont, New York, against 62 competitors from 10 nations—and the following year, John Parrington, also of Adelaide and with Hough, won it again in Ireland.

And so, the 1966 world 505 championship was sailed in Adelaide. Jim Hardy, with Max Whitnall as crew, won the championship for Australia for the third time in a row, beating the great Danish sailor Paul Elvstrom into second place.

Bill Northam of Sydney, in his sixtieth year, won yachting's first Olympic gold medal in the 1964 Olympics in Japan, with a crew that had intelligence, precision and experience in Pod O'Donnell and Dick Sargeant.

The Australian team—Mercedes 111 (Ted Kaufman), Balandra (Sir Robert Crichton-Brown) and Caprice of Huon (Gordon Reynolds)—won the 1967 Admiral's Cup—the international ocean racing teams' championship held every second year at Cowes, Isle of Wight, England.

By 1967, Australia's racing yachtsmen were riding a wave of success that perhaps lulled them into a false sense of security in their newly-found place in the international field.

For, as in many other sports, international standards began to steadily rise. In the 1967 America's Cup challenge, the US defender Intrepid, skippered by Bus Mosbacher, easily whipped the Australian challenger Dame Pattie in four straight races.

The Americans, no longer taking the Australians lightly as competitors as they had in 1962, closed ranks, enforced provisions in the America's Cup rules denying the Australians use of American-woven sail cloth. Olin Stephens, the Madison Avenue genius of Twelve Metre yacht design, produced Intrepid, the outstanding Twelve of the post War years.

Although Dame Pattie, was a competitive boat designed by Warwick Hood and skippered by Jock Sturrock with a much freer hand in crew and equipment selection than under Sir Frank with Gretel in 1962, the Intrepid—Mosbacher combination was far superior.

The 1968 Olympic team failed to win any medals at Acapulco, Mexico.

Ron Jenyns of Brisbane finished fourth in the single-handed Finn class; Carl Ryves and Dick Sargeant of Sydney fourth in the Flying Dutchman class; the Dragon crew headed by John Cuneo of Brisbane was fifth;

the Star class crew of Dave Forbes and Dick Williamson of Sydney was sixth and the veteran 5.5 Barranjoey, chartered by Bill Solomons, with Mick York and Scott Kaufman crewing, was seventh.

While there were no medals, the realisation was born that more first-class international competition must be sought in off-Games' years. In those days there were few benevolent sponsors and certainly no benevolent governments.

And so, financed by raffles, gambling nights and wine bottlings, the Olympic classes and other international classes intent on winning world championships, began a regular trek to the northern hemisphere.

Besides gaining valuable international experience, they enjoyed some successes as well. In 1969 John Cuneo, with John Shaw and Ross Bradbury as crew took Jock Robbie, a boat sponsored by a syndicate of Royal Queensland Yacht Squadron members, to Majorca and finished second in the Dragon Gold Cup.

Three Australian 5.5 metre class yachts—

ADMIRALS CUP 1967 . . . Mercedes III (above), Balandra (below) and Caprice of Huon (bottom right), victors by a record margin

NICHOLAS II . . . sponsorship a boon

Pam (Gordon Ingate), Crest (Carl Halvorsen) and Kings Cross (Frank Tolhurst) went to Scandinavia in 1969 for the world championship. Although they did not gain a place, in the main titles, Ingate did win the highly-prized Scandinavian Gold Cup in Norway and the Australians convinced the northern hemisphere 5.5 sailors that the next world championship should be sailed in Australia.

That championship, held off Palm Beach, Sydney, in 1970, was won by David Forbes steering Carabella—owned by Kevin McCann who, with Jim Gannon, crewed for Forbes.

Dinghy class sailors, too, began to restlessly search for international competition. In 1968, the 100 members of the Jollyboat Owners' Association, based at the unpretentious but lively Port Melbourne Yacht Club, raised $2,500 to send Roger Byrne and Bill Binks to USA where they won the world championship.

In 1969 David McKay of Cronulla, in a boat he built and mostly designed himself, won the world Moth class championship in the USA. The same year, Syd Lodge and John

Bolton of Perth went to England and won the world championship in the Hornet Class—a very strong class in England where it was designed but to that point sailed only in Perth and Melbourne.

In 1970, John Gilder and Doug Giles of Adelaide won the world championship for the two-man 470 class at Tel Aviv, after training heroically all winter on icy St Vincent Gulf. They won again the following year at Cherbourg, from a fleet of 60 from 14 nations.

As with the 5.5s, the fund-raising and hard training effort to put a winning crew on the starting line on the other side of the world paid its dividend with the 420 world championship being allocated to Adelaide in 1973.

Again, an Australian crew won. Anders Wangel, a professor of medicine at the University of Adelaide, with Gilder's former crew Doug Giles, won comfortably from crews representing 11 nations. Gilder was runner-up.

The Australians swept the major placings with the best visitor, Jean Chaussade of France, back in tenth place.

This double-edged trend continued in both dinghy and one-design keel yacht classes with participation in championships in other parts of the world leading to world championships being allocated by class controlling associations to Australia.

This meant massive voluntary effort by Australian class associations to fund and organise the championships, but the interflow of talent and experience—the chance for local sailors to race against the world's best—was well worth the effort, and certainly lifted the standards of sailing in Australia.

And so Rodney Pattisson and Iain MacDonald-Smith, the incomparable British crew, won the world Flying Dutchman championship for the third time on St Vincent Gulf in 1970. The great Danish sailor, Paul Elvstrom, won his 11th world championship in the Soling Class, off Palm Beach, Sydney in 1974 with Australia's David Forbes runner-up.

And John Cassidy and Warwick Crisp of Perth won the world Fireball championship in lumpy seas and big winds on St Vincent Gulf, also in 1974. Chris Law of Britain won the Finn Gold Cup from a strong international entry on Waterloo Bay, Queensland in 1976.

The 1972 Olympic yachting at Kiel,

DAME PATTIE . . . a competitive boat

Germany re-established the Australians among the world's best in the Olympic classes following the years of drought since Bill Northam's gold medal win in 1964.

Significantly, the two gold medals won by Australian crews went to those headed by Dave Forbes and John Cuneo, blooded at previous Olympics.

Both had campaigned earnestly on international circuits since Acapulco in 1968, and benefited tremendously from experience in Europe just before the 1972 Games. The Australian Yachting Federation gained permission from the Australian Olympic Federation to send the yachtsmen before the main body of the team in time to compete in European regattas.

The team, managed by David Linacre of Melbourne, was the best-prepared and organised Australia had sent away.

Forbes knew exactly what he needed to win and, after finishing 28th in the Kiel Week regatta and tenth in the European championship in the Star Class, boldly discarded all his

equipment. He chartered a European Star with an American made mast and boom, recut a mainsail himself and with crewman John Anderson made the whole boat mechanically perfect.

By the time the Games started, they had the fastest boat in the fleet. They read the tricky winds well and returned consistently high 3-8-2-3-4-1-3 placings to win.

Cuneo re-thought his whole approach just before the Olympics. He had managed only 14th in the Dragon Gold Cup prior to the Games and could not get his boat, Wyuna, going in the choppy Baltic seas. But he sorted out his tuning problems with the help of Olympic team reserve Mike Fletcher, the sailmaker and tuning specialist, who also persuaded him to re-organise his crewing techniques.

Fletcher felt Cuneo was trying to do too much himself within the boat instead of concentrating on helming and making full use of his crew in John Shaw and Tom Anderson.

They began the Olympics sensationally, winning the first three races. Cuneo crashed to 19th in the fourth race and a non-finish through lack of wind in the fifth put him under pressure. But he stole a third placing in the sixth heat and in the final heat finished fourth after pushing the US boat, the only competitor with a remote chance of beating him, back to 12th position.

John Bertrand of Melbourne who stayed on in the USA to work for a sailmaker after crewing on Gretel 11 in the 1970 America's Cup, finished fourth in the Finn Class.

Mark Bethwaite, and Tim Alexander, like Bertrand bright young stars of the team, were in the running early, but finished eighth after two bad placings in the last two heats.

Overall, the Australians were the most successful yachting team at the Olympics. But Australian Olympic Class yachtsmen were smart enough to realise they had to do more to remain competitive through to the next Olympiad.

Forbes and Cuneo won their gold medals largely as a result of personal drive and financial outlay. To win again, in the face of

DAVID FORBES . . . a gold medal

steadily rising competitive standards, demanded a more organised approach.

And so an Olympic planning committee was established as a sub-committee of the Australian Yachting Federation to co-ordinate Olympic team preparation for 1976 and, in particular, to attract, sponsorship to assist the best Olympic class sailors to travel the long and expensive miles between Olympics to contest the international regattas—and remain competitive.

This committee, headed by Kevin McCann of Sydney with Ken Berkeley as secretary, raised more than $170,000 in sponsorship and in co-ordinated fund-raising efforts instituted an annual regatta for the Olympic classes that helped build tremendous esprit de corps—as well as improve the standard of competition.

And so the 1976 Olympic Games team arrived at Kingston, Ontario, knowing it was fully competitive because of the continuing international participation of its members since 1972.

And yet, the results were not as spectacular —no golds, but two bronze medals—the 470 crew, Ian Brown and Ian Ruff of NSW, and John Bertrand in the Finn Class.

Forbes slumped to 11th in the Soling Class. Later, he blamed the break he had the previous season sailing in the Six Metre American-Australian Challenge Cup match, for his loss of form.

The Flying Dutchman crew, of Mark Bethwaite and Tim Alexander, finished ninth; the Tempest crew, Joern Hellner and James Byrne, were also ninth, and the Tornado class crew Brian Lewis and Warren Rock of Perth, fourth—unlucky to miss out on a medal. They broke their mast while leading the first race.

The team was accompanied by Frank Bethwaite as meteorologist and Mike Fletcher as coach was certainly the best-organised lineup Australia has ever sent to the Olympic yachting events.

And if the Olympic planning committee had not been so diligent in its efforts to prepare the team, it would probably have slid right out of contention, as did so many Australian competitors in other sports at those Olympics.

Following the success of the OPC, the Australian Yachting Federation formed a special

GRETEL II . . . innovative and fast [Old Spice]

development committee, headed by Ken Berkeley, with the aim of improving the whole sport of yachting—mainly by obtaining coordinating and channelling sponsorship money to significant sectors of the sport.

The committee is looking at new coaching schemes, improving junior sailing and developing women's sailing as a fully autonomous part of the sport.

In 1977, the Australian Yachting Federation sent an official team to the first world women's sailing championship in England where, Lyndal Coxon, a 22-year-old medical student from Sydney, won the singlehanded Laser Class.

Australia's offshore sailors have justly earned a reputation for excellence in strong winds and rough seas.

They are bred that way because it takes guts, endurance and raw courage to win in Australian waters. Very few Sydney-Hobart races as the top long ocean race on the Australian calendar are sailed without the fleet encountering a sou'westerly to gale force spin-

ning off the Roaring Forties in Bass Strait or off the Tasmanian coast.

Boats, as well as men, are tuned to more robust winds than those that predominate in European and North American waters and that is why the Australians usually have problems when the weather falls light.

The Australians were the first to bring a serious team approach to the Admiral's Cup.

To justify the expenditure of $100,000 or so on transporting three yachts and their crews to England and back, they have to take it seriously. And so they were the first to train and campaign as a team.

Initially the Admiral's Cup, established in 1957, tended to be regarded as an offshoot of Cowes Week in England, the result of lesser importance than the winning of individual races.

Now, with other countries including Britain following the pattern first set by the Australians of selection trials, team training and team meetings to exchange navigation and tactical information, it has truly become the ocean racing championship of the world—and therefore much harder to win.

The Australians took the Cowes scene by surprise when they won the 1967 Admiral's Cup at their second attempt by a record margin of 104 points with consistent performances from Balandra (Sir Robert Crichton-Brown), Mercedes 111 (Ted Kaufman) and Caprice of Huon (Gordon Reynolds).

They were well placed to win again in 1969 with a team of Ragamuffin, an exceptional performer newly-launched by Syd Fischer, Koomooloo, owned and skippered by Denis O'Neil as a modified version of Mercedes 111—and Mercedes 111.

They went into the last race of the series, the Fastnet, with a small points lead from Britain and America. But at the end of that race, a vast and complete calm settled over the whole fleet, leaving the smaller Australian yachts hopelessly becalmed near the Scilly Isles.

The Americans, with two big yachts, Palawan and Carina, and the innovative lifting-keel Red Rooster, skippered by its designer Dick Carter, finished before the calm winning the Admiral's Cup by 14 points from Australia with Britain another 11 points behind.

The 1971 team lost a very real chance of winning the Admiral's Cup when Koomooloo, then owned by Norman Rydge Jr, sheared the rudder from its stock on a hard run home in the Fastnet race won by Ragamuffin, the only Australian yacht to win the British classic.

The third member of the team was Salacia 11 (Arthur Byrne), almost a sister-ship to Ragamuffin and an outstanding yacht, taking second place in one of the shorter Admiral's Cup races.

By 1973, the Cup had firmed as a major international event with 16 teams competing. However, it was not one of the "big three"—Britain, US or Australia—that took the series but a very well drilled German team.

Its Saudade, helmed by Hans Beilken, former One Ton Cup winner, was outstanding, winning both of the short, inshore races. Australia finished second, with Ginkgo (Gary Bogard), Apollo 11 (Alan Bond) and Ragamuffin (Syd Fischer), Britain was third.

The winds tended to be light, not enough for the two outstanding offwind performers,

Ginkgo and Apollo 11—both designed by Bob Miller—to show their capabilities.

The 1975 series was sailed almost entirely in light, flukey winds. The Australian team—Bumblebee (John Kahlbetzer), Mercedes IV (Ted Kaufman) and Love and War (Peter Kurts)—failed completely to come to terms with these conditions and made some bad tactical errors as well. Britain won, with 980 points from Germany (875) and the USA (846). Australia finished a dismal ninth, the first time in six challenges she had been out of the first three.

While competing for the Admiral's Cup continues to be the major goal in Australian off-shore yachting, a new compartment of the sport—level rating—is attracting strong competitors. The level rating concept was born in 1965 as the inspiration of Jean Peytel of France for competition between yachts of similar size racing without handicaps.

This was done by selecting a handicap rating, now 27.5 ft under the International Offshore Rule, to which all yachts had to conform. This gave room within the rating formula to experiment with hull shape and sail area, providing the answer came to 27.5 or less.

The yachts it provided were called One Tonners, after the trophy they race for—an ornate creation fashioned from a 22lb. block of silver originally presented to the Cercle de la Voile de Paris in 1898 for small yachts conforming to the restricted One Ton class rules.

The idea was successful, and other level rating classes followed—Half Ton, Quarter Ton, Three quarter Ton and Two Ton. With the yachts in each class theoretically the same speed, the racing is as close as in the one-design dinghy and keel yacht classes.

And the level-rating classes have provided hot-house development in ocean racing design that has been the major influence on all ocean-racing design over the past few years.

Syd Fischer, the tough Sydney sailor, won the One Ton Cup in 1971 with Stormy Petrel, in Auckland. Chris Bouzaid of New Zealand had won the Cup at Heligoland, Germany, in 1969. Bouzaid won again, off Sydney, in 1972, skippering Wai-aniwa. Second, only fractions of a point behind, was the Sydney yacht Pilgrim (Graham Evans).

The Half Ton class (rating 21.6 ft.) quickly won a strong following in Australia, and its close racing produced another world champion crew, headed by Tom Stephenson of Melbourne during 1975. Stephenson's win in the selection trials was the first real breakthrough of the Sydney domination of Australian ocean racing.

Stephenson went to the USA a long time before the world championship, chartered the best Half Tonner he could find—a Doug Peterson design called Foxy Lady—and prepared meticulously for the world championship held on Lake Michigan, Chicago.

He had a strong crew in Rob Hose, Tony Michael and John Green, with the widely-experienced Sydney sailor Hugh Treharne as tactician. The Australians won two races and finished clear winners with 189.5 points from the US yacht Checkered Demon (Loys Sharbonet) on 169.

New Zealand designers and boatbuilders have, for nearly a century strongly-influenced the Australian scene. The level-rating One Tonners, Half Tonners and Quarter Tonners designed by Aucklanders Bruce Farr and Paul Whiting were, dominating their respective classes in Australia by 1977.

Both designers favoured a light, shallow, dinghy-style hull with seven-eighths instead of the more usual masthead rig. These yachts were competitive to windward against the more "traditional" designs with their masthead rigs.

But reaching across the wind and running before it, they were markedly superior, fast and easy to handle.

Catamaran racing has been very strong in Australia since its introduction in 1954 by Melbourne boat builder-designer Charles Cunningham and his son, Lindsay.

Today, the do-it-yourself fleets they inspired have been joined by a host of factory-produced fibreglass classes that give thrilling performances and good racing to hundreds of followers.

A British design, the Tornado, was selected as the first catamaran class in the Olympics. It won international status after a trials series that was contested by a Cunningham design. However, the Melbourne father-and-son team were more than compensated for this disappointment

[Old Spice]

AMERICA'S CUP CHALLENGE . . . Australia (left) and Southern Cross trialling out for the 1977 challenge

RAGAMUFFIN . . . Syd Fischer's consistent performer

ment by having one of their creations win the International Catamaran Challenge Trophy (popularly known as the "Little America's Cup") in 1970 after three unsuccessful attempts.

The trophy is contested by International C class catamarans, perhaps the most exciting sailboats in the world with few restrictions including 25 ft overall length, 14 ft beam and 300 sq ft of sail including the spars.

The Cunningham-designed Quest 111, sailed by Bruce Proctor and Graham Candy, defeated the Danish defender Sleipner, 4-3, after a nervously close series.

Quest 111, skippered by Proctor, with Graeme Ainslie crewing, retained the trophy on Port Phillip Bay in 1972 against the US challenger Weathercock.

Australia retained the trophy, with Miss Nylex, designed by Roy Martin and powered by a solid aerofoil wing instead of a sail, against a New Zealand challenge in 1974.

Two years later the soft-sailed Aquarius V, owned by Alex Kozloff and skippered by Robert Harvey won the trophy for the USA.

The Cunningham-designed Nicholas 11 failed to regain the trophy in mid 1977 in California losing 4-0 to Patient Lady 111 skippered by Duncan MacLane with Skip Banks.

The America's Cup, sailed in the now old-fashioned Twelve Metre class for an outlay of $1 million-plus per boat, in a freakish event that stands alone as yachting's greatest prize.

It is the type of challenge the Australian gambling nature finds hard to resist, and while it remains unwinnable, entrenched in the New York Yacht Club Australia has mounted the most formidable challenges since the War.

After Dame Pattie's chastening defeat of 1967, Sir Frank Packer commissioned Alan Payne to design a second Gretel—and Gretel 11, like Gretel, Payne's first challenger for Sir Frank in 1962, was innovative and fast enough to have won.

It was only lack of battle practice and the shattering psychological blow of losing the second race on a protest after crossing the finishing line first that cost Jim Hardy and his crew the America's Cup in 1970.

The US defender Intrepid, altered since its 1967 win and skippered by Bill Ficker, won the first race after Gretel started badly, then lost a man overboard. Gretel 11 was first to finish in the second race but was disqualified after a protest by Intrepid for colliding at the start.

Intrepid won the third race, in a moderate-fresh breeze that suited her. Gretel snatched the fourth. As the wind dropped into the lighter wind range that favoured her, she proved faster, and Hardy and his afterguard took ad-vantage of a tactical error when Intrepid failed to cover on the last leg.

With the score 3-1, Intrepid was still psychologically favoured and won the deciding fifth race after the closest contest in recent memory.

Alan Bond of Perth challenged in 1974 with Southern Cross, a Bob Miller design. The boat was fast in fresh winds, but light air prevailed in Newport that year and the new US defender Courageous skippered by Ted Hood disposed of Southern Cross, skippered by Jim Hardy, in four races.

However, the belief that the America's Cup can be won led to two Australian challenges for 1977. Gordon Ingate captained a modified Gretel 11 for the Royal Sydney Yacht Squadron and Bond tried again, with a new design by Bob Miller—who changed his name be deep poll to Ben Lexcen—and Johan Valentijn. The boat was Australia and the skipper Noel Robins.

The dual challenge perhaps summed up the attitude of Australian racing yachtsmen to international competition. The problems imposed by distance competing in the northern hemisphere and receiving the latest information on trends and techniques are immense. But the Australians are great triers, and will no doubt mount another challenge, despite Australia's spanking 4-0 loss to Courageous skippered by the flamboyant Ted Turner.

PETER COLE . . . ALAN PAYNE . . . JIM HARDY

17 BOXING

By RAY MITCHELL

RAY MITCHELL— World renowned for his incredible boxing knowledge, he has also won acclaim as author, editor and television personality and has acted in every capacity, other than medical officer, in the sport.

Fight fans usually judge a boxer on his last ring performance, often assessing his whole career on that final fight.

This is unfair because a champion normally loses his last contest, or, at best, is below his best form.

Thus Jimmy Carruthers is judged on his comeback fights, beginning seven years and four months after he became the first world champion—of any division—to retire without a defeat or a draw to mar a perfect record. Fans forget that he was a great bantamweight in the early 1950s.

So it was with Lionel Rose, our greatest bantamweight (8.6) since Carruthers. Lionel started to lose favour in 1970, lost a little more in 1971, then nose-dived to disaster in his comeback of 1975—after more than four years of inactivity—ending with two "inglorious" knockout defeats in 1976.

But what of Lionel Rose at his best? Remember how awe-struck you were when he demolished Rocky Gattellari in December 1967? Remember how thrilled you were when he won the world bantamweight title from the formidable Fighting Harada in Japan in February 1968? Were you one of the million or so who thronged Melbourne streets to be part of a reception in the 19-year-old's honour when he returned with that world title?

Remember how proud you were of him when, after two successful world title defences overseas in 1968, he won the A.B.C. Sportsman of the Year, several overseas Boxer of the Year and other Australian Sportsman of the Year awards, named Australian of the Year and awarded an M.B.E.?

You were glad to know him then, just as you were when he defended his title successfully against Englishman Alan Rudkin at Kooyong on March 8, 1969. That was the richest fight in Australian history, bringing—with TV rights—$300,000.

Lionel Rose had charisma. From the boxing viewpoint he had everything. There have been harder punchers, tougher fighters, better boxers, but Australia never produced a pugilist who had so much of every department of the sport.

He lost 11 of his 53 professional bouts, but four of these came in his comeback phase. A further five came from his losing of the world bantamweight title to his first retirement.

I first saw him in his seventh professional fight. At that time he had passed his 17th birthday by only five weeks, but such an impression did he make that I wrote of him as a definite world champion of the future.

To me, Rose at his best—and we always must judge a boxer at his best—was THE flower of the Australian pugilistic garden in the past decade.

My number two of the past 10 years was Lionel Rose's firm friend Johnny Famechon, world featherweight title-holder from January 1969, when he outpointed Jose Legra, to May 1970 when he was outpointed by Vicente Saldivar.

There was much speculation about a possible match between Famechon and Rose in 1969, and every boxing promoter and would-be-promoter in Australia would have given his eye-teeth to have promoted such a contest. It would have broken all attendance and gate records.

Who would have won: Rose, the complete all-rounder, or "Fammo", the wizard of speed?

Enigmatically, in view of my placing Rose as number one, I would have tipped "Fammo" to win by a points decision, by virtue of his speed of foot, but he would have had to stay at long range. If he had conducted the bout at close quarters he would have lost to Rose.

Famechon, one of the top "Mr Nice Guys"

of boxing, was lightning on his feet, and when at his best, would thrill fans with his brilliance in boxing skill and evasion. Yet there were times, in even his best fights, when he would become negative and cause irritation.

Famechon was knocked down a few times, but nobody ever beat him inside the distance—because when he rose from a knockdown, he was more difficult to nail than a shadow to a wall.

Famechon lost only five of his 67 fights. Probably his finest hour was when he knocked out Fighting Harada in the 14th round of their second meeting, fought in Tokyo.

He lost his last fight—and his title—in Rome, with come-backing Mexican southpaw Vincente Saldivar being a points winner. It is my opinion that Famechon would have won if he had thrown his right hand more often. Only three times did he land with this blow and each time he knocked Saldivar back.

[News Ltd.]

ROCKY MATTIOLI . . . mature, tougher, stronger

What a pity he did not have one more fight —a return with Saldivar. Famechon surely would have won that.

During the last 10 years there have not been as many outstanding contenders as in some other decades, but one for whom I have a soft spot was Charkey Ramon—real name Dave Ballard.

Having refereed 19 of his 35 professional fights, I knew his every move and intended move. He was Australian and Commonwealth junior-middleweight (11 stone) champion.

He should have been world champion at the weight.

Charkey was a fighter cast in the Les Darcy mould. He hit hard enough to knock out 21 of his 35 opponents, and he lost only once—a points decision to 12-pound heavier Fred Etuati in Ramon's 16th paid fight.

Ramon won the Australian title on June 28, 1972—one week after his 22nd birthday— by knocking out Paul Lovi in the third round. He won the Commonwealth crown by halting Englishman Pat Dwyer in the eighth round on October 30, 1972.

In March 1973 he met world rated Jacques Kechichian in Noumea. Ramon clearly winning on points. Before the decision was announced Kechichian raised the Aussie's hand. Of the three officials only one awarded Kechichian a round.

On June 7, 1973, Ramon outclassed Canadian Donato Paduano in a Commonwealth title defence. Paduano had beaten Luis Rodriguez, one-round conqueror of Tony Mundine, and nobody had ever halted Donato—until Ramon did it.

Ramon toyed with the Canadian; he used him as he would a sparring partner in the gymnasium. It was not until the 11th round that Ramon opened up with full power. When he did Donato fell apart. One more punch would have dropped him.

Ramon broke a collarbone while surfing. The injury kept him out of action for a while. That clear, he then suffered a severe collarbone break that did not heal properly. A medical specialist told him he could throw his shoulder out with one punch, so Charkey Ramon retired.

In my book Charkey Ramon undoubtedly

LIONEL ROSE . . . the best

LIONEL ROSE by Minary of Fighter

151

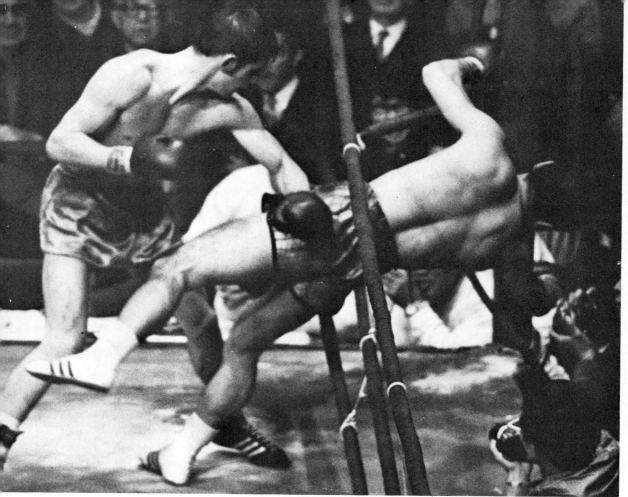

JOHNNY FAMECHON . . . victor over Fighting Harada

would have beaten the then world junior-middleweight champion Koichi Wajima. As Jacques Kechichian said dazedly after his loss to Ramon: "He too strong. He just keeps coming."

It seems Hector Thompson always has been with us because he has been on top in Australia for so long, but also because everyone tabbed him as a sure champion from the time he started pelting punches for pay early in 1970.

Since then Thompson has collected the Australian and Commonwealth junior-welterweight (10.0) titles, the Australasian lightweight (9.9) and welterweight (10.7)—and the Australian welterweight crowns.

He also has fought for two world titles: lightweight and junior-welterweight.

He was unlucky in both—unlucky on June 2, 1973, because in world lightweight champion Roberto Duran he was meeting one of the three greatest lightweights of all time, and unlucky on November 15, 1975 on two counts: Firstly he was stopped because of a cut eye, and although behind on points, was coming home strongly and secondly because he met champion Antonio Cervantes one fight too early.

One fight too early? Cervantes lost his title to Wilfredo Benitez in his next fight—and showed unmistakable signs of being well past his best.

But Thompson, conqueror of two former world champions, Alfonso Frazer and Pedro Adigue, is to try again for the world junior-welter title. As this is being written Thompson has been promised a shot at Saensak Muangsurin's W.B.C.—recognised title, and if he wins that he will chase the W.B.A—recognised title-holder—Antonio Cervantes.

Thompson would beat Cervantes now. Three times he beat tough Carlos Gimenez who met Cevantes for the vacant title in June 1977, and Gimenez would have beaten Cervantes, but for suffering a cut eye which terminated the bout.

Hector Thompson is class. He boxes well, has an exceptionally good defence, is a dangerous body puncher, is extremely tough—three of his four stoppage losses have come through injuries—and hates to lose, thus being dangerous until the final bell. In his 74 professional fights he has lost only six.

Paul Ferreri is one of those boxers about whom fight fans say: "He's hard to beat, but who cares?"

Ferreri is a southpaw. He is fast, clever without being flamboyant, not a particularly heavy puncher, hard to hit solidly and usually does just enough to win.

His record shows 51 victories, five draws and only five losses in 61 fights. Only one of those losses came within the distance, and that to Carlos Zarate for the W.B.C.—recognised world bantamweight title.

That was on August 28, 1976, and a cut eye brought the termination of the bout in the 12th round.

At that, Ferreri went further than any other of Zarate's opponents. Carlos has the fantastic record of 45 straight wins in his unbeaten career, with 44 of those being by knockout. It is the most amazing record in history.

Ferreri won the Australian bantamweight title in October 1969. He won the Commonwealth title in September 1972, relinquishing the national crown in 1975, but winning it back in 1976.

He lost the Commonwealth title to Sully Shittu in Ghana in January 1977 in a disputed decision and is listed as the official number one contender for Shittu's title.

There have been times when Paul Ferreri has thrilled the fans, such as when he beat Kid Snowball in 1971. Snowball brought out the best in Ferreri by sheer aggression and threat of dynamite hitting. In fights such as that one, Ferreri excelled himself.

Ferreri not only is one of the top 10 Australian pugilists of the past decade, he also is one of the best bantamweights this country has developed in the past half-century.

In 1970 a 16-year-old Italian-born fighter who migrated to Australia as a child started

CHARKEY RAMON . . . should have been world champion [Fighter Magazine]

to thrill television fight fans. His name: Rocky Mattioli, christened Rocco and nicknamed Rocky after his godfather, former unbeaten world heavyweight champion Rocco Marchegiano (Rocky Marciano).

Mattioli rose too fast. By the time he was 18 he was right up there with the best welterweights in the country—and ran the risk of burning himself out. So he retired for 16 months.

When Rocky Mattioli came back in April 1973 he was more mature, stronger, tougher and he hit harder.

Three fights later he stopped Jeff White to win the Australian welterweight title. That was on May 17, 1972. It was quite a night to remember.

In the 12th round Mattioli decked White with a solid punch to the jaw. White was on his feet at eight but was dazed and the fight was stopped.

Italians swarmed into the ring. They came

through the ropes, over the ropes and under the bottom strand. They chaired Rocky.

Suddenly there was a loud crack. The supports under the centre of the ring snapped. The ring went down in the middle so that it was like the letter V.

The Italians left the ring faster than they had entered it!

In 1975 Mattioli relinquished his Australian title to campaign in Italy for a world title. On August 6th 1977 he won the W.B.C.—recognised world junior-middleweight title by knocking out champion Eckhard Dagge of Germany in the fifth round.

To date 24-year-old Rocky Mattioli has had 52 professional contests, winning 35 by KO, 11 on points. He has lost four, only one inside the distance, and that because of a cut eye.

One of the most exciting fighters to arrive on the Australian scene is Tony Mundine.

Win or lose, Mundine makes the heart beat faster. He has been cheered, lauded, abused and denigrated, but he still pulls in the crowds.

He has held three Australian titles—middleweight (11.6), light-heavyweight (12.7) and heavyweight. He is the only Australian in history to win Commonwealth titles in two divisions.

Of his 64 fights he has won 47 by KO, with 40 of his fights against imported boxers. Of these he has won 30 by KO, four on points. Overseas he has had eight fights, winning five by KO, one on points.

Early in his career there were many who freely tipped him to win a world title. There were even some who believed he would beat the great world champion Carlos Monzon, but when he got his chance he was knocked out in the seventh round.

Why has he been abused and denigrated at times? One reason lies in the fact that many

TONY MUNDINE . . . exciting

overseas boxers imported to meet him fell far below him in class, but as Mundine has said: "I only do the fighting."

Probably the biggest reason for the downgrading of Mundine by some fight fans is that he has been knocked out seven times. They were not mugs who knocked him out.

Mundine won the Australian middleweight title in April 1970. In February 1972 he conceded 44 pounds in weight to Australian heavyweight champion Foster Bibron — and knocked out Bibron in the 11th round to take the title.

In April the same year he knocked out Bunny Sterling in the 15th round to win the Commonwealth middleweight title — and Bunny was no rabbit.

In November 1973 Paris flocked to see Mundine outpoint former world middleweight champion Emile Griffith. Paris had taken Tony to its heart a few months earlier when he

flattened Frenchman Max Cohen in the fourth round.

But in February 1974 Mundine himself took the full count against bullet-headed American negro Bennie Briscoe.

At Buenos Aires on October 5, 1974, Mundine was knocked out by Monzon in the seventh round. After being flattened in the first round by "Sweet" James Marshall at Brisbane Festival Hall on May 2, 1975, Tony Mundine announced his retirement. His titles went into the melting pot.

Four months later he was back, this time as a light-heavyweight. After one warm-up fight he knocked out Steve Aczel of Australia to take Steve's Australian and Commonwealth light-heavy titles. Since then he has made four successful defences of the Commonwealth diadem.

In June 1977 he knocked out Australian heavyweight champion Maile Haumona in

HECTOR THOMPSON . . . Buries a left into Baby Cassius' face

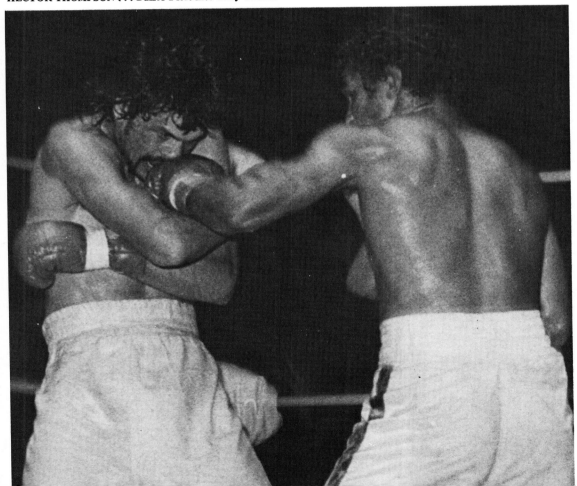

the 10th round of a billed non-title fight, but as the contest was over three-minute rounds, Mundine won the title.

Those seven KO defeats prevent Mundine from being recognised as the best middleweight or light-heavyweight Australia has produced, but it is doubtful if any Australian champion in either of those two divisions has been more exciting to watch.

Who was the Australian champion who, as challenger, competed for nine different titles — an Australian record — and won five of them?

The answer is Jeff White, to me one of the most courageous and under-rated champions Australia has had.

He was not a hard puncher, but he was

JEFF WHITE . . . underrated

persistent. He fought like former world triple champion Henry Armstrong, but without Henry's power of punch.

Freddie Wicks, who lost the Australian lightweight title to White, told me: "In the first few rounds I thought: 'This fellow can't punch. I'll beat him', but he just kept coming, boring in, not giving me any peace and he wore me out."

White's title-collecting started with the winning of the Queensland State junior-lightweight (9.4) and lightweight in 1969.

In the same year he beat Con Russell in a bout billed for the vacant Australian junior-lightweight title but as Russell was ranked only number four contender, this was not recognised as a legitimate Australian title fight.

The following year White took the national lightweight title from Wicks, and the Australian welter crown from Alan Moore. In between he fought champion Percy Hayles for the commonwealth lightweight title, losing by an official half a point.

He outpointed Lionel Rose in a lightweight title defence in 1971, outpointed Alan Moore's brother Paul in a welter title defence, but was stopped by champion Ralph Charles in a Commonwealth welter title attempt.

White was out-weighed by Charles. A smart boxer can outpoint a heavier fighter, but when the lighter man is an aggressive fighter who relies on his aggression, stamina and strength alone to win fights, he cannot beat a heavier man who also relies on strength, — particularly if the heavier man is a solid puncher.

White was out-gunned and he never again appeared to be as good a fighter as before.

Yet he still went after titles, losing to the amazing boxer Manny Santos in an Australasian lightweight title tilt, and going under by two points to Hector Thompson for the Australian junior-welter title.

Jeff White lost nine of his 35 fights — 13 of those fights were title tilts — but I always will have a soft spot for Jeff. He was guts personified.

Lionel Rose, Johnny Famechon, Charkey Ramon, Hector Thompson, Paul Ferreri, Rocky Mattioli, Tony Mundine and Jeff White. These are the eight Australians I rank the standouts of the past decade. If only we had more space we would add Henry Nissen, flyweight, and Bob Dunlop, light-heavyweight.

18 CYCLING

By JOHN HOGGETT

JOHN HOGGETT . . . Sports Editor of the "Sydney Daily Mirror" in 1975 and 1976 and currently Sports Editor of the "Sydney Daily Telegraph". Covered the 1976 Montreal Olympics for the "News Ltd" group including all the cycling. Highly regarded throughout the industry as a reporter with great all-round sporting knowledge.

Pedalling down memory lane through the fates and fortunes of Australia's leading cyclist during the past 10 years is almost a nightmare—more torturous than the most rugged section of any King-of-the-mountain near the end of a strenuous road tour.

Every downward push of the pedal rolls off another name . . . Waddell, Ryan, Nicholson, Johnson, Danny Clark, Hilton Clarke, Oliver, Bylsma, Gilmour, Don Allen, McVilly, Hoole, Bilney, Sutton, Sefton and Remo Sansonetti.

And every upstroke brings an uproar for a name left out . . . somebody else's personal favourite.

You don't need a push start to be told that so-and-so (the amateur) wouldn't sit on with the big boys (the professionals). The God-given talents of the pure speed machine—the sprinter—are pitted against the guts and determination of the distance and road riders.

All boiled down one thing is clear—Australia has produced many topliners capable of holding their heads high in any competition in the world against any competitor.

The wealth of talent produced in this country, usually starting as amateur juveniles, sub-juveniles or juniors, some working their way through to Commonwealth and Olympic Games representation and most ending up in the "pay for play" arena of the professionals, is just part of that wondrous thing that in past decades made Australia renowned as a sporting nation.

Maybe the rest of the world has caught up to a degree recently with more sophisticated methods of extracting the almost ultimate from their raw talent.

But make no mistake. The raw material is still here. Just as it was in the past. With assistance where it counts (usually in the pocket, these days!) that tradition stretching back through Ploog, Cox, Strom and Arnold, Mock-

ridge, Patterson, Opperman, Grey and Spears will continue.

Any era in any sport produces a few outstanding stars shining brightly above the rest of the galaxy and they tend to get all the accolades. But I feel the performances of some of the lesser lights against international competition—along with the champions—should be recorded in a chronology such as this.

As a jumping off point for the past 10 or so years I can think of no better dividing line than the 1966 Commonwealth Games in Jamaica. In that time Australian cyclists added to the country's honour roll a tally of five Commonwealth Games gold medals, 10 silver and six bronze; three world professional championships and two runners-up; and three Olympic Games silver medals.

While Jamaica produced no gold, five cyclists did collect six minor medals. Phil Bristow claimed the silver medal in the 1000m time trial behind Trinidad's Gibbon (1 min 9.6 sec) with a ride of 1: 10.9, team-mate Richard Hine picking up the bronze one-tenth of a second away. Hine picked up a second bronze behind England's world rated Hal Porter in the 4000 m pursuit and team-mate John Bylsma took the silver. Hilton Clarke had to settle for silver in the 10 miles when he finished a breath behind England's Ian Alsop, and Daryl Perkins came in third in the 1000m sprint with Trinidad's Gibbon again victorious.

Edinburgh 1970 saw Australia collect six medals—and two of them were gold. John Nicholson downed team-mate Gordon Johnson in the 1000m sprint final, and Johnson went one better to strike gold when he teamed with Ron Jonkers to win the tandem.

Up-and-coming youngster Danny Clark was second in the 4000m pursuit and road riders Ray Bilney and John Trevorrow gained

Ready for the bell lap in an Interstate track event

silver and bronze respectively behind New Zealand's Bruce Biddle over 102 miles. These three and another Australian, Dave Watson, broke away from the field with about 40 miles to go. Their sustained pacing gave the main bunch no chance of hauling them in.

Watson was forced to drop out with lung congestion and Trevorrow could not maintain the pace of the other pair close to the finish. Bilney looked the likely winner with 10 yards to go, but Biddle hurled himself and his bike at the line to get the judges' verdict by the narrowest of margins.

Three gold, four silver and two bronze was the cycling team's haul back across the Tasman Sea following the 1974 Commonwealth Games in Christchurch.

Defending champion John Nicholson showed why he was rated so highly in Europe with an easy gold in the 1000 m sprint. New South Welshman Dick Paris, also originally selected in the road team, showed he made the right choice by picking up a surprise gold in the 1000 m time trial, clocking 1 min 11.85 sec to just better Nicholson (1:11.92).

The third gold went to road rider Clyde Sefton, the silver medallist at the Munich Olympic Games in 1972, who was only named as a reserve when the team was selected, but obtained a start after Paris withdrew. Sefton's team-mate Remo Sansonetti took the bronze.

Minor medals were picked up by 18-year-old Garry Sutton—a bronze in the 4000 m pursuit behind defending champion Ian Hallam, of England, and a silver in the 4000 m teams pursuit along with Kevin Nicholls, Gary Reardon and Murray Hall.

With an average age of 19 they did extremely

well to finish so close to the experienced, world-ranking English team. Hall added another medal to his collection when he took the silver in the 10 miles and the tandem team of John Rush and Danny O'Neill also struck silver.

Although our 1968 Olympic team to Mexico failed to get among the medals despite top performances, Munich 1972 made the world sit up and take notice. Three silver medals won instant overall acclaim and did much to boost the sport at home.

Commonwealth Games sprint champion Nicholson duelled with Daniel Morelon in the 1000m sprint final, but had to bow to the Frenchman's superiority. Morelon had previously won the event in 1968, took the bronze in 1964 in Tokyo and went on to gain the silver behind Czechoslovakian Anton Tkac in Montreal in 1976. Morelon has been rated as the best-ever sprinter in cycling.

Tasmania's Danny Clark went close to snatching gold in the 1000m time trial. One of the early starters in his race against the clock Clark rode a sizzling 1 min 6.87 sec and then had to wait in mental agony as rider after rider failed to reach his mark. But it was not to be his day and finally Dane Niels Fredborg, the 1968 silver medallist, clipped 0.43 sec off Clark's time.

And finally there was Clyde Sefton, the boy from South Purrumbete, 40 km south-west of Colac in Victoria. He became the first Australian to be placed in an Olympic road race when he finished second to Dutchman Hans Kuiper.

Kuiper stole a march on the field near the end and opened up a small break to cross the line first in 4 hr 14 min 37.0 sec. Sefton outsprinted the cream of the world's amateur road riders in the main bunch's mad dash for silver to cover the 184.2 km journey in 4 hr 15 min 4.0 sec.

On the world championship scene Gordon Johnson took out the 1970 professional sprint title at Leicester, England—the first Australian to win the coveted rainbow jersey for this event since Bob Spears at Amsterdam in 1920. Johnson changed allegiances immediately after the 1970 Edinburgh Commonwealth Games on the offer of $1000 and declared: "I'll win the world championship." He was also runner-up in 1973.

Nicholson turned professional in 1974, but at the world titles had to settle for second place in the sprint title behind Pedar Pedersen of Denmark. But in 1975 he reversed the placings and in 1976 retained his title.

But over this decade or so one cyclist, although he has not won a gold medal or a world championship, stands astride as the most outstanding. That is the boy from George Town, Tasmania, Danny Clark. His ability to win events from six-day races down to 1000m sprints puts him into the same category as the great Sid Patterson and the late and great Russell Mockridge.

As an amateur Clark won nine Australian senior championships and three Commonwealth Games test races besides his Commonwealth Games 4000m pursuit silver medal and Olympic 1000m time trial silver.

In 1973 he won every individual track championship—the 1000m sprint, 1000m time trial, 4000m pursuit and the 10-mile. His other amateur titles were the sprint, time trial and 10-mile in 1971; the time trial and 10-mile in 1972; and in 1973 at the Commonwealth Games trials he took out the time trial, 4000m pursuit and 10-mile event.

But Clark never got to the Christchurch Games. On November 7, 1974, he announced he was turning professional following a dispute between cycling officials and his father, Terry.

Clark said he was angry because his father had been dropped as a trainer with the Australian team at the Games after being introduced as such to spectators during competition at an event in Hobart that year.

Leading amateur official Bill Young said that Terry Clark had been named as a trainer, but when he failed to turn up for the road titles in Adelaide and the Games trials in Sydney they had no alternative but to replace him.

So, on November 11, 1974, Danny Clark contested his first professional event at Camperdown Velodrome, Sydney, in the NSW mile title. But he could only finish fourth to evergreen professional Keith Oliver.

Clark had to wait for his third event of the day, the 25-lap scratch race, before recording his first pro win and first pay. Sixteen days later he showed his versatility when pitted against Oliver behind motor bikes in a special event.

Despite his lack of experience at this type of

KEITH OLIVER . . . leads Ezio Cardi (Italy) at Camperdown

racing at which Oliver is an expert — and riding on the outside — all the determination that has made him such a topliner showed through when he rounded his opponent in the last 100 m to win. Five days later he became the first rider in 10 years to win the Melbourne Cup on Wheels from scratch.

At the Australian professional titles in 1975, the only one he contested, Clark won the 10 km and 15 km, finished second to Nicholson in the sprint, third to Bylsma in the pursuit and teamed with fellow-Tasmanian Frank Atkins to take out the 100 km teams madison.

Later in the year at the world championships in Montreal, Clark finished fourth in the sprint title after being eliminated by titleholder Pedar Pedersen in the semi-finals. Pedersen lost his crown in the final to Nicholson.

Although commitments to racing reduce his appearances in Australia these days, Clark has managed to win the nation's top professional handicap wheel races from scratch — the Austral, Lavington, Burnie, Devonport and Latrobe.

But Europe and the glamorous six-day racing circuit and its associated big money is where Clark's future now lies. Not since the days of the legendary Australian team of Strom and Arnold has an Australian made such an impact on the hard-core European cycling fans.

Billed as Team Australia with fellow countryman, road rider Don Allen, they have become a major drawcard. The pair has competed in 14 six-day events and never been out of the top five. They shocked the cycling world when they took out the Ghent six in November 1976 and caused one critic to comment: "It was like a French cricket team beating Australia."

All-in-all Clark looks likely to be the dominating Australian cyclist well into the next decade and most top European riders acknowledge it is only a matter of him setting himself for a certain world title to add another line to his long list of achievements.

Nicholson and Gordon Johnson, with their world championship wins, have proved themselves to be in the top echelons of world cycling. But they do not have the all round ability of Clark.

Nicholson is a pure sprinter and there is a great possibility more world titles will come his way. His initial kick puts him at top speed

JAN BYLSMA . . . outstanding pedaller   [News Ltd.]

160

GARY SUTTON . . . heading for all time greatness

very quickly over the final 200 m of a sprint event, which is why he rides nearly all his races from the front, stalling his opponent to the last possible moment before hurtling himself over the last stretch to the line. But past 1000 m his initial momentum has left him and brings him back to the field.

Johnson, on the other hand, liked to ride his sprint events from behind. He used his opponent as a yardstick building up his pace from a slower start than Nicholson, putting his whole body into action so that after 200 m he was still accelerating. That arched back driving down into his legs to send him skimming round a track was pure power. Johnson was pretty successful at distances up to 10 miles, but past that his stamina began to tell.

Nicholson's list of achievements on the Australian scene stress how much he was a pure sprinter. He won only two amateur senior titles — the 1000 m sprint in 1970 and 1972. He also has won the 1975 and 1976 Australian professional sprint titles. By the same token Johnson won the 1967 Australian amateur sprint title, retained it in 1968 and added the 10-mile, the sprint, 1000 m time trial and 10-mile in 1969, and the 10-mile in 1970. As a professional he won the 1972 sprint and 10-mile titles, and the 10-mile again in 1973.

By the same token Johnson won the 1967 Australian amateur sprint title, retained it in 1968 and added the 10-mile, the sprint, 1000 m time trial and 10-mile in 1969, and the 10-mile in 1970. As a professional he won the 1972 sprint and 10-mile titles, and the 10-mile again in 1973.

Victorian Barry Waddell must also rate in this period, although he had won a string of Australian road and track titles before 1966. In the twilight of his career those huge legs carried him to the 1966 10-mile pro title, the one and 10-mile in 1967, the pursuit and five mile in 1968 and the five mile again in 1969. He was a great crowd pleaser and a tremendous six-day and handicap rider, winning many events.

The year 1966 also saw the last of the great Sid Patterson when he took out the pro one and five mile titles just to show the youngsters how it was done.

And then there's Graeme Gilmore, a Tasmanian who turned professional straight out of junior amateur ranks, won many of the country's top handicap events and found himself back with the scratch riders very quickly. He won the 1967 Australian road championship and in 1968 showed his versatility by taking the one mile title. Gilmour took himself off to Europe and after serving a long apprenticeship he is one of the finest six-day riders there, partnering the best.

Newcastle's bob Ryan is something of an enigma. Ask most Australians who he is and they couldn't tell you. Yet he took out six successive NSW sprint championships and the Australian sprint championship in 1967-68-70-71-73. In the last he beat Johnson in the final. He also won the 1969 one mile title, and has partnered some of Europe's top six-day riders to victory in Australia. Ryan made a couple of sorties overseas, but did not stay very long. If he had persevered there is no reason why he could not have been as successful as Gilmore.

There is NSW favourite Keith Oliver, capable of beating any rider in the world on his day — a top six-day rider, a top handicap rider, one of our best behind the motor bike, always a danger in a road race or tour as he proved by winning the Victorian Sun nine-day tour, two Sydney Sun tours and recording fastest time in the Warrnambool to Melbourne.

Hilton Clarke, who won three amateur 1000 m time trials and a 10-mile title, as well as five professional titles in a span from 1966 to 1976, must be regarded as one of our outstanding pedallers.

So must John Bylsma, who won the amateur 4000 m pursuit title in 1966-67-68-69-71-72 and finished fourth in that event at the Munich Olympic Games. He went on to win the professional pursuit in 1973 and 1975.

Another pursuiter more recently on the scene must also rate — New South Welshman Garry Sutton. He has won the title in 1974-75-76-77 and the 20 km in 1974 and 1976. He is also a leading road rider and tipped to be one of our leading figures over the next few years.

And so we travel to almost purely road riders and Clyde Sefton must rank at the top of the tree in this period. His Olympic silver medal and Commonwealth gold are reference enough.

Sefton has such a strong finishing sprint he is capable of winning some of the glamorous road races on the European circuit. His effort at Christchurch proved his capabilities.

Just past the half-way mark of the 184km event he and Englishman Phil Griffith broke away from the field. They raced neck and neck round the 10.2km circuit, but coming to the 1 in 12 gradient Cashmere Hill for the last time, Sefton careered away and hurtled down the other side to victory.

The fact he was included in the team only after Dick Paris pulled out to concentrate on the time trial is incidental.

Sefton's build up to the selection trials was hampered by a knee injury. He won the event by 29 sec with another Australian Remo Sansonetti, 10 min 10 sec behind Sefton in third place.

Sansonetti himself has also shown he has that little extra to make it to the top in the tough European road circuit with some top performances. He has won three Australian road titles.

Don Allen, Danny Clark's Team Australia six-day partner, Ray Bilney, Graeme McVilly, Kerry Hoole and Dick Paris have all put up outstanding road performances and also must be rated in the top bracket.

GORDON JOHNSON . . . sprinting from behind

DANNY CLARK . . . versatile

19 POLO

By RICHARD SLEEMAN

RICHARD SLEEMAN, a young journalist with "The Australian" newspaper, has covered sport in most parts of the world during the past five years. Born into a family keen on thoroughbred racing and breeding, his interest in polo was fired up on visits to Argentina, Europe and the United States.

Looking back through the records of great polo matches of the past 10 years, one word seems to stand out like the proverbial sore thumb . . . BEER!

Beer? At the polo? Oh surely not old man. You must be jolly well daft. Champagne's the thing you know. Indeed, champagne may well be among the first choices in a word association test with polo, but there's no mistaking the amber fluid in connection with grand matches staged in Australia.

Ranking highly among the most thrilling of polo encounters on Australian soil was the second in a series of Australia-United States "Tests" in the Easter of 1976.

And when discussion among the chicken and champagne set perched on rugs alongside a Mercedes, Bentley or Jaguar gets around to those goddam yanks, beer invariably raises its frothy head.

Two young American millionaire brewers were among that free-wheeling American squad that walloped Australia three matches to nil.

They were brothers James and Robin Uihlein, heirs to the Schlitz brewing company, producers of the brand that boasts it made Milwaukee famous.

James and Robin demonstrated, with some gusto, that they didn't stick absolutely to the family flavour.

More than a few glasses of antipodean ale passed their lips during the course of the tour.

"I'm afraid polo around the world is regarded as a rich man's sport. James and I are trying to live that image down," Robin was quoted as saying in a newspaper report which pictured the brothers galloping through a couple of jars.

They described Australian beer as "very smooth, and a little stronger and heavier than American beer." If that was the case, then the Americans gained their recompense with a brand of polo certainly "very smooth, and a little stronger and heavier than Australian polo."

After a crowd of 40,000 had watched the United States clean up at Sydney Showground on a Thursday night, the tourists went to Warwick Farm three days later to take on Australia's Richard Walker, Jamie Mackay, Jim McGinley and Arthur Bragg.

The United States led 4-1 at the half-way stage, but Australia fought back to hit the lead when Mackay scored in the fifth chukka.

In the see-sawing polo that followed:

● America battled back to even the scores, with goals by Joe Barry and then McGinley squaring matters again.

● Barry slammed home a 60-metre drive which seemed certain to give the Americans victory until McGinley again came to Australia's rescue with a 40-metre goal to send the match into extra time.

● Long tall Texan Barry's 140-metre-plus driving paved the way for Bill Linfoot's winning goal in a sudden-death seventh chukka for the United States to scrape home 9-8.

The visitors clinched the series by beating Australia 11-6 at Warwick Farm a week later. Back home to the brewery went James and Robin Uihlein who mixed brewing and tasting with $100,000 a year careers in professional polo.

Whether they hit the ball as hard or as often as the mercurial Argentinians of 1972 is difficult to say. Almost certainly the best team seen in Australia in the past decade was a four member group of gauchos playing under the banner of the Argentine resort city of Mar Del Plata.

Mar Del Plata, famous for its casino, wealthy residents and golden beaches, also boasts a very fine polo team.

The squad riding rough-shod across the

ROYAL PATRONAGE . . . presentations to Sandy Tait, Richard Walker, H.R.H. Prince of Wales, Sinclair Hill and Ken Austin

Australia pampas in the Easter of 1972 comprised the captain, Alex Mihanovich, Eduardo Moore, Alfredo Goti and Martin Braun.

In 14 matches in Australia, the Argentinians won 12, including two of the three Tests.

Quarantine restrictions prevented them from bringing their ponies, but on borrowed chargers, they gave Australian polo buffs a rare treat.

The Argentine won the first Test against Australia 12-8 at Warwick Farm in April in probably the finest match seen here.

Long-serving polo player and administrator, Ken Austin, umpire for that memorable match, recalls the day vividly.

"It was a sizzler, all right," he said. "My horses were getting so tired keeping up with the players, I went through three mounts."

Competing for the ball at full gallop.

RICHARD WALKER . . . seven-goal rating

The 28-goal ranked Argentinians downed their 23-rated rivals because of more accurate striking for goal.

Australia's Sinclair Hill (captain), Richard Walker, Sandy Tait and South Australian Hugh MacLachlan held the tourists to 6-3 at half-time, but wayward aim finally let them down.

Two goals—one by Braun and another by Goti—typified the Argentine mastery.

Braun slammed home a tremendous near-side hit after Mihanovich had intercepted a lofted shot. Goti triumphantly lifted the last goal in following some superb horsemanship.

During the fiercely contested Test, Hill

SANDY TAIT . . . Australian representative

and his grey pony came a cropper, but the Australian managed to escape injury.

At Scone a week later, the Argentine lost 8-7, before bouncing back against Australia at the Wells Station polo grounds in Canberra to win 7-6 in extra time.

The "Superpoms," Alan Kent, Paul Withers, Howard Hipwood and John Horsewell, who came to Australia in the Easter of 1977, vie with the Argentine and the United States for the honour of being labelled best touring team.

Although there was a real live aristocrat, Lord Vestey, with the squad, the Englishmen were mostly calculating professionals who took what was billed as a centenary series with wins in the first two Tests.

Hipwood masterminded his team's 6-4 defeat of Australia in the second, adding four goals, having won the first Test 6-5 under floodlights three days earlier.

With these losses to touring international teams all too clearly remembered, it would be easy for an outsider to disregard Australian polo talent.

Easy . . . but most certainly incorrect!

In Sinclair Hill alone, Australia has a player talked about in the same breath as the legendary American Tommy Hitchcock and Australian 10-goaler Robert Skene.

An observer at England's billiard table-like Cowdray Park best described the outspoken grazier/politician/polo professional.

"Hill has the incredible knack of hitting a large number of virtually impossible shots a long way. By these means, he is able to keep up a constant supply of well-placed shots from which his forward players are not slow to reap the benefit," the observer said.

"There is possibly no greater No. 3 in England today than Sinclair Hill. He has shown he can lift his game to dazzling heights."

It is in many ways a pity the salad days of the sixties and Hill from the Hill are gone. While my family trudged around Sydney Showground collecting sample bags, and complaints from my brother who always wanted the most expensive show-bags, I sat entranced on the Showground Hill watching the magician on horseback lead his North-West teams in the Daily Telegraph-sponsored Gold Cup.

There was a certain atmosphere then that nostalgia seems to have strengthened.

Typically, Hill remembers the Showground days without quite so much sentiment.

"I used to play before 65,000 at the Royal Easter Show and have to pay to entertain them. It was ridiculous," he said in a recent interview.

Hill, both host to and guest of royalty for years, has stirred a hornet's nest with his campaign for professional polo.

His main antagonist, Goulburn grazier

Competing at close quarters.

Richard Walker, enjoying a seven-goal rating and next to Hill the most gifted player in Australia, is strictly an amateur.

Walker gained much personal satisfaction leading unsponsored Goulburn to an 8-5 win over Hill's Triumph team in the inaugural Kooralbyn Australian championships at Warwick Farm.

Walker is undoubtedly a magnificent player possessing a killer instinct to augment his natural flair.

Although there is little love lost between Hill and Walker, they are Australia's right royal polo pair.

Honest-to-goodness royals like Prince Philip and Prince Charles are of course no strangers to Australian polo fields, culminating in Prince Charles scoring the winning goal in a special Silver Jubilee clash late in 1977.

They have played here several times, once in March 1970 even trying out their ponies in Sydney's Centennial Park.

Their polo feats in Australia are probably best remembered for quick-witted Prince Charles's "swipe" at a ranger on horse-back in Centennial Park.

As the ranger's big black gelding edged onto the makeshift field, Prince Charles inquired of its rider: "Would you like a stick, then?"

With polo files full of Princes, millionaires and those on the fringe, it's a strange twist that beer should be among the main talking points of the past 10 years.

Ah well, that's the way the Mercedes Benz!

SINCLAIR HILL . . . world-rated and synchronised with chief antagonist Richard Walker (right)

[News Ltd.]

20 ROWING

By PETER MUSZKAT

PETER MUSZKAT has been covering international sporting events since 1959, first for the "Sydney Daily Mirror" then for Australian Associated Press, and more recently for "The Australian" and the "Sydney Telegraph". His biggest assignments have been three full-scale Kangaroo Rugby League tours of England and France, a Wallaby Rugby Union tour of the British Isles and a Pacific Conference Games.

Just fleetingly, seven husky New South Welshmen and a lone Victorian looked like providing a medal-starved Australia with a very real chance for gold in the 1976 Olympic city of Montreal.

As they powered their Empacher fibreglass eight-oar shell to a heat victory over the 2,000-metre course, leaving the 1972 gold medallists, New Zealand in their wake, the Australians gave promise of going that one all-important step further than in Mexico eight years before.

Only nine hundredths of a second separated the Australian eight at the 1968 Mexico Olympics from this country's first rowing gold medal in the event.

There had been three Australian gold medal successes in Olympic sculling—two by Henry (Bobby) Pearce in 1928 and 1932, and one by Mervyn Wood in 1948.

But for all their similarities, the purists insist there is a decided difference between rowing and sculling, and the solo triumphs of the late Bobby Pearce and the current New South Wales Police Commissioner Merv Wood are part of another chapter.

Australia has always ranked among the top-dogs of world sculling, way back to last century when professional races were all the rage, and more recently when showman Stuart MacKenzie dominated the famed Henley Diamond classic in England and went within a whisker of adding to our Olympic successes on Ballarat's Lake Wendouree in 1956. MacKenzie was pipped for gold by Russia's Vyacheslov Ivanov, who went on to become the only man in history to win the Olympic sculling crown on three successive occasions.

The laurels haven't been nearly as great in rowing, yet Australian eights are always treated with healthy respect by the giants of the sport at international level—East Germany, West Germany, the United States, Russia, Czechoslovakia, Great Britain and New Zealand.

A bronze medal in Helsinki in 1952 was followed by a place in the final in 1956 and the silver medal in 1968.

So it was little wonder Australians held their breath in anticipation of their 1976 crew becoming only the sixth nation to take the gold in the blue ribband event of world rowing. But fate and circumstances conspired against them.

The success in the heat, which qualified the crew for the final without further competition, backfired when it was discovered the number two man, Mal Shaw, had suffered a crippling back injury.

He had to be replaced, but there were no further races for the Australians to blend the new man into a combination that coach Mike Morgan had been developing for three months.

Predictably, the Aussies wound up fifth in the final, trailing the gold medallists from East Germany, Great Britain, New Zealand and West Germany, and beating only Czechoslovakia to the finishing line.

Yet at an Olympics that proved a bitter disappointment to a once-proud sporting power without a single gold medal success to Australia, the rowers, as usual, acquitted themselves admirably.

Their efforts in Montreal capped a successful transition from oarsman to coach by Morgan, who coincidentally had been the number seven man in the "near-miss" Australian eight of 1968.

Morgan was still young enough to be in the crew of 1976, but his skill and determination had won for him the coaching appointment from a curiously-mixed Australian administration—occasionally superbly efficient and professional, and at times, frustratingly backward and petty.

The graph of achievements for Australian rowing crews followed a wobbly course between 1966 and 1976, and the results were directly related to the fluctuating efficiency and foresight of the men in control.

After Australia had bombed out disastrously with a full contingent in Tokyo in 1964— in not reaching one final—officials embarked on a costly and far-sighted programme, promoting Test series between Australia and New Zealand, as well as sending crews to the world championships in Yugoslavia (1966) and North America (1967).

That way, the stage was set for "Callaway's Heroes" to emerge with their 1968 silver medal showing. Heroes because the man at the helm that year, veteran coach Alan Callaway, was the mastermind behind the total operation.

MICHAEL MORGAN . . . looming as Australia's greatest coach

[News Ltd.]

Appropriately enough, Callaway had been a war-time naval commander, and such a campaign was right up his alley.

Sadly, a mixture of complacency and poor judgement had neutralised most of the glory by the time the 1972 Olympics in Munich had come around. For some inexplicable reason, Australian administrators sought no international competition for their crews between Mexico and Munich, resulting in a washout for a crew sorely lacking in experience.

Once again, the wily Callaway was at the helm, but even he couldn't make up for the problems that beset the 1972 Australian crew.

Just prior to the Munich Olympics, which were to provide their own special chapter of horror before a shocked world-wide audience, Australian rowing suffered two major tragedies.

Ian (Zac) McWhirter was found to be suffering from terminal cancer as the Australian eight geared up for the Olympics, and naturally had to vacate his number six seat in the crew.

And Brian Denny, Australia's most experienced oarsman at the time, and the nominated stroke of the Australian four-oar crew, was electrocuted at work before the team left for their pre-Olympic campaign in Europe.

Having learned a bitter lesson, Australian administrators again mapped out a series of overseas campaigns, all geared towards a renewed bid for gold in Montreal.

It was an ambition that went pretty close to succeeding, as Australia's best heavyweight oarsmen were groomed—first at the world titles in Moscow in 1973, then at Lucerne, Switzerland the following year, and finally at Nottingham, England in 1975.

The rest of the world sat up and took notice when the Australians qualified for the eights final at Nottingham after matching the semi-final time of the hot favourites, East Germany, along the way.

But the Australians weren't psychologically tuned for success at the time, and finished last in the final, a long way from the winning East Germans.

Too much emphasis had been placed on the purely physical aspects of the Australian preparation, and their mental approach simply wasn't up to scratch.

Mike Morgan was quick to seize on this problem, and researched it thoroughly before

Precision, Coordination, Courage . . . requisites for success

applying a totally new and advanced line of motivation to his Olympic crew of 1976.

Unfortunately, Morgan had to overcome several shattering experiences during the always tense count-down to the Olympics. Shortly before he left for the Olympics, Morgan lost his father.

And not long before, he had been deprived of two members of the New South Wales crew he had coached to a resounding King's Cup victory on the Nepean River, west of Sydney.

He had been very happy with the prowess of Tony Brown and Bryan Weir and was clearly distressed when they were dumped from the Olympic squad in favour of two interstate rowers — Peter Shakespear of Western Australia and Brian Richardson of Victoria.

The selectors also added Mal Shaw to the successful New South Wales King's Cup crew. An Olympian in 1972, and one of Australia's most seasoned international campaigners,

Shaw had been passed over for the NSW crew of 1976.

As in 1974, he was a late addition to the Australian squad, and ironically, it was his back injury that disrupted the crew's combination immediately before their big chance for gold in the Olympic final.

Anomolous team selections have provided an unfortunate undercurrent for a number of recent overseas campaigns, the latest being the staggering omission of Australia's most accomplished current oarsman, Chris Shinners, from the crew to contest the 1977 world titles in Amsterdam.

Once again, it was a case of a winning NSW crew being tampered with after effortlessly retaining the King's Cup, and Shinners was replaced in the bow seat by West Australia's Steve Saunders.

The crew's morale was further affected by a last-minute and unexpected change of coach.

1976 OLYMPIC EIGHT . . . Stuart Carter (cox), Islay Lee (stroke), Ian Clubb (7), Tim Conrad (6), Robert Paver (5), Gary Uebergang (4), Athol Macdonald (3), Malcolm Shaw (2), Brian Richardson (bow) — Shaw replaced through injury by Peter Shakespear for final

Unlike the New Zealanders, who experience the same disadvantages of competing out of season in a foreign hemisphere at world championship regattas, the Australians appear to have no established pattern, or continuity in their nomination of crews for overseas.

From 1973 to 1976, Australia sent abroad 13 crews in seven different classes, and apart from the heavyweight eight, there was no certainty of any other class being chosen. In contrast, during the same period, New Zealand sent away 11 crews in only five classes and they maintained a very definite pattern of continuity.

The results told the story. Of the 13 Australian crews, only two made a final. Only one of the 11 New Zealand crews missed out, and they returned home with one silver and three bronze world championship medals for their efforts.

Apart from the silver medal triumph in Mexico, Australia's reputation on the international rowing scene has been fanned chiefly by the Victorian dominated lightweights from Melbourne University.

Under the guidance of their coaching genius Peter Philp, himself an Australian representative oarsman in 1966, the University's coxless four won the first world lightweight crown in Lucerne in 1974 and followed up with a close third placing in the same event at Nottingham a year later.

Australia is gradually developing in women's rowing, although no representatives were sent to the Montreal Olympics last year.

It all began with a female sculler and coxless pair representing in Lucerne in 1974 and a coxed four in Nottingham in 1975.

This year, Australia is sending away its

best women's crew ever, a coxed four, to the world titles in Amsterdam, but it could be many years before enough progress is made to seriously threaten the supremacy of women from the Iron Curtain countries.

Tim Conrad, an Australian representative in 1973, 1974 and 1976, is coaching the current women's four, and already their improvement has been encouraging.

On the domestic front, New South Wales has become the dominant force, steadily overhauling Victoria's one-time stranglehold on the coveted King's Cup—symbol of interstate rowing supremacy.

The NSW crew's four-lengths victory in Perth in 1977 made it four in a row, and one more success in Franklin, Tasmania, next Easter would create a record for successive King's Cup wins, as well as topping Victoria for the greatest number of victories overall.

Before the King's Cup came into being, Victoria had won the Australian eight-oar championship twelve years in a row from 1894 to 1905. But now, there can be no disputing that NSW and more specifically Sydney, has become the hub of Australian rowing.

From 1967 to 1977, NSW has won the King's Cup on seven occasions from 11 starts, and while the build-up continues towards a fully-professional coaching establishment, the gap is likely to widen between the standard of the champions and the also-rans from other States.

Since the introduction in 1972 of national championships on an annual basis, run in conjunction with the King's Cup regatta, the NSW domination has been even more pronounced. In those years, NSW has never failed to win at least 60 per cent of the events.

NSW has also been agitating to have the King's Cup thrown open to competition by club crews—a change successfully applied to the last two President's Cup events for scullers. Under the new qualification laws, each State can enter three scullers, compared with the previous single representative in former years. The change has made for better racing, with NSW scullers finishing first and second after thrilling duels on both occasions.

1977 NSW EIGHT ... Stuart Carter (cox), Islay Lee (stroke), Ian Clubb (7), Gordon Clubb (6), Tony Brown (5), Ian Paver (4), Stephen Handley (3), Dave Clarke (2), Chris Shinners (bow)

A streamlined administration has given the NSW Rowing Association a decided edge over its counterparts in other States.

Nine members of a management committee are elected each year to control the sport, while other States persist with the delegate system, giving every club a voice, but proving cumbersome and restrictive as far as decision-making is concerned.

In the past two years, professionalism in the truest sense of the word, has been introduced to the sport at club level in Sydney.

Drummoyne showed the way in 1976 by snaring New Zealand's super coach Rusty Robertson, whose legion of international successes included a gold medal in the four plus cox in Mexico (1968) and a further gold for the eights in Munich (1972).

Robertson has become the supremo at Drummoyne, in charge of the club's heavy-weight eight, as well as formulating a uniform coaching policy and style. He is also heavily involved in lectures and recruitment drives, and in arranging vacation activities for school-boys. Not to be out-done, the Sydney Rowing Club, so deeply steeped in tradition, has countered Drummoyne's initiative with a very professional coaching panel system this year.

Mike Morgan is the club's new director of coaching, with responsibilities of taking charge of the heavyweight oarsmen, as well as supervising the training programme and coaching methods adopted by a panel of expert coaches—Pat Hannan, John Welch and Reg Stride. It is obvious other Australian clubs will have to follow the lead of Drummoyne and Sydney, even if the fully-professional approach adopted in the Iron Curtain countries is never quite achieved.

Like the United States and Great Britain, Australia is lucky to have ready-made rowing nurseries in much of the school system, providing a continuous stream of new talent for this enormously demanding sport.

The Great Public Schools Regatta once ranked with the major events on the Sydney sporting calendar, but lost considerable public support since a restriction on pre-race publicity was enforced by the respective college head-masters.

Each year, the eight competing G.P.S. crews contesting the Head of the River eights, turn out some outstanding prospects that clubs snap up eagerly to boost their ranks. Because of the demanding nature of the sport, the turn-over is understandably fairly high by comparison with less strenuous pursuits.

The next step in development is the highly successful Colts representative system, providing opportunities for promising young oarsmen under 23 to be blooded for future international representative honours.

On the score of equipment, Australia is lagging far behind Europe in boat development and building techniques.

The German's unmatched skill and prowess give them a huge advantage, and the decisive thinking of the NSW Rowing Association in purchasing a West German Karlische shell in 1974 for use by NSW and Australian crews, has already paid handsome dividends.

While the professional approach continues, rowing should flourish, and only good can come from the efforts of Morgan and Robertson, who have responded to the guidance of the NSWRA by starting a coaches' forum to promote some degree of uniformity at all levels—school, club and international.

21 SURFBOARD RIDING

By IAN HANSON

IAN HANSON — Joined the "Sydney Daily Telegraph" as a cadet in 1972. In 1973 he became a Rugby League and surfing writer until 1977. Hanson is now the sports editor on the "Manly Daily". He covered the Australian surf titles for the "Sunday" and "Daily Telegraph"'s at Bancoora Beach in Victoria over Easter weekend in 1977. He has been in every NSW State senior or junior R and R final since 1968, and in 1976 won the Manly-Warringah Branch surf belt title.

Robert "Nat" Young could ride a wave on an ironing board and make it look spectacular.

Young, known world wide as surfing's innovator of the 1960s, put Australian surfboard riding on the international map.

And he was supported by a curly-haired wizard named Bernard "Midget" Farrelly.

Young, nicknamed "the animal" because of his aggressiveness in the water, was a tall, strongly-built athlete from Collaroy, on Sydney's northern beaches.

Farrelly, the leader of the Freshwater gremlins, won the first official world surfing title in small, sloppy surf at Manly on May 17, 1964. Farrelly gave a brilliant performance riding the last possible wave he could catch before the permitted time expired.

During the championships at Manly world title conditions were formalised.

It was the first of only six world championships contests to be held.

The third in 1966 went to Young who outgunned the bigger names from the US and Hawaii.

Young, at 18, won an unofficial world championship in 1962 at Ocean Beach, San Diego.

He was the first champion who was not a native of the host country.

It was in fact a great break through in efforts to achieve unprejudiced judging of international contests.

From then on Australia and Young led the way on waves all over the world.

Boards, concepts, design and styles changed constantly and Young, with the radical George Greenough and Bob McTavish, led the way in new innovations.

Young mastered every surfing spot in the world from his home beach Collaroy to the big seas at Sunset Beach, Hawaii.

Since Young there has been a steady stream of big name surfers who have conquered riders and the ocean in most international surfing contests.

Victorian Wayne Lynch has been hailed as one of the most radical of all Australian champions.

Lynch is a "goofy footer" or a surfer who rides with his right foot forward instead of his left.

He won the 1968 European championship at Le Barre, Biarritz, France.

He defeated Young which shows how good he really was.

Born in Lorne, Victoria in 1952, Lynch later developed new techniques such as the 360 degree turns on the face of a wave.

Lynch won four Australian junior titles from 1967 to 1970.

In the 1970s surfing has become highly professional with contests such as the Sydney Surfabout worth over $25,000 and the surfing circuit in Hawaii and South Africa producing contests with prizemoney well over $20,000.

Queensland's Michael Peterson won more professional contests than any other surfer. He had hidden ability to come from behind and snatch victory with brilliant performances.

At the same time surfers like Wayne Lynch, Ian Cairns, Peter Townend, Paul Nielson, Terry Fitzgerald, Peter Drouyn, Mark Warren and Mark Richards rode their way to the top.

Richards is a sensational surfer — a Newcastle schoolboy who reached the top of the world. He's called "the aeroplane" because of his wavey arm style.

He is beautiful to watch and is one of the few surfers who can master a small board on any sized wave right to the beach.

He treats surfing as a competitive sport and even trains for big events.

"NAT" YOUNG . . . could ride a wave on an ironing board

IAN "KANGA" CAIRNS . . . rode his way to the top

"MIDGET" FARRELLY . . . brilliant performer

"I make sure I'm in peak physical condition before the big events.

"I go out to win and I make sure I'm in the best condition to do so. I not only surf but run and do weights " he says.

Now the world "champion" is decided on the professional circuit and Australia constantly dominates the top 10 ratings.

One man, the smooth-talking, smooth-riding Townend from the Queensland Gold Coast, is undoubtedly the "Mr Consistent".

He has finished second in big contest finals on more occasions than any other surfer, but overall he tallied enough points to lead the top 10 in 1977.

Others worthy of mention include the late Bobby Brown from Sandon Point, NSW. Ted Spencer, Keith Paul, Robert Coneeley and top woman rider Judy Trim from Dee Why.

22 SURF LIFESAVING

By IAN HANSON

IAN HANSON — Joined the "Sydney Daily Telegraph" as a cadet in 1972. In 1973 he became a Rugby League and surfing writer until 1977. Hanson is now the sports editor on the "Manly Daily". He covered the Australian surf titles for the "Sunday" and "Daily Telegraph"'s at Bancoora Beach in Victoria over Easter weekend in 1977. He has been in every NSW State senior or junior R and R final since 1968, and in 1976 won the Manly-Warringah Branch surf belt title.

The year 1967 holds special significance in the long, action-packed history of Australian Surf Lifesaving.

It saw the start of the modern era of a sport which has thrilled thousands of people around the beaches of Australia's vast coast line.

It was Easter Sunday at South Australia's picturesque surfing beach Southport.

Lifesavers from every State in Australia gathered to pit themselves against the surf in the traditional swimming, boat, ski, board and beach events.

The Southport national carnival, unlike any other Australian championship, was the forerunner to some of the most sensational competitive surf carnivals ever seen.

For the first time since the Australian titles were officially held in 1920 an event appeared on the programme which had never before been conducted on national level.

It was the gruelling four-leg Iron Man race.

A handful of Australia's fittest surfers met the starters gun that day to make history as the first Iron Man of surfing. It was an all-round test of ability which required the competitor to swim, paddle a board and ski and finish off with a beach sprint.

Spectators and lifesavers alike stood amazed as the field headed out to sea for this grinding, gut-busting "pentathlon" of surfing.

It was obvious right from the start that one man, 25-year-old Maroubra surfer Barry Rodgers, would finish victorious and hold his head high throughout the surfing world.

He opened up a commanding lead in the swimming section and went further ahead paddling his ski and board. In fact he eased up at the finish and won by the length of the straight.

Rodgers, winner of the Australian open surf race title in 1963, had the ability to crack a broken wave, a feat accomplished by only a handful of surfers.

The deep chested, broad shouldered "Adonis" emerged from the surf that day to the cheers of a crowd who dubbed him the king of Australian surfing—and from that day on he was known as "Mr Surf".

Rodgers marked himself as the best all-rounder in lifesaving: he had mastered an event he stole from the Americans during a tour with the Australian team in 1965.

For the next two years Rodgers streeted all to retain the Australian title at North Cronulla (NSW) in 1968 and again at Clifton Beach (Tasmania) in 1969.

He still remains the only man ever to win the national Iron Man title three years running.

The year 1967 also saw the emergence of a handful of youngsters who were to become stars of the most hotly-contested decade in lifesaving carnival history.

Gone were the days of the surf champion who trained on a schooner of beer and a mile a day . . . the Olympic surf age had arrived.

At Southport a snowyhaired, slim-lined youngster from Merewether in Newcastle, Scott Derwin, won the coveted Australian open surf title thus following in the footsteps of Newcastle's Jeff Dawson winner of the title in 1964 and 1965.

Dawson was rated by Rodgers as the best surfer he has ever seen and Derwin wasn't far behind.

But a name popped up in what were termed non-championship races to practically rewrite Australian surf lifesaving records. It was that of raw-boned 16-year-old Victorian Graham White from Lorne.

White won both the open surf and open junior surf events. The following year at North Cronulla his chlorine bleached shiny white

[News Ltd.]

GRAHAM WHITE . . . explosive, outspoken champion

locks appeared under the same black and white quartered cap — and he took Sydney by storm.

His speed and surfing know-how set the surfing world alight — he again left the cream of Australia's swimmers and surfers in his wake. White showed stamina never seen before at an Australian surf carnival.

The strongly-built Victorian repeated his performance in the two non-championship races and added the junior championship to his fast-growing list of successes.

Although only a junior he backed up to run second in the open surf to Chris Bradford — the 1967 junior champion.

Over the next nine years White stamped himself as an explosive, outspoken champion and he dominated distance pool swimming and surf events.

White represented Australia in the 1968 Mexico Olympic Games and finished fourth in the 1500 m. The following year at Clifton Beach he became the first man to win four surf races

at an Australian championship carnival — an incredible feat.

This time he added the prestige open surf championship to his other three wins in a performance which placed him up with the biggest names of Australian surfing.

He was the best by far.

White left behind such accomplished surf-swim stars as Derwin, Greg Rogers, Tony Shaw and Rick Wilkinson. In 1970 White continued to dominate the scene and again he added a new title — this time the senior belt championship.

Unbeaten in major championships for two years White left Australia for 12 months study at an American university.

But he returned in 1972 for the Munich Olympic Games trials and couldn't wait to get to the Australian surf titles at Blacksmiths Beach, near Newcastle.

He had no trouble in regaining his open surf crown won in 1971 by Wilkinson from Rogers and fellow 1968 Olympic Games colleague Mark Anderson.

White repeated the dose at Burleigh Heads the following year to win his fourth open surf

KIRRA R and R TEAM

title—one less than the legendary Bob Newbiggen.

When the 1974 nationals in Glenelg (South Australia) came around White was favoured to equal Newbiggen's record.

But it wasn't to be. He was still swimming as well as ever, but faced one of the most star-studded fields ever assembled for an open surf race.

The field included Olympians Graham Windeatt, Mark Anderson, Robert Nay and Neil Rogers and top line surf swimmers Ian Montgomery, Peter Raeburn, Lance Johnston and Steve Smith.

Conditions suited the stillwater champions —Glenelg was like a millpond and the water was freezing. Windeatt set a cracking pace out and around the buoys with White, Nay and Rogers close on his heels.

On the way back to the beach White put in everything he had and set out after Windeatt, but the Collaroy star held on to his lead and robbed the defending champion of a dream he hasn't accomplished. Third home was Rogers, a Munich and Montreal Olympian.

Windeatt annexed the double by winning the open belt final from Alan Saxby and Peter Tibbitts.

White's defeat came with his change of clubs from Lorne to Mooloolaba on the Queensland sunshine coast. Over the next three years White was to move twice again and they certainly proved lucky.

In 1975 at Dee Why he was a member of the precision Southport senior R and R team which won the national blue-ribband event, and in 1977 he repeated the effort when a member of the successful Kirra R and R team.

Mention has already been made of the Rogers brothers Greg and Neil—both Olympians. The pair together with another brother Ron, all from Clovelly, were known as Australia's leading surfing family.

Ron and Neil both won open belt race titles—Ron pulling out all the stops in a tremendous effort to beat the great White and Greg Price (Nobbys) in 1972 at Blacksmiths Beach and Neil staging one of the closest duels ever seen to down Peter Tibbitts by a touch at Clifton Beach in 1976.

Tibbitts had won the title at Dee Why and has to be one of the greatest belt swimmers in

BARRY RODGERS . . . iron man　　　[News Ltd.]

surfing history. He went on to easily win the 1977 title at Bancoora Beach in Victoria from Lance Johnson and Peter Raeburn.

He was one of the few non-Olympians to succeed in a class of swimmers who could match most stillwater champions anywhere in the world.

Among the new brigade of Olympians were Max Metzker, former world 800 m and 1500 m world freestyle record holder, Steve Holland and Mark Kerry—all finalists at the Montreal Games.

Metzker produced two of the finest exhibitions of swimming and surfing seen in flat conditions to win the coveted senior-junior double at Clifton Beach in 1976 and he had to defeat Holland to do it.

The young 15-year-old from Maroubra downed Holland in the junior title and Windeatt and Nay in the seniors. But it was only a last minute decision which saw Metzker line-up in the senior event.

His mentor, "Mr Surf" Barry Rodgers, told Metzker the open title was the only title. He spread-eagled the field and then backed up to shoot past Holland on a wave to score in the junior event.

It was one of the biggest upsets of the three-day carnival, but then as former world Olympic gold medallist Brad Cooper once summed up: "There's too much luck in the surf."

He made the comment after Ian Montgomery caught a wave to win the 1973 NSW State title. After Cooper had led most of the way.

In 1975 Graham "Goldie" Dyson from the Wanda club toppled Olympians Kerry and White in a "boots-and-all" open surf race at Dee Why. Dyson, a powerful wader and supremely fit, led practically all the way in a memorable performance.

One of the biggest upsets of the seventies came at Bancoora when Paul Gately beat Ron McKeon and Garry Steed in a brilliant exhibition of surfing and wave riding.

Gately, a former cadet champion, was in the right place at the right time to catch a wave and he'll be remembered as a true surf champion.

It is impossible to mention so many names in a sport where there are so many competitors and so many stars, but these men all swam and surfed like dolphins.

Queensland's Robert Littler is by far one of the finest lifesavers ever produced in Australia.

Bondi's Leigh Emery was a belt swimmer—extraordinaire—as was Cronulla's Graham Elliott.

North Bondi's veteran Peter Smiles is one of the best surf swimmers never to win an open championship—he was uncanny. Kevin Neilson, Fred Annesley, Norm Rabjohns, Graeme Brewer, Robbie Williams, Graham Ankin and Guy Oakley were all mighty surf swimmers.

Freshwater's cadet Darren Bogg was undefeated in the 1977 season in which he won the metropolitan title a week after gaining his bronze. He then took out the State and Australian titles in a cakewalk.

Maroubra's Dennis Heussner was a sensational surfer who excelled on a long board and then on a ski.

Scarborough's Ken Vidler won two Australian Iron Man titles and is rated along with the great Barry Rodgers. Vidler was a champion's champion—a true perfectionist who also won a national ski title at Dee Why.

Experts will argue for ever and a day about who was the best ski paddler ever produced —Vidler or Freshwater's Murray Braund.

The two never met at their peak. Braund won two single and two doubles titles with Greg Jarmaine, but relinquished his crown to Vidler when he went to Canada for two years.

Another to master the tricky board and skis was 1975 national long board and malibu champion—Steve Warren from North Cronulla.

Others were Howard Hughes, Dick Cahill, Jack Trail, Peter Milburn, Doug Andrews, Steve Lenton, Geoff Dews—all of whom are household names in the craft section of Australian surfing.

Every sport has its bridesmaid—in Rugby League Manly Warringah were for so long the bridesmaids and never the brides, but their luck changed. The same applied to John Holt of Cronulla.

For seven years Holt tried in vain to capture the Australian Iron Man title.

In 1970 he took the Australian junior championship at Ocean Grove and the following November defeated the best in the world to be unofficial world champion, but no matter how hard he tried Holt couldn't break the hoodoo when it came to nationals.

He was forced to wait until 1977 when again it looked as though he would be out of luck.

Olympian Holland opened up a commanding lead in the swim section and Holt was fifth, with the defending champion Vidler ninth going into the board leg. But like the true surfers they are Holt and Vidler cracked a wave to go past Holland and stage a neck and neck battle to the death on the skis.

Unlike 1976 when Vidler beat Holt by an inch it was Holt's turn to win when he lunged at the line to hold off a determined bid by Vidler.

All surfing events don't revolve around swimming.

Beach sprints, flags, relays and, of course, the famous grand parade and march past — a glittering display of banners and costumes.

Several beach sprinters have dominated

the last decade, but none more so than Brian Gardiner, twins Graham and Greg Lawson, Bob Cairncross and Paul Burke.

Gardiner, a State Rugby League representative with Queensland, won the title for North Wollongong and also Maroochydore.

In 1967 Graham Lawson from North Burleigh won the national final, and the following year his twin Greg Lawson made it an all-family affair.

In beach flags one name stands out — Bob Pickard of Freshwater (NSW) and Leighton — Fremantle (West Australia).

Pickard was once described by a Sydney newspaper Sports Editor as "the quick brown beach fox". He was agile and crafty and this ability won him three national titles.

Over the last 11 years two clubs have dominated the march past — one of the most time-consuming, concentrated events of all.

Collaroy has won eight Australian titles

COLLAROY MARCH PAST TEAM

and Bundaberg three and on those three occasions Collaroy finished second.

Boat rowing has long been one of the most thrilling summer pastimes for Australian lifesavers. Crews like nothing better than to crack big waves to the beach. But nothing thrills surf carnival crowds more than to see a wave throw a boat and its crewmen reeling back to beach after failing to negotiate the break.

Rowers take their lives in their own hands when they step into a surf boat, but they are trained to perfection and are fit enough to handle any situation that arises.

There's a saying in boat rowing that a crew is only as good as its sweep. Sweeps dominate the records of Australian championships.

The Ballina crew swept by Max Sidney won three national finals in a row in 1967-68-69 to equal a record set by Cronulla.

Other sweeps to stand out — Warren Molloy (Queenscliff and Warriewood), Ron Payne (Newport and Freshwater), Ken Murray (Caves Beach) and Merv Gladstone (Bronte).

Clubs to excel in national carnivals have been Point Lonsdale, Coogee, City Of Perth and Woolamai. In complete contrast the Rescue and Resuscitation event is one of the most interesting but less spectacular surf carnival events, but one which holds the most prestige.

The Kirra club has certainly led the way in the R and R competition, winning four national premierships. Their coach Arch Nicholson and captain Bob Littler are two of lifesaving's most dedicated men.

Other top R and R teams and coaches have been North Cronulla (Warren Rennie), Southport (John Ogilvie), Coogee (Len Harris) and Bondi (Harry Nightingale).

It's men like these who keep the lifesaving movement alive. They give up hours, days, weeks and years to train lifesavers in resuscitation, drill and swimming.

They are responsible for the up-bringing of so many young Australians, men who serve their country in a voluntary sport which has saved many a life and made Australia famous.

BALLINA BOAT CREW . . . champions

23 BASEBALL, SOFTBALL, SNOOKER, PARAPLEGICS
By KEVIN MITCHELL

KEVIN MITCHELL—One of the younger brigade of sporting journalists, is quickly making his mark for all round coverage with the "Sydney Sun". He is also a handy left arm spin bowler with the Randwick District Cricket Club in Sydney.

BASEBALL

Baseball took an historic decision early in 1973—direct competition with cricket as a summer sport.

The move was greeted with some consternation, detractors claiming successful cricketers wouldn't sacrifice a place in a grade team to play a sport they could play in winter.

They were wrong.

Many cricketers did switch—and baseball entered what might conservatively be described as a mini-boom. The transition has not been without trauma, of course, and the division it has brought about between summer and winter advocates has not been healthy for the game.

But one can't deny the audacious move has pulled baseball out of the doldrums; it's been a positive step that took some nerve throughout its execution—and it looks like giving baseball a well-deserved chance to establish itself on some sort of professional footing.

That baseball hasn't captured the imagination of the Australian sporting public as it has in the United States and Japan has often puzzled those close to the sport. It has just about everything one could ask for in a ball game—speed, action, excitement, skill . . . facets that have traditionally been winners in this country.

Look at Australian Rules and Rugby League, for instance. Cricket, of course, has been the main hurdle—one that doesn't exist in the United States and Japan. Yet Test cricketers like Neil Harvey, Norm O'Neill, Bill Lawry, Ian Craig and Ian and Greg Chappell have proved cricket and baseball do mix. The public, apparently, is reluctant to accept this. But things are changing.

And a man at the forefront of the revolution is Dick Shirt, a former Australian team pitcher who has soaked up plenty of American know-how and is trying to get baseball moving in a big way.

His Auburn club in Sydney's Western Suburbs could be the launching pad from which the sport takes off. Successful Friday night promotions there the past two seasons indicate the public can be educated to accept regular night 'ball at a suitable venue.

"I'd really like to see people streaming out each week in the summer months to see Friday night baseball at the Park", says Shirt. "In Adelaide they get 3,000 to 4,000 to their Wednesday night games. It could happen here."

Australia has had some fine players over the past ten years. Perhaps the best of the lot has been Kevin Greatrex, now at the tail-end of his illustrious career. Probably the best batter seen in this country for many years, Greatrex has stood at first base for South Australia for 14 seasons and has been in every Australian team picked since 1968.

David Mundy, a former Sheffield Shield cricketer with South Australia, has also played 14 series with the State team and has been a regular national team selection at third base. A fine hitter of the ball in both games, Mundy played alongside the cricketing Chappell brothers in baseball and cricket.

Whereas the Chappells saw their future in willow and leather, Mundy stuck to baseball—with great success.

Short stop is regarded by some as the most important position on the field and Australia is well-served in this spot by Victoria's John Hodges. Hodges went to New York in 1973 as a raw 16-year-old for a spring training session with the New York Mets and came back a polished star.

Others who have tried their hand in American baseball include Barry Stace, who has pitched for NSW, Western Australia and the

[News Ltd.]

(Above) DICK SHIRT . . . former Australian pitcher

(Below) SID THOMPSON . . . benefited from a season
with Philadelphia Phillies

[News Ltd.]

[News Ltd.]

KEVIN GREATREX . . . best batter for many years

national team after a year in Kansas City; Shirt
who first went to the U.S. in 1964 for a stint with
the Cincinatti Reds; NSW pitcher Sid Thompson, who benefited tremendously from a season
with the Philadelphia Phillies and is now
settled in America, coaching a semi-pro team
in North Carolina.

American coaching ideas, techniques and
equipment have given baseball a new face in
this country over the past couple of seasons.
Two of the most important have been the
"lively ball" and the aluminium bat.

Mosman (Sydney) coach John Pachett
summed it up neatly. "People who don't know
a thing about baseball want to see players belt
the ball as far as it can go. With these innovations they can see as much of that sort of baseball as they like. That didn't happen three or
four years ago."

SOFTBALL

When American nurses stationed in Australia during World War ll turned their thoughts to recreation, they picked up a big white ball and a bat . . . and softball was off the ground in this country.

There are now 150,000 registered players throughout Australia—and the number is growing. In the past 10 years we've beaten the best, staged the world championships, introduced sponsorship and established this country as the best amateur team in the world.

And some outstanding players have graced the game in that time.

Gladys Phillips is widely regarded as the greatest softball player this country has produced. She retired in 1970 after captaining the Australian team for more than a decade from third base. People who saw the Victorian at her height say she was unrivalled in nearly every facet of the game.

Victoria has produced many fine players, not the least of them the late Eleanor McKenzie, who also represented Australia at cricket and basketball. She bowled in the cricket team, was guard in basketball and, on the diamond, stood commandingly at first base. She had a fine sporting tradition to live up to also, being the niece of former Test cricketer Keith Miller.

Many thought Eleanor would be hard to replace. But Sybil Turner, of NSW, has taken over the job with distinction. Originally a catcher, she switched to first base when she entered the Australian team.

Sybil's career is linked very closely with that of Christine Bennett, her schoolmate at Carlingford High, where they played baseball. They both entered the NSW senior team at 13 and together in the Australian side at 17. Now 21, they are two of the sport's most talented players.

Bennett is a utility player, having switched from the pitching mound to third base—which in one way is a great loss as she can hurl the ball at an incredible 75 miles an hour.

Schools, of course, are the ideal nursery for softball players. One man who has a big hand in spreading the sport is Geoff Mould, sports master at Sydney's Matraville High and coach of the Australian schoolboys Rugby team that recently returned from the U.K. after a triumphant unbeaten tour.

Mould was responsible for Judith Phillips taking up softball when he was teaching in Byron Bay. Judith went on to represent NSW and Australia and is the current national team vice-captain.

No list of great softball players would be complete without the name of Midge Nelson, Victoria's national team catcher. Also a hockey international, Midge was awarded the British Empire Medal for her services to sport.

SNOOKER

On January 21, 1968, a 38-year-old ex-coalminer flew out of Sydney bound for Bolton, Lancashire.

It was the first of many such trips he was to make, but none would be as important. Eddie Charlton had shelled out £200 to challenge a cocky gentleman called John Pulman for the world match play snooker championship . . . and "fast Eddie" was sure he could play snooker better than anyone in the world.

He lost—but he returned to Australia something of a hero. The games had been close and were marked by some highpower psyching by the Englishman. That was enough for St. George Leagues Club, where Eddie was a member.

They agreed to stage the world open snooker championship between title-holder Rex Williams and the Australian, which Charlton won, drawing 14,000 people—still the biggest attendance in the history of the game.

That, effectively, marked the rebirth of snooker, and Eddie Charlton was on the way to his first million. He won't say if he's there yet, but he must be mighty close—and snooker players everywhere should give the big man with the droopy eyelids a rousing cheer when he does pass the magic figure.

Charlton is the outstanding Australian snooker player of the past 10 years. He's won 17 of the past 18 national titles and doesn't look like losing his supremacy for a long time.

EDDIE CHARLTON . . . has reigned supreme in Australia

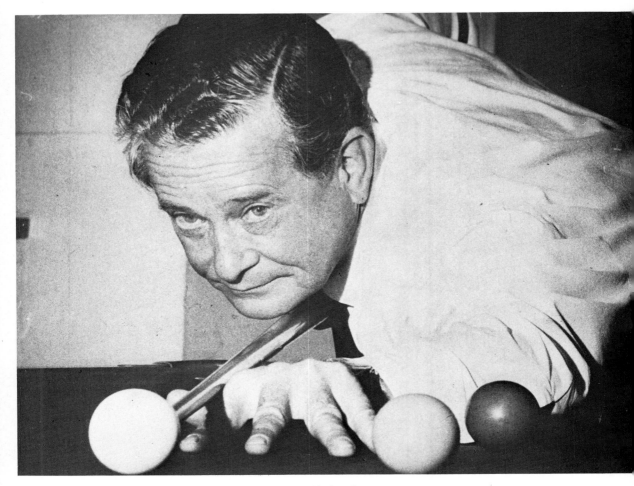

HORACE LINDRUM . . . gave up active competition early in this decade

He's turned snooker from a dead duck into a million dollar business almost overnight, making it a viable profession for at least 50 other players—though few have skimmed the cream off as sweetly as Charlton.

As he is the undisputed number one, it seemed reasonable to ask for his assessment of opponents over the past decade.

"In 1968 there were really only five professionals on the Australian circuit—Norman Squire, Warren Simpson, Newtown Gahn, Horace Lindrum and myself—though Horace had just about given up active competition. Overseas there was Fred Davis—the greatest snooker player I've ever come up against—John Pulman and Rex Williams," Charlton recalled.

That's not really much in numbers, but the standard was excellent. Not a struck match between most of them . . . though Charlton reigned supreme in Australia.

Others who started to emerge after that fateful January in 1968 were Alan McDonald, who was resident professional at Souths Leagues Club in Sydney and NSW amateur champion four years on end—Rex King. 1970 proved another turning point in the game.

Charlton organised—and won—the first Australian professional snooker championships held for more than 30 years.

They drew more talent from overseas— John Spencer, Gary Owen, Paddy Morgan and Dennis Wheelwright. Of those, Owen, Morgan and Wheelwright were to settle in Australia,

WARREN SIMPSON . . . in 1968 one of five Australian professionals

adding a competitive edge that had been decidedly lacking.

Irishman Morgan became a great drawcard, his Gaelic wit spicing many a tournament. Wheelwright was installed as the resident pro at Revesby Workers Club and Owen, who won the world amateur championship in 1968 and 1969, threw out a strong challenge to Charlton's hitherto unquestioned supremacy.

More players were to filter through to the circuit, which had been almost incestuous in its limited format—Ron Mears, Ian Anderson, Phil Tarrant, Jim Charlton, Eddie Charlton jnr . . . and a young wizard called Gary Lackenby.

"He could have been anything," says Charlton. "But, after I'd coached him for a year, he dropped out of the game entirely. He's back in it now, but I feel he may have lost that little something."

Charlton is adamant snooker is not a game you can "let go." He practises five hours a day nearly every day of the year . . . and manages to squeeze in some pretty packed flying and playing schedules.

And, while Charlton says Davis is the best player he's come up against, the man he finds hardest to beat is Ray Reardon. The affable Welshman is Charlton's nemesis—though the Australian champion would never concede ascendancy to him.

"He's damn tough to beat," says Charlton. "He's got a great temperament and is a good long potter of the ball. Perhaps his only weakness—and it's one I share with him—is that he's not always consistent."

Charlton sees a great future opening up for snooker. But it would be surprising if he didn't hold such a view.

"The future is tremendous," he enthuses. But he also sees changes; indeed, he advocates one that has drawn irksome condemnation from fellow pros—a smaller table. "The 6 ft by 12 ft table is too big," says Charlton.

"We should be using the 5 ft by 10 ft table they use in the United States, Japan, Europe and, would you believe, Russia, for billiards and pool. Russia, I was surprised to discover recently, is developing billiards on a massive scale. They have millions of players in the game right now."

Charlton leaves for the United States at the

end of the year to sell his new-look snooker to the Americans. If it takes off, and, if the pros in the United Kingdom, Canada, New Zealand and South Africa can be persuaded to switch to a smaller table, the prospects of a considerably enlarged world championship are real.

It would add some credence to a game that awards its world title to the best of only about 50 professionals.

And Charlton is a man who proved almost exactly a decade ago that dreams are often the substance of reality.

PARAPLEGICS

To see men and women strive for excellence, perhaps supremacy, in sport brings a warm rush to the heart of any sensitive soul.

When those participants are handicapped —some terribly—the poignancy of the whole endeavour is overwhelming. It reminds one what sport is all about—or used to be . . . and it cuts a healthy swathe through arguments for more money, better conditions, more adulation, status and the sundry other demands of our modern mercenaries.

Because paraplegic sports competitors aren't in it for the glory, money or prestige. They compete for the sake of competition.

Kevin Batts, who has managed every Australian paraplegic touring team in the past decade puts it admirably. "Psychologically, competing in sports lifts them. They can share their problems. They have a new incentive to become involved in life again," he says.

Australia has had many wonderful performers in international paraplegic sport over the past 10 years.

Not the least of them in courage and ability is Wayne Patchett, paralysed from the neck down. He managed to hurl the discus 12.6 metres to win the class 1A gold medal for that event at the 1976 Paralympics. He also holds the world record for hurling the Indian club, with a distance of 25.23 metres in England in 1975. Wayne, a 26-year-old computer engineer who lives in the Sydney suburb of Guildford, became a quadraplegic after a river accident seven years ago.

Vic Renalson, from Long Jetty, could be

VIC RENALSON . . . two golds for Australia

excused for turning a sour countenance towards life. A car accident made him a paraplegic, but he developed his already hefty frame into a mini dynamo and won a heavyweight weight-lifting gold medal for Australia with a lift of 432 pounds.

Years later, he'd dropped to middleweight—not through choice, but circumstance after another car accident. The loss of one of his legs only strengthened his resolve to compete and succeed; which he did when he won a gold medal at the Jubilee Games in London in 1976. Vic, as an able-bodied athlete, had represented Australia as a wrestler.

Ray Fowler—ex-ninth Div.—is another in Vic's vintage and could also hold his own with able-bodied competitors. A runner-up in the 1972 Paralympics archery, Ray shoots scores that are world class. He was a competitor at the 1956 Games in England and again at Rome in 1960.

Also at those Rome Games was Daphne Hilton—nee Ceeney—who won two swimming golds . . . though she got not a tenth of the publicity of another Australian who was gobbling up the gold at that time—Dawn Fraser.

Pauline English though, is perhaps the name that has captured the imagination of the Australian sporting public more than any other in paraplegic sport.

Pauline was 14 when her father Jim urged her to take up swimming—"You are not going to spend the rest of your life loafing around" he told her.

Paralysed from the waist down since she was three, Pauline trained under ex-Olympian Don Talbot in the Sydney suburb of Hurstville.

Four weeks later this incredible young lady had broken two Australian records at the New South Wales paraplegic and quadraplegic games in Sydney and a month later at the Zurich titles. Pauline entered four events—for four wins and four Australian records.

Gold eluded her at the 1974 paraplegic Olympics in Heidelberg, but she was delighted with three bronze medals.

"An Olympic gold medal is what I really wanted," Pauline told her father . . . and this is what she finally achieved at the 1976 Paralympics in Toronto when she won the 25 metres butterfly.

RICHARD OLIVER . . . World Record Holder for Class 4 100 m in 18.1 seconds

BOB McINTYRE . . . named in Top 10 in International Basketball after 1976 Canadian Paralympic Games — Australian Records Class 5 in 100 m and 800 m events

24 MOTOR RACING

By JOHN WALLIS

JOHN WALLIS: A professional journalist John Wallis now 42, began his newspaper career with the "Sydney Daily Mirror" at 18. He has worked on various metropolitan newspapers in Sydney and Adelaide and for the past 14 years has written a regular motor sport column for the "Mirror".

It was a damp, gloomy April day in 1969 and only a handful of press and radio men turned out at Sydney's Oran Park racetrack to witness the unveiling of a new race car, the Allan Moffat Trans-Am Mustang.

Moffat had shown he knew how to race with some hair-raising performances in a Cortina. But the 29-year-old Canadian wasn't a Geoghegan, Matich or Beechey, so the press weren't all that interested.

Had they known the full extent of that first day's testing, every pressman in Australia would have been on hand.

For those few laps in front of a handful of press heralded the start of a new era in motor racing — the era of Moffat.

Within a year Moffat rocketed himself into headlines throughout Australia, mixing controversial antics with top line, heart stopping driving that had the crowds flocking back to the racetracks.

With bespectacled Moffat on hand, record crowds flocked to Bathurst, Sandown, Calder and Oran Park.

At one Oran Park meeting 53,000 people tried to force their way into the circuit to see Moffat take on Bob Jane and Ian Geoghegan. They were unsuccessful as the track could hold only 28,000 or so. But the resulting traffic jam, that spread from Camden on the southern outskirts of Sydney, right back to Liverpool, brought as much publicity as the race itself.

And since that day in 1969, when he unveiled his Trans-Am Mustang in its now famous flame red colors, Moffat has been involved in just about every "Great Race" held in this country. Winning or losing he has captured the imagination of the fans. He is "Mr Controversial" with his outspoken comments and his racetrack attitude of total dedication that makes him sometimes look a win-at-all-costs driver.

The stories are myriad . . . "Moffat pushed him off . . . Moffat was pushed off . . . It's Moffat's fault . . ." There is even a rumour he was involved with another driver in a stand-up fist fight following a race at Warwick Farm, the now-defunct Sydney motor racing circuit.

Allan Moffat will race anywhere and has won everywhere, but he considers Bathurst the ultimate challenge. The 6 km Mt Panorama circuit with its hills and dales and its crushing, car-destroying Con Rod straight is the real test of driver and machine.

And it was at Bathurst on Easter Monday, 1972, race fans saw probably the greatest race ever staged.

It wasn't the legendary Hardie Ferodo and it wasn't a field of many cars doing battle. It was a race between just two men and their machines. But it is one that has already been described by the critics as the most heart-stopping ever seen.

It was a race between Moffat in his famous Mustang and Ian Geoghegan in his new works Ford Falcon GTHO. Some 15,000 fans had braved the icy conditions of the mountain.

They had come to see the third round of the Australian Touring Car championship which had drawn Moffat, Geoghegan, Bob Jane in his Camaro and Norm Beechey in the Monaro, among others.

Practice set the scene for the battle royal as Moffat and Geoghegan duelled for pole position during the two Sunday sessions.

Moffat finally grabbed the spot with a best time of 2 min 25 sec, ahead of Geoghegan, with Jane next.

It was wet and windy at dawn on Easter Monday and the mist on the top of the mountain was thick, so thick you couldn't see the track 50 ft in front of you. Spectators were huddled in little groups trying to keep warm.

I remember going round the track in an official vehicle and thinking I had wasted the journey. The meeting would have to be cancelled.

But the fog cleared and the racing finally got under way, in rain and sleet that kept the spectators stamping their feet . . . until event six.

By then the rain had cleared and the big cars proceeded to shake the mountain to its roots for 13 of the most unbelievable laps of racing ever seen.

For the entire journey Geoghegan and Moffat ran nose-to-tail and side-by-side, hurtling down the main straight neck and neck at more than 150 mph, neither giving an inch.

Neither driver would give in and at one stage it looked as if the race would end in disaster when the two huge "V" cars touched at more than 100 mph.

But their skill kept them on the road and the race ended with a breathtaking dash by Moffat in a vain bid to catch Geoghegan over the last short dash along pit straight.

And once again controversy raged after the event. Moffat claimed Geoghegan's car had sprayed oil all over his windscreen during the event and that he had been forced to drive "blind" for much of the race.

He demanded Geoghegan be outed and there were heated scenes in the pits with accusations flying thick and fast before officials ruled the result should stand with Geoghegan the winner.

The race almost began with a pile-up. Colin Bond's Torana was stuck on the starting line with throttle troubles after the warm-up lap and several cars had to swerve to avoid him.

In the confusion Bob Jane slipped through to send his big Camaro thundering up the mountain with Moffat, Geoghegan and Beechey hard on his heels.

The big field streamed on its way, but all eyes were on the end of Con Rod straight to see who would come over the famous "hump" first.

A roar went up when the red Mustang came pounding down to Murray's Corner just ahead of Jane, Geoghegan and Beechey . . . the race was on. Moffat dived his Mustang under the big Camaro as the cars swerved their way through Forest Elbow at the start of the main straight. Could they catch him?

[James Hardie]

ALLAN MOFFAT . . . another victory presentation, this time from Seven Network general manager Ted Thomas

Geoghegan certainly thought he could. He wound the big Falcon right up and set off to swallow up the Jane Camaro.

He brushed past the Victorian and began closing on his arch rival Moffat as the cars swung past the pits to complete lap two.

Beechey retired his Monaro with gearbox trouble on lap three and Jane had dropped into limbo back in third place. But they had been forgotten. All eyes were on the Geoghegan-Moffat duel.

They came past the pits to start lap four neck and neck. Then a great cheer came up from the crowd as Geoghegan took the white Falcon past Moffat up Mountain straight.

The local hero was in front. Everyone was happy. But not for long.

[James Hardie]

BATHURST WINNERS . . . (from left) Peter Brock (1972, 1975), Allan Moffat (1970, 1971, 1973, 1977), Bruce McPhee (1968), Colin Bond (1969), Bob Morris (1976) and John Goss (1974)

Up the mountain the two cars sped and then across through McPhillamy Park and over Skyline, where the track disappears completely from a driver's view before diving down into a series of sharp Esses.

It was here Moffat made his move again. He jammed the Mustang back a gear and, clipping the edges of the track, sent his machine hurtling past Geoghegan to take the lead again.

Many claim the cars touched, but it was Moffat who held the lead as they came past the start-finish line.

But Geoghegan had not finished his race. He pressed close to the tail of the Mustang and was finally rewarded two laps later when Moffat went wide on a corner, letting him past. From there on the crowd was treated to some of the greatest driving ever seen on a race-track.

Geoghegan held his lead come what may as Moffat tried every trick in the book to get past. He ranged up on the outside at every corner, filling Geoghegan's rear view mirror.

He tried to find a way past through the Esses and he attempted to outbrake the big Falcon at the end of the main straight as the cars came to the "hump" at nearly 160 mph.

But Geoghegan wouldn't give in. Ice cool the big man wrestled the Falcon round the Mountain lap after lap. By the ninth lap they had lapped the rest of the field, but no-one bothered to watch the other cars go by. All were watching for Geoghegan and Moffat.

Then came the last lap.

Geoghegan led by half a length as they went past the pits. But Moffat moved up almost bumping the tail of the Falcon as they braked for Hell Corner at the end of the pit straight.

Up the mountain he ranged up to try to force Geoghegan into error. But to no avail.

SYMBOLIC . . . Rory out to give General Motors a lion's share of the prizemoney
[James Hardie]

Down Con Rod straight for the last time, Moffat tucked in behind Geoghegan, getting a "tow" to conserve himself for one last desperate effort.

He made his move as they came over the "hump". He swung the Mustang out as they came into the braking area, holding his foot off the brake pedal until the last desperate moment.

Smoke came from the tyres as the Mustang locked up a brake and the crowd was on its feet cheering as the Mustang's nose appeared to be fractions ahead as they swung into the right-angled Murray's corner for the last time.

But Moffat had been forced to go for the outside run. Geoghegan held his line and held off the challenge to win by less than a car's length.

Then came the drama. Moffat pulled up at the Control tower and immediately claimed he had been continually sprayed with oil from Geoghegan's car. He protested, showing officials a windscreen that was smeared with oil film. It

NOSTALGIA . . . former world champions Jack Brabham (left) and England's Stirling Moss at Bathurst comeback
[News Ltd.]

was so bad, he said he had been forced to peer out the side at times.

Pictures were taken, a hearing was set up and officials met till 7 p.m. hearing evidence before they decided the results should stand.

And so ended the greatest touring car race Australia has ever seen. It was a race of two men and machines . . . a virtual sprint from start to finish and it will be remembered by everyone who saw it.

Strangely it was one of the last major Easter meetings held at Bathurst. A meeting was tried there in 1973, but failed and the Australian Racing Drivers Club decided to give it over wholly to the motor cycle racers, concentrating their Bathurst efforts on the Hardie Ferodo in October.

And many claim the Hardie Ferodo is the world's greatest touring car race. Certainly it is a battle of men and machines, an endurance race that demands superhuman will to win.

It has produced many great battles, and now ranks on the international calendar with the world's great races.

It has drawn international stars and seen upset wins, but above all it has been a battle of men over machines and the 1976 One Thousand has been hailed as the greatest of them all.

For 1976 was the year of Stirling Moss and Jack Brabham. The year that the world's two racing legends came out of retirement to take on the mountain, co-driving a Torana.

They focused the world's publicity spotlight on Bathurst and gained headlines from London to New York.

But it was Englishman John Fitzpatrick who ended up with the winner's garlands. And in so doing he produced one of the greatest displays of controlled driving ever seen, nursing a shattered car to the line to win the race for the Ron Hodgson team.

In the most emotional scenes ever witnessed at Mt Panorama, he nursed a crippled Torana to victory cheered on by a record crowd and his pit crew, some of whom were weeping openly.

The car should never have finished. It had no brakes, a broken rear axle and no clutch for the final 10 or 15 laps.

Fitzpatrick beat the odds. He coaxed the car round the course, trickling it up the mountain for the final time then virtually letting it coast down to the finish line to victory.

Again, it was a great race and again it involved Allan Moffat to a large extent.

He had won the Australian Touring Car Championship and was the popular elect in his huge Falcon to take out his fourth Bathurst.

This year he had teamed with expatriate Australian Vern Schuppan, to lead the Ford challenge against the horde of Toranas, who were relying on Colin Bond in the Holden dealer team car, Peter Brock and, of course Brabham and Moss.

Brabham and Moss received the publicity, although some of it was rather critical. "Can the oldies come back . . . Life begins at 40, but 50?" were among the more cynical remarks.

They proved they could, although the race for them was run virtually at the start when Brabham stalled on the grid and was crashed into by another car. Their shattered Torana was hauled off the grid and got back into the race nearly three hours later after a major rebuild.

But it was Moffat who had the early limelight on the track. He took pole position with a fastest lap of 2 min 25 sec, and with Schuppan led for most of the first 86 laps. It was then, with a comfortable lead and most of the crowd getting ready to hoist their Ford banners, that disaster struck.

The Falcon rolled into the pits with a broken fan pulley, smoke and steam belching from the engine compartment. A head gasket had blown and Moffat's race was run.

But for the crowd, the real race was still to come. It turned out to be an epic struggle between the Toranas, producing the closest finish to Bathurst ever seen.

When Moffat left the scene, it looked as if the Holden dealer team had finally broken through for a win. Bond and John Harvey were more than one and a half laps ahead of the Fitzpatrick-Bob Morris car with Brock another lap down.

And things looked even brighter when Brock pitted his car with a broken axle, losing more time. Rain, which had been threatening all day, began to drizzle down, but no-one slackened speed.

With 123 of the 163-lap journey gone, Morris handed the Torana over to Fitzpatrick, a series of pit-stops having put them just ahead of Bond's car.

PETER BROCK . . . leading Torana driver

But disaster struck the Englishman only two laps later when he was forced back into the pits with a punctured front tyre. Bond sailed by and set up a lap lead. The chase was on.

Fitzpatrick, Britain's top sedan car driver, responded, and with 15 laps to go, caught the Bond car.

But the tearing, grinding sprint to catch

CHAMPIONS . . . Bob Morris (right) makes a point with a pensive Colin Bond

the leader had done its damage. The Hodgson Torana was ready to fall to pieces. Still, the drama had not stopped. Suddenly Bond came into the pits with a broken fan belt and a blown head gasket. Fitzpatrick coasted to a comfortable lead and the dealer team decided to press on with their crippled car and settle for second.

It looked as if Fitzpatrick and Morris could not be beaten. The mechanics, headed by Bruce Richardson, were busy packing up and getting ready for the victory celebration when, with four laps to go the Torana came by much slower than before. Next time round it was down to a crawl and there was smoke billowing from it.

The gearbox had gone and the clutch was slipping. Could he hold on. The Torana stuttered and stumbled around the track to take the last lap board at almost a crawl, with Bond's car closing rapidly.

There were emotion-charged scenes in the pits. Richardson sat down on a toolbox and unashamedly wept as his wife tried to comfort him; Bob Morris was crying; Ron Hodgson walked away from the pits, unable to watch.

And all the time Fitzpatrick was coaxing the car up the mountain. It was a snail's pace climb with the motor sounding as if it was going to stall every time he crashed the crippled gearbox into another gear.

Then came the announcement from the top of Mt Panorama . . . "Fitzpatrick has got to the top of the hill. He can coast home from here".

And the fans erupted into a frenzy of cheering. Police had to forcibly hold sections of the big crowd back as they tried to swarm onto the track before the car reached the finishing line.

Meanwhile, Bond was closing fast. He was pushing his battered Torana to the limit. But it was too late. Fitzpatrick took the flag just 58 seconds ahead.

"It couldn't have gone another lap," he admitted later.

"I couldn't make it go too fast because the brakes had just about had it. And with the broken rear axle it wouldn't steer properly. I just pointed and hoped it went that way."

The 1976 Hardie Ferodo will not go down as the most thrilling. It will probably be recorded in history as the slowest last lap finish. But it will certainly be remembered as one of the Best Of The Past Ten Years.

ALLAN MOFFAT . . . 'Mr Controversial' in action [James Hardie]

25 WATER POLO

By KEN LAWS

KEN LAWS, the assistant sporting editor of the "Sun" newspaper in Sydney, has played water polo for 16 years, representing NSW in 1965, 1966, 1969 and 1970. He has served for many years on the committee of the NSW Association and helped organise the 1976 Australian titles in Sydney. He played 10 years of first grade with the Balmain club in Sydney, winning six premierships.

New South Wales, Western Australia and Victoria have long been the strongholds of water polo in Australia, but the best player in Australia today learned the game in South Australia.

Charlie Turner is not only the best of the last 10 years, but it stretches back to when I started watching the sport in 1956. His speed, shooting power and strong legwork are awesome. The 1976 Olympics proved Turner as world class. In the first game the 24-year-old forward tore a ligament in his left shoulder against Hungary on the way to taking out the gold medal.

Australia was only beaten 7-6 with Turner playing on. Although hampered by his shoulder injury and in pain, he scored 18 goals—a magnificent achievement. Players in the team claim that, had the mercurial Turner been fully fit, Australia would have made the top eight.

Turner learned to swim in England where he competed for the Barracuda Club of London. He showed great promise as a backstroker, winning the Southern County title in his age group. His family migrated to Australia when he was 13 and that's when he first picked up a water polo ball.

Turner started in the lower grades with the Chrysler Club in Adelaide and made a dramatic rise, playing first grade at 14, before winning a place in the South Australian team a year later. He played in the Australian titles for South Australia from 1968 to 1974 and was picked in his first National team in 1973.

That European tour was the turning point in his career. Turner found European players did far more legwork than their Australian counterparts and when he returned to Australia he started a training programme that has developed the best pair of legs in Australian water polo.

You've heard the expression in motoring "it can turn on a sixpence", well that's what Turner can do in the water, where from experience I'll tell you it's a lot harder than on dry land. You could say he's aptly named Turner.

Turner has now made four tours with Australian teams and gives a lot of credit for the improvement in his game to the coaches Ron Wootton and Tom Hoad. In 1975 he switched from Adelaide to join the Sydney Club Universities to represent NSW in the last three Australian titles.

At 24, Turner has already played more than 100 National series matches, and water polo followers and officials are hoping he keeps going for another eight years to spearhead our next two Olympic sides.

My other best players in the last 10 years are David Woods and Tom Hoad and there hasn't been a goalkeeper to match Mick Withers.

As a youngster Woods had one great advantage over other aspiring water polo players—he could throw a stone from his front door to the best training pool for water polo in Australia—the Dawn Fraser Swimming Pool at Balmain.

While youngsters in other areas would take a bat and ball to a park in summer, Woods and his mates would go to the pool and play a rough and tumble game with a water polo ball in front of the goals. That game—called pairs— had no referee and virtually no rules, and Woods and his mates would play it for hours. It was there he probably built his great strength and endurance.

At the same time Woods was swimming with the Balmain Club. He won many titles and developed into a good medley swimmer, taking the State Open title when he was 17. Woods started competition water polo when he was 14

CHARLES TURNER . . . fouled by Cuba's Gerardo Rodriguez as team mate David Neesham looks on in foreground —Olympic Games 1976

[News Ltd.]

and made first grade with the powerful Balmain Club as a strapping 6 ft 2 in, 16-year-old. Later that season he made the NSW team, which he was to grace every year until 1976 when he retired.

The 1961 NSW team, which went to Adelaide under former Olympian Keith Whitehead, was one of the youngest of all time and brought in a new era to NSW water polo. Three youngsters making their first tour — Woods, Nick Barnes and Bill Phillips — went on to represent Australia. Barnes and Phillips made the 1964 Olympic team, while Woods was an unlucky omission.

The 15½ stone Balmain powerhouse had to wait until 1965 to make his first Australian tour. He played the next European tour in 1967 and was a member of the ill-fated 1968 team to the Mexico Olympics, but barred from playing by the Olympic Federation.

Woods was a member of the 1972 Olympic team and set one of many firsts in his long career when he became the first Games athlete to be married at the Olympic Village. He wed Sydney girl Judy Kerrison with his cousin Gary Pearce, also in the Olympic team as a rower, best man.

Woods captained the Australian team to the World Championships in Cali, Columbia and retired from first class water polo after making the 1976 Olympic tour.

He started his career as a free-scoring centre forward, but quickly picked up a grasp of the halves and backs as well and early in his first-class career could be switched into any role. His main attributes were his great strength and endurance.

In the 1962 Australian titles, Woods played one of the gutsiest games of water polo I ever saw. NSW played arch rivals Victoria in a match they had to win to force a play-off for the title. Victoria's trump card in that series was veteran centre forward Keith Weigard.

In a bold move, Woods was switched from the forwards to mark Weigard. For the whole match the 18-year-old Woods swam Weigard

[News Ltd.]

DAVID WOODS . . . many firsts in a long career

all over the pool, with Weigard using every trick he knew to try to slow down the Balmain boy. But at the finish Woods was still going, Weigard wasn't, and NSW took the match and went on to take the title.

"Woody", as Queensland player "Polo" Wilson christened Woods, gave another brave effort which wasn't recorded in the record books during an Australian title series in Perth. The day before NSW played Western Australia one of the locals star players decided to show Woods a bit of local hospitality to try and slow the NSW captain down.

The local invited one of his teammates to dinner as well with the West a hot favourite to beat NSW. But next day, with Woods playing a blinder and his two dinner mates not going quite so well, NSW scored an upset win.

Woods has also made his mark as a coach. He was captain-coach of NSW in 1969 and in 1970 the "Blues" won the Australian title in a cakewalk. The nearest any team got to Woods' team was four goals. In 1978 Woods will be back to first-class water polo as a coach when he takes the NSW team to Melbourne.

"Mr Water Polo"—that's what they often call Western Australia's Tom Hoad. I've never

seen Hoad in the goals, but that's the only thing in water polo I've never seen him do. He could shoot with either hand, play any position, holds an international refereeing ticket and is the current Australian coach.

As a player, "Toadie" was one of the fiercest competitors I've seen in any sport. Not a tall man, Hoad made up his lack of size with a training programme that made him the fittest player in Australia.

Hoad played for Western Australia for 14 years and represented Australia at the 1960, 1964, and 1972 Olympics.

If you raced any of those teams over 50 metres, Hoad wouldn't run in the first three. But over 10 metres starting from the water, Hoad would be unbeatable.

It was that explosive acceleration that made him always one of the most dangerous players in the Western Australian side. Naturally a left-hander, Hoad practised so hard with his right hand that at the finish of his career he could shoot just as well either hand.

His determination and dedication to fitness have made Hoad an outstanding coach. He was one of the best tactical players ever seen in Australia and has the ability to impart know-

199

[News Ltd.]

MICK WITHERS . . . "walks on water"

ledge. In the West he has concentrated on the younger players, handling the under 18 team in the last two years and his work is starting to pay dividends at senior level.

Mick Withers could "walk on water". I don't mean he was blessed or lucky—he just had such good legs he could move along out of the water to his costumes, not using his hands. It was those powerful legs that made him a brick wall in the goals.

The stocky 5 ft 10 in goalie wasn't born with that ability. Withers acquired it by churning out lap after lap of the hardest work you could possibly give a pair of legs. "Work until

your legs feel numb and then keep going" was the advice he always gives youngsters who want to play in the goals.

Withers, born in England, came to Australia when he was 10. A long-service player for Victoria, he transferred to Sydney in 1968 and joined the Balmain Club where he took over the goals from State man Hermie Bakels.

Withers played in the 1964 and 1972 Olympic teams and from 1966 to 1970 was regarded as being in world class. Perhaps his only failing as a goalkeeper was that at times he got out of the water too far and the ball slipped through underneath his arms—but only occasionally.

[News Ltd.]

ALAN CHARLESTON . . . hard to leave out

players out . . . men like Western Australia's Allan Charleston, Les Nunn, Billy McAttee, Graeme Samuel, David Neesham and Eddie Brooks, Victoria's Leon Weigard, Ian Mills, John O'Brien, Tony Harrison, and New South Wales's Andy Kerr, Bill Phillips, Nick Barnes, Don Sarkies, Peter Montgomery and John Harrison.

When the editor of this book asked me to do this chapter on water polo, he asked for the best players in the last 10 years. But as any player will tell you probably the most important man in the game is the referee. Who was the best referee in the last 10 years?

For mine, the position is vacant.

ANDY KERR . . . in the top group

[News Ltd.]

I played in the backs for Balmain when Withers was in goal, and he had the ability to make even me look good. It's remarkable how much difference a top goalie can make to a side. With someone like him behind you, backs can play a very confident game. Many times I used to give forwards a bit of extra room so they would shoot, knowing Withers was there.

The beauty of his goalkeeping was the nine times out of ten he wouldn't deflect the ball for a corner throw, but pull it in to give his team possession. He was able to do that more than any other goalkeeper I've seen and that's what made him head and shoulders above the rest.

There will undoubtedly be plenty of argument about why certain players have been left out of my best in the last 10 years, but no one can dispute that the four players I've picked were champions.

I must admit it was hard to leave a lot of

26 GLIDING

By NOEL BURNETT

NOEL BURNETT aged 34 years is a top competition pilot himself. He has been gliding almost nine years. He will be the Assistant Team Manager for the Australian Team which will compete in the 16th World Gliding Championships (the Olympics of Gliding) in France in July, 1978. He is editor of "Australian Gliding", the magazine of the Australian Gliding Federation.

At the outbreak of the Second World War gliding in Australia was still in its infancy with small groups of enthusiasts pooling their resources to build and fly what are today regarded as very primitive gliders. The sport of gliding had been developed in Germany in the 1920s but it had been slow to spread to Australia. Interest in the sport was concentrated in Europe and several competitions were held in the 1920s and 1930s at various places in England, Germany, France and Switzerland. This culminated in the holding of the first recognised International Gliding Championships which were held on the Wasserkuppe in the Rhone mountains in Germany in 1937.

After the War the early interest in gliding was rekindled locally and a major boost occurred with the formation of the Gliding Federation of Australia in 1948. The Federation was formed by gliding enthusiasts in cooperation with the Government instrumentality then controlling aviation, the Department of Civil Aviation. The Federation was given powers to control the conduct of the sport in a farsighted move by the Department. As a result of this decision the basic framework of gliding in Australia was determined. Henceforth gliding was to be organised into a club movement rather like the earlier Aero Club movement. An individual who wished to fly joined a club which provided instructors to teach him how and gliders in which to fly and all of the other necessary aids such as winches to launch the gliders.

On the World scene again the first post-war contest was held at Samedan, near St. Moritz in the Swiss Alps in 1948, and it was given for the first time the title of a World

Championship. The next World Championship was in Sweden in 1950 and then in Spain in 1952. Australia did not compete until the Spanish contest where Merv Waghorn flying a pre-war design Weihe single seat glider was placed 13th out of 39. From then on World Championships were held on average every two years, generally in Europe. Australia was represented at all subsequent contests but until the 1965 Championships in England, the 10th World Contest, it had never been able to send a full team of four pilots as most of the stronger European nations did. We generally sent our pilots to learn rather than try to win.

In 1968 Australia was still regarded, and properly, as a minor force in World Gliding. The interest in competition flying had been slow to develop, the first National Championships were not held until 1957 and the 1968 National Contest held at Benalla in Victoria was only the eighth such contest.

The 11th World Championships were also held in 1968 in Leszno, Poland. Australia was represented for the first time by two young pilots; up to then the movement had not been able to afford to provide any substantial financial assistance to our team and as a result our representatives had tended to be those who could afford to compete and not necessarily the best local pilots. These two pilots, John Rowe and more particularly Malcolm Jinks were to dominate the competition gliding scene in Australia for the next ten years. Both pilots came from Waikerie in South Australia where good gliding conditions and the encouragement of an active group of serious pilots had combined to produce in these two all the qualities of a top competition pilot. Malcolm and John had both learnt to fly very early; by the age of fourteen both were competent solo pilots. Malcolm won his first National title in

The ASW 17 Open Class glider in flight

Dawn greets the gliders and tug tied down at Black Springs, SA, in winter

1965 at the age of twenty, he won again in 1966 and 1967 and John's turn came in 1968.

Though these two were clearly the best in Australia, in 1968 the World Championship in Poland exposed them to much tougher competition; in weather conditions that they had not experienced in Australia. John came 29th and Malcolm 32nd out of 48 competitors. Lessons were learned however and hopes were raised that Australia would soon be able to earn its place among the top gliding nations.

In 1970 the Americans conducted the 12th World Championships at Marfa, Texas. We were again represented by Malcolm and John and by two other pilots Bob Martin, also from

Waikerie and Max Howland from Queensland. Once again the team returned without having captured any major honours. Our team manager reported that we still had a lot to learn, although Malcolm did place 16th while flying an aircraft that was really not competive against those being flown by the top pilots, particularly the Americans and Germans. The top American pilot George Moffat won the Open Class in this Contest and a brilliant young German, Helmut Reichmann the Standard Class. Helmut had won so convincingly in his first Championships that it was felt that he had developed a secret way of using the weather conditions. At any rate Helmut, by profession a University Lecturer, was obviously someone who could communicate his ideas and he was invited to come to Australia for the 11th National Championships to be held in 1971 at Benalla again.

Helmut's visit was to prove invaluable. He flew each day in the contest and held discussions on each day's flying afterwards with the competing pilots. The knowledge passed on in this way spurred the top local pilots on to better things.

Also competing at Benalla was another pilot with a German name, Ingo Renner. Ingo had migrated to Australia a couple of years before. He had learnt to fly in Germany but made his first cross-country flight in Australia. Ingo had done well in his first Nationals the year before and did so again at Benalla.

In the Open Class Malcolm Jinks won yet

MALCOLM JINKS . . . dominates competition gliding

Kestrel 17 soars above Waikerie, SA

INGO RENNER . . . world champion 1976

again but a real surprise occured in the Standard Class: a woman pilot, Sue Martin the wife of Bob Martin who had flown in America in 1970, won the title. There were then and still are few women who are serious competition glider pilots. Sue had taken on the men and beaten them at their own game. We will hear more of Sue later.

The visit by Helmut Reichmann was an attempt to improve the standards of the local competition pilots which had succeeded. Now a group of visionaries in the Gliding Federation, lead by its President Bill Iggulden, decided to try to convince the World body controlling gliding the C.I.V.V. that Australia should be the host country for the 1973 World Championships. They saw that in this way Gliding in Australia generally would benefit. The movement was now large enough to tackle this enterprise, or would be by then. In the event the C.I.V.V. accepted the bid but asked that the Championships be held in 1974 and granted Yugoslavia the 13th Championships to be held in the Northern Summer of 1972.

Preparations for the World Championships were put in hand and Waikerie was selected as the site. In anticipation of this the National Championships in 1972 and 1973 were held there. In 1972 Ingo Renner demonstrated that he had learned a lot from Helmut and won the Open Class easily. Malcolm flew in Standard Class and won again, his sixth Australian title.

Ingo and Malcolm were of course selected to compete in Yugoslavia along with Tony Tabart and Maurie Bradney. At last our pilots broke through: Ingo came 6th in the Standard Class in very difficult conditions, Helmut Reichmann and George Moffat in fact both placed well down. Maurie Bradney was unfortunate to place 35th out of 51, he did not score any points on one day of the contest when he had his camera stolen from the glider after he had outlanded. The cameras are used to take pictures of turnpoints on the ground to prove that the glider had been around the required course—no cameras no points. Malcolm· was placed 14th and showed that he was now knocking on the door, and Tony Tabart was placed 22nd out of 38 in his first attempt.

The next Australian Championships at Waikerie in 1973 were a full dress rehearsal for the World Championships. As far as was possible the Championship was staged by the same group of people that would officiate the following year. When the contest was over Ingo had won Open Class again, flying an outdated glider while Maurie Bradney showed his effort of the previous year was no fluke by winning the Standard Class. At the closing ceremony for the contest the Australian Team to compete at Waikerie was announced: Ingo Renner, Maurie Bradney, Tony Tabart and a newcomer Paul Mander. The announcement was not popular, Malcolm Jinks was not in the team despite placing second to Maurie, to make matters worse Malcolm would have been flying, if selected, from his home airfield. Of course no official reason was given for the selection but many people privately believed that the team selectors wanted some new blood in the team: perhaps they were encouraged by Ingo's showing in his first World Championships.

The holding of the 14th World Gliding Championships at Waikerie was the most important thing ever to happen to Australian gliding. For years the average gliding enthusiast had read about such events and more recently had helped support the Australian team financially. Now he could attend a World Championships and even be part of the ground organisation. The spin-off from the Championships was enormous. For example, many foreign pilots decided to sell their gliders locally rather than take them home and in one fell swoop the number of modern Open Class gliders in Australia quadrupled. The general public also became more interested in gliding as a result of the publicity generated by the Contest and many people joined the movement and began to learn to fly.

The World Championships was a success for Australia in every way. This was only the third time the Championships had been held outside Europe and many people from overseas were wary about Australia's ability to organise and stage an event as prestigious as a World Championship. But when it was all over everyone agreed it had been the best World Championship ever. Sixty-three overseas pilots had a taste of the superb gliding weather Australia has to offer. Over the two-week period of the Championships, 11 Contest days were held, a record number far exceeding the European average of six days. By the end of the contest half serious suggestions were being made that Australia should become the permanent site for future World Championships.

Australia's success in organising the event was very nearly duplicated in the flying itself. Ingo Renner flew brilliantly and consistently so that by the 8th day he lead the contest, he retained this position for three days, but just when everyone was convinced he would win Helmut Reichmann who had been closing the gap after a slow start took out the coveted title on the last day. Ingo had to be content to take a very close second place. Helmut's win was duplicated in the Open Class by George Moffat, thus the 1970 Champions won again in 1974, an unheard of occurrence. For Australia Tony Tabart placed 13th, Paul Mander 16th and Maurie Bradney 19th.

The next World Championships in 1976 took place at the other end of the Earth, in

TONY TABART . . . represented Australia in 1974 World Championships

Finland just a few hundred kilometres below the Artic Circle. By then Ingo Renner had won his fourth National Title and Malcolm Jinks had returned to the winners' circle to win in 1975 and 1976. Both made the Team. John Rowe also returned to his earlier form placing second to Ingo twice in a row and was selected for the Team with the fourth spot going to newcomer Alan Wilson.

Ingo was determined to avenge his narrow defeat in 1974 and this time he was successful,

JOHN ROWE . . . set a world record in January 1977

The ASW 19 . . . a recent Standard Class design built from fibreglass in Germany

after 11 attempts Australia had a World Champion.

The Contest in Finland was plagued by bad weather: only 7 days were flown in Open Class and 5 in Standard. Weather conditions were totally different from Australian conditions and the Europeans obviously had an advantage but Ingo demonstrated that he was now the World Master. Malcolm Jinks placed 16th again, but was very unlucky as on the morning of the last day he was in fourth place and should have finished there as the last day's task should have been cancelled for Open Class as it was for Standard Class. In the event the very fluky days saw some pilots who had been in the top five places relegated to finish in the high teens, a most unsatisfactory result. John Rowe placed 21st while Alan Wilson had to withdraw from the contest when he damaged his aircraft in landing.

Kestrel 70 over Cooma

Ingo was to prove he deserved the title of World Master when in May 1977 he was invited by the organisers to compete in the sixth Smirnoff Sailplane Derby. This event is a race across the United States from Los Angeles to Washington D.C. In that Contest Ingo was flying against five World Class pilots which included George Lee the U.K. pilot who had won the World Title in Open Class in Finland in 1976 and George Moffat twice World Champion in 1970 and 1974. Ingo won handsomely, in fact he won 8 out of the 10 contest days.

As this article is being written preparations are being made for our Team to go to the next World Championships to be held in France in July, 1978. Ingo and Malcolm have continued to dominate by each winning their class in the last two National Titles and are joined on the team by Tony Tabart who has come second to Malcolm the last two years and newcomer John Buchanan.

Well that's what has happened in the competitive scene in Gliding from Australia's point of view in the last ten years—what else has occurred? Ten years ago no-one could even imagine that an Australian pilot could set a World Gliding record: the Germans held the speed records and the Americans the distance and height records.

Once again, Sue Martin showed the men how to do it. In 1970 she set a Women's World Record for distance to a goal and return with a flight of 656 kilometres and in February, 1972 set two World Records for speeds around a 100 and 300 kilometre triangle. Two of these records have since been broken overseas but Sue still holds the 300 kilometre speed record at 114km/hr.

In January, 1975, the men got into the act, Ingo Renner, with a passenger flew a World Record distance in a two-seater glider of 970 kilometres. He flew from central Victoria to the Darling Downs region of Queensland. Malcolm Jinks then broke the record for speed around the 500 kilometre triangle with a speed of 140km/hr the previous record had been established in South Africa eight years previously and was the longest standing speed record. Malcolm's record stood for 21 months before being broken by a Rhodesian pilot who completed the task at an average speed of 143 km/hr. Then in January, 1977, John Rowe made a brilliant flight to set a new World Record for speed around a 750 kilometre triangle. John achieved an average speed of 134 km/hr and this record still stands.

So in the last ten years Australian pilots have improved their performances so much that we are now regarded as a top gliding nation, our National Championships are regarded as a major World Class event. We have won a World Title and have set several World records. All of this has encouraged the rapid development of the sport. Ten years ago there were only about 2,000 glider pilots in Australia; this has increased to over 5,000, the number of gliders has increased from just under 200 to over 800. In the last two years alone nearly 300 gliders have been imported, about 50 two-seat trainers and 250 single seaters.

A revolution in glider construction took place in the early 1960s when the German factories began to build gliders from fibreglass rather than wood and fabric, this material allowed aircraft wings to be produced that were perfectly smooth and the improved performances obtained were substantial. Ten years ago there were only 10 such gliders in Australia but in the last two years alone almost 250 were imported.

In the space available in this book it is impossible to cover every aspect of gliding and I have not tried to. However, to indicate just what is achievable in this wonderful sport let me just highlight two World Records. The greatest distance ever flown in a glider is over 1,600 kilometres, this was flown in America in 1977, while the highest average speed ever achieved in a glider is 165 kilometres per hour also flown in America in 1974—don't forget these feats were achieved without any form of mechanical assistance and the energy used was obtained freely from the sun.

27 BASKETBALL

By LINDSAY GAZE

LINDSAY GAZE has represented Australia in basketball since 1960—the last six years as coach. Currently he is also the general manager of VABA Stadiums, co-ordinating the sport nationally and organising tours in and out of Australia. As coach of the Victorian team he enjoys an unbeaten record while he also channels the fortunes of the Melbourne Club.

Over the last 10 years basketball in Australia has grown from a very minor recreation to the largest Olympic sport with over 300,000 participating in organised competitions.

During the same period the playing standards have made similar improvements.

Australia was unranked in Olympic competition in 1968 and by 1976 had climbed to its best-ever finish in eighth place in the Montreal Olympics. Several factors have influenced the tremendous progress of the sport during this period.

The basketball population explosion was made possible through an increase in the number of facilities and although Church and Youth club halls are still used, the sport is now centred around attractive new Municipal stadiums.

The expansion in the number of school gymnasiums provides further opportunities for increased participation.

In the early 1970s the Federal Government policy of recruiting teachers from the United States indirectly assisted the playing and coaching standards.

Many American teachers came to Australia with an excellent background in basketball, and those who did not join clubs usually implemented excellent coaching programmes within the schools.

The national and State associations were not content to merely let things happen, and after a barren period between 1964 and 1968 set about establishing a regular programme of international competition and coaching exchanges.

The Melbourne Club "pioneered" a tour of the United States in 1967, arranging games against some of the top-ranked University teams. When they returned with a 9-11 record they demonstrated Australia could produce teams capable of at least being competitive.

The Melbourne Club made a second tour in 1968, extending their tour beyond the United States to Europe and once again showed basketball in Australia was on the way up.

Wins against Springfield College, Assumption College and a third-place finish in the Real Madrid tournament in Spain were the best results to date for an Australian club team.

The benefits of obtaining this type of competition became apparent to all Australian clubs as the Melbourne team became a dominating influence in local competition. They won four State titles, six national titles and were never out of the final of either tournament from 1966.

By 1970 other club and State teams were starting to develop international competition and although the United States was the prime target, competition between teams from the Philippines, Singapore and New Zealand became more common.

It was in 1967 when Lindsay Gaze, a player on the Melbourne team, had a most important conversation with Dale Brown the assistant coach of the Utah State University team.

Brown suggested if ever he thought an Australian player could make the grade in the United States, he should contact him for advice regarding scholarship opportunities. It wasn't until 1970 that Gaze responded with a recommendation. There was a young player in Melbourne who showed great promise. He was rather small at only 6 ft 1 in, but he had good athletic potential and was a fine shooter. His name was Eddie Palubinskas.

Brown accepted Gaze's recommendation and by arranging a basketball scholarship at Ricks Junior College in Idaho, provided a start to a most spectacular career.

In his first year at Ricks, Palubinskas averaged 22 points a game and led the entire

ANDY CAMPBELL . . . at 7 ft. 2 in. he towers over the Prime Minister

coach, recalling Palubinskas to help their mission in Munich.

Failing to qualify for the final 16 in the Mexico Olympics and a twelfth place finish in the 1970 World Championship in Yugoslavia meant Australia was not considered to be a serious threat in Munich.

However, a new attitude emerged when Australia defeated Italy and Yugoslavia—the current World champions—in pre-Olympic exhibition matches.

Unfortunately for Australia luck was not to favour them in the early games.

The loss of all five starters, Palubinskas, Ken James, Rocky Crosswhite, Richard Duke and Ray Tomlinson on fouls undoubtedly cost the game in a very close finish against Spain.

A one-point loss against Czechoslovakia could have easily been a three or four point win if two free throws could have dropped at the 90-second mark.

However, Australia won world recognition when they produced their best effort against Brazil.

Showing the benefit of prior experience Australia was able to expand a six-point, half-time lead to 14 points and when the pressure was applied late in the match they had the composure to hold on for an historic 75-69 win.

Comfortable victories against Japan and Egypt helped Australia improve their ranking and further victories over Poland and West Germany gave them a ninth-place finish.

During the Olympics, Palubinskas established himself as one of the finest shooters in the world, finishing the second-leading scorer in the Games only one point behind Japan's Taniguchi.

Following the Olympics Palubinskas accepted a scholarship to attend Louisiana State University where former Utah State assistant coach Brown had moved and to take over as head coach.

During the next two years he gained national prominence in the intense competition of American major college basketball, and although L.S.U. failed to win a Conference Title, Palubinskas came under notice of professional scouts.

Palubinskas was drafted in the fifth round by the Atlanta Hawks of the National Basketball Association and thus became the highest

nation of Junior College, University and Professionals in free throw shooting converting 142 of 151—a remarkable 94 per cent.

In his second year he was almost as prominent averaging 21 points a game and hitting 90 per cent from the free throw line. It was no surprise offers poured in for Palubinskas to accept a scholarship to a major University for his remaining two years of eligibility.

He has risen to become eighth in all-time history of College basketball for free throw shooting.

Meanwhile Australia prepared for the 1972 Olympics with Gaze, the newly-appointed

draft choice by any foreign player in the history of the N.B.A.

He was also drafted in the seventh round by the Utah Stars in the rival American Basketball Association.

The success of Palubinskas in American College basketball attracted other Australian players to seek similar opportunities and there was no shortage of coaches willing to give them a try.

There are now sufficient numbers of players who have accepted scholarships to American schools to cause Australian coaches concern.

They are starting to complain their best young talent is being exported and, if the trend continues, then they will have no chance of building a future.

There are calls for the Government to help provide scholarships for national prospects and for the provision of better facilities so that

EDDIE PALUBINSKAS . . . proved in world class, scoring against Cuba in the Montreal Olympics

offers from America will become less attractive.

Three of Australia's tallest and best young prospects are now studying in the United States and like most other players thinking if they can perform well and gain national recognition, they also might get a crack at the pro's where the average salary is around $100,000 per season.

Colin Heard, at 6 ft 6 in, set records during his two years at Menlo Junior College in California helping them achieve State honours and is due to accept a scholarship at Lewis and Clark College this year.

Gerry Doyle, 6 ft 8 in, will commence playing at Kansas State College this year after graduating from Allen County Community College whose coach said Gerry was the best player they have had at the school and is certain to do well at Kansas State.

The best professional prospect is 7 ft 2 in Andy Campbell, the tallest player produced in Australia. As a virtual unknown, in three years won selection on South Australia's State junior team, Australia's Olympic team in 1976 and then a US scholarship.

He is set to follow in the footsteps of Palubinskas at Louisiana State University.

No coaches or club officials will begrudge the loss of their stars to the United States if they can make their way to the professional ranks. The rewards are great and the incentive to younger players following will improve.

But only the extremely talented and physically capable have a chance. Despite his undoubted talents and athletic ability, when the final test was made Palubinskas was told "You're a bit too small and we are looking for a bit more physical strength".

The loss of a professional contract for Palubinskas was one of the best decisions for Australia. Once again he returned home to make another effort to lift Australia's ranking in the 1976 Olympics.

With four players—Ian Watson, Rocky Crosswhite, Palubinskas and Ray Tomlinson—returning from the 1972 team and a foundation of competition with top American teams leading up to the Games, Australia was poised for their best result.

Confidence was boosted when they beat the Canadian College champions twice in pre-Olympic exhibition matches and followed with

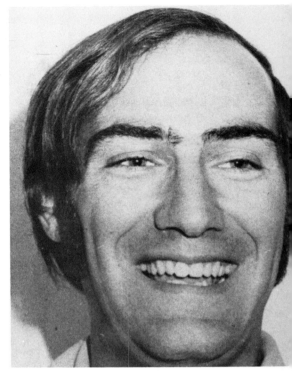

ROCKY CROSSWHITE
FOUNDATION . . . Rocky Crosswhite, Ian Watson, and Ray Tomlinson form a solid basis for future competition

a 20-point win over Puerto Rico in another exhibition.

Australia shocked Russia with their consistency and accurate shooting and late in the second half had a good chance of forcing an upset. The size and power of the Russians eventually took its toll, but only one other team, Yugoslavia, performed better against the pre-Olympic favourites.

The vital match for Australia was against Mexico, who had qualified for the Games by beating such perennial powers as Spain, Brazil and Bulgaria in the pre-Olympic tournament.

Both teams desperately needed the win to elevate their standing into the top bracket and were confident they had the players to do it.

Veteran Mexico forwards Arturo Guerrero and Manuel Raga were in peak form, but their deadly accuracy was matched by the Australian pair Eddie Palubinskas and Andris Blicavs. There was never much separating the teams, until midway through the second half when Mexico established an eight-point lead.

IAN WATSON

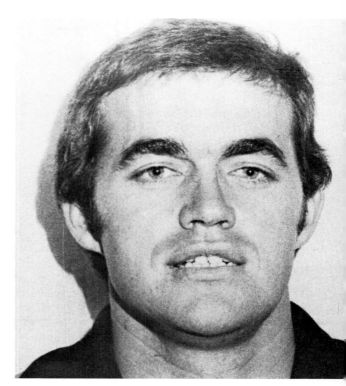

RAY TOMLINSON

Australia refused to submit and in a desperate finish held on to level the scores at the end of regulation time.

An extra five-minute period was called and it wasn't until the final eight seconds that Australia was able to break the basket-for-basket deadlock winning 120-117, an Olympic record aggregate score.

Other records were set in this game also.

Palubinskas scored an amazing 48 points making 20 from 24 shots from the field and eight from 10 from the free throw line. Blicavs was perfect from the field hitting nine from nine.

It was the longest game and highest percentage shooting contest in the Olympics as Australia connected on 67 per cent and Mexico 47. Australia's percentage was even better at the free throw line hitting 22 from 26, whilst Mexico made 13 of 14 attempts.

The win guaranteed Australia at least eighth place finish—their highest standing in World competition.

This position could have improved if luck had been kinder. Tony Barnett, a starting forward, broke his ankle in the next match against Japan, putting him out of the remaining games. His absence undoubtedly made the difference between winning and losing against Italy.

Italy were the current holders of the European title and heavily favoured, but Australia surprised by leading throughout by as many as 14 points.

However the adjustments which had to be made to cover Barnett's absence and the physical pounding the smaller Australians had to contend with eventually took its toll.

With two minutes remaining Italy gained the lead for the first time and although Australia fought valiantly they lost narrowly and with it the chance to play off for fifth place.

The excitement of reaching an improved position in the Olympics and obtaining individual honours was encouraging for Australian officials, but there was an undertone of disappointment because the women's team had been denied the opportunity to participate in the 1976 Games.

Women's basketball has progressed at a similar rate to the men during the last 10 years and now ranks amongst the best in the world.

Lack of funds has always been a handicap, but through individual effort and a keen national desire, Australia has managed to scrape together enough to send teams to the last two World Championships where they finished ninth and10th respectively in 1971 and 1975.

Included in their results in the 1975 World Championship in Columbia, Australia had a great win over Japan, the silver medallist and only a narrow loss to the United States cost Australia a place in the top group of six teams.

In December 1975 the champion Victorian team Telstars showed they were getting the measure of the Americans when they completed a 16-game tour of the United States with an undefeated record against their top teams.

When women's basketball was admitted to the Olympic Games programme for the first time in 1976, there was a great upsurge in enthusiasm amongst players and officials throughout Australia. Their record of achievement in World Championships and international tours justified a confidence in their prospects at Montreal.

The enthusiasm turned to despair when the Australian Olympic Federation Justification Committee refused permission for Australia to send their team to the Olympic Qualification Tournament.

The Australian team was so confident about their chances that they were prepared to raise all of their own expenses, but the A.O.F. stood firm on their decision.

The disappointment of failing to get the chance to play in the first Olympic Games tournament has been converted to determination to reach that high honour in the future.

A NSW team repeated the record of the Victorians in December 1976 by completing an undefeated tour of Canada and the United States and set the foundation for another tilt at the 1979 World Championship and the Moscow Olympics.

One of the features of basketball during the last 10 years has been the expansion of junior competition between the States and more recently the development of international competition. Combined with the opportunity to travel with club teams it is not unusual for young boys and girls to have seen all capital cities before the age of 18.

Tournaments are conducted under intense competitive conditions and players strive for championship honours in all age grades. But there are an equal number of tournaments conducted on a "social" level allowing teams of all standards to meet in friendly competition without the stress of winning at all cost.

This attitude of "friendly recreation" is the philosophy of mini-basketball and it is in this area that the sport is experiencing a tremendous explosion.

It is unknown just how many mini-basketballers there are in Australia as registration figures are not kept, but through sponsored clinics in 1976 approximately 80,000 new players at the primary school level were introduced to the sport, many of whom are now actively involved in regular match programmes.

Junior mens' tours from the USA commenced with the invitations from The Kings School, Parramatta NSW, to Lake Oswego and Lakeridge High Schools from Oregon.

This successful tour through NSW and Victoria commenced in 1973. Since then some 14 American junior teams have visited five States in Australia. Reciprocal tours by Australian schools and clubs started at the end on 1973.

In all tours the emphasis has been on a cultural exchange using basketball as a means of seeing another country, but the side effects of incentive and experience can be seen through the improvement of playing standards.

One can't look back over the last 10 years without also having a vision of the future. One of the most important factors that will affect the immediate future happened in February, 1977 when Australian basketball gained $250,000 sponsorship support from the Trustees of the late George Adams—Tattersall.

It had been noted at the Montreal Olympics only two sports—basketball and hockey—improved their rankings from the previous Olympics. Tattersalls provided their support to basketball for the purpose of assisting the sport to become medal contenders in 1980.

During the last 10 years the improvement in basketball has been dramatic. In the future it will be more subtle, but now Australia has joined the elite basketball countries of the world they intend to stay there with medal prospects in Moscow looking more than extremely bright.

28 HOCKEY

By JOHN DWYER

JOHNNY DWYER played hockey for Queensland and Australia for almost 10 years and was a member of "The Originals", the 1956 Olympic team. When a leg injury forced him out of the game just prior to the Rome Olympics he became sporting editor of radio station 4IP. He moved to Sydney eight years ago to join "The Sun", and is now licensee of "The Friendly Inn" in New South Wales' picturesque Kangaroo Valley.

When the infant hockey was born in Australia, officials then entrusted to its nurture lovingly called it "the game that grows".

At first it might have seemed a misnomer. Its anaemic infancy threatened a possible early demise, or at best a lifetime of struggle for survival in the face of great adversity.

But that same loving care of the early officialdom saw the game through its embryo period until over the last 10 years hockey has grown into vibrant adulthood, worthy to take its place high on the list in this sport-loving nation.

So high in fact, that today you will see the advertising slogan, "Play Hockey, Australia's top Olympic sport".

And that, officials say, is no idle boast, for they can point to an Olympic record of which they can be justifiably proud.

For at the 21st Olympiad in Montreal last year, wasn't it the hockey side which brought home Australia's only silver medal?

And wasn't it that same hockey side which had the nation glued to its television sets in the hope of our only gold strike?

New Zealand won that gold rush which is now part of history, but more of that later.

To say the leaps and bounds of progress have been made only over the past 10 years is stretching things a little too far. Sure the numerical increase has been steady, and sure it has shown a great improvement over the last decade.

Australian Hockey Association secretary, Mr Harry Nederveen, says there are almost 20,000 registered senior men players throughout the country and the junior total adds another 45,000, with the game being played from Darwin down to Tasmania and throughout every State right over to Perth, where it is at its blooming best.

Ten years ago the number of senior players was little more than half that. But the import-

ance of the growth has not been in numerical strength alone, it has also risen tremendously in stature.

And to look for the beginning of the flexing of biceps we must go back to 1956.

For it was in 1956 in Melbourne Australia got its first chance to play hockey at Olympic level.

And it was in Melbourne that skipper Ian Dick's "Originals", as they were to become known, put up the first show of strength . . . the first indication of things to come.

In finishing fifth out of 16 competing nations "The Originals" erased the memory of some humiliating defeats in the rare tilts Australia had had at international level.

No more would we see the blaze approach of the famous Indian side which toured Australia in the 1930s when the legendary Dyan Chand and his cohorts ran riot to notch a dozen goals against the bewildered wearers of the green and gold.

Matches taken at such casual ease that the Indian goalkeeper could walk contemptuously away from his net to the spectators over the fence, nonchalantly signing autographs secure in the knowledge it was only if his countrymen saw fit would he get a touch of the ball during the entire game.

And the progress continued with John McBryde's 1964 Olympic team bringing home our first hockey medal—a bronze—from Tokyo. Then the preparations were on in earnest for the next Olympiad in Mexico City in 1968.

It was a well balanced unit Don McWatters led, and one which brought this country's best result to date—a silver medal.

Australia impressed the hockey nations of the world by working their way into the final against Pakistan and they lost few, if any, admirers in going down 2-1.

CLUB HOCKEY . . . in Melbourne, one of the many grassroots venues for Australia's international success

This was the team that contained players like Pat Nilan and Ron Riley.

Nilan had been a member of the team in Tokyo, but this was Riley's first appearance in the Olympic uniform—and what a duo they proved to be.

Nilan at inside-left and Riley in the centre-forward position formed a combination to equal anything in the world.

In fact, they came home from those Games with the popular reputation of being individually the best in the game in their respective positions.

Nilan and Riley brought a finesse to the game which this country had never seen before.

During his career Nilan played 86 games for Australia and wore the Olympic blazer in 1964, 1968 and 1972.

Riley, too, played in three Olympics, 1968, 1972 and 1976 and his total appearances for Australia reached 70.

[News Ltd.]
BOB PROCTOR . . . save of the century

Behind Nilan and Riley in the centre-half position when Australia won that silver medal in Mexico was the last of the famous Pearce brothers from Western Australia, Julian.

Or more correctly, the youngest of the famous Pearce brothers, Julian.

When Julian won his Australian cap he became the fifth member of the family to do so.

Starting off this hockey fairy tale come true were the older members of the family, Cec and Mel, who were playing for Australia in the early 1950s when about the only international competition Australia was getting was every two years against New Zealand.

Mel stayed in the game long enough to become one of those 1956 "Originals" spoken of earlier.

And joining him in that 1956 Olympic team in Melbourne were the middle members of the Pearce family, Eric and Gordon.

So Australia had the almost unbelievable situation where three members of the one family were together in an Olympic team.

And Eric and Gordon stayed in the game

at international level long enough to repeat the dose.

When the plane arrived in Sydney from Mexico City, there proudly showing their silver medals were the three Pearce brothers—Eric, Gordon and Julian.

The Olympic scene shifted to ill-fated Munich four years later and naturally Australia was there well-equipped, eager and confident to joust.

The result could not come up to the previous two efforts, although the fifth position gained again left Australia a force to be reckoned with among the top hockey nations.

Again it's four years on and the medal quest shifted to Montreal, where a new name "astro-turf" reared its head.

The synthetic surface was new to skipper Robert Haigh and his boys, but they settled in to it well.

It was new too to New Zealand and to India and Pakistan where the playing pitches are packed down like turf wickets anyway.

To all European hockey nations "astro-turf," or its equivalents, were quite familiar surfaces, yet it was to be Australia and New Zealand who were to battle it out for the precious gold medal.

And on the way to that final against New Zealand Australia was to reach some unprecedented heights.

Heights such as a 6-1 drubbing of the once lords of Olympic Hockey, India. A far cry indeed from those days of the 1930s, when goals dripped from those magic Indian curved sticks like droplets from a leaking faucet.

But there were reversals, too, among the triumphs on the way to the final and Australia was destined to meet India again in a play-off to decide who would make the semi-finals.

And here we saw just what a professional approach the Australians now have to their hockey.

An approach where anything within the rules is worth trying in a bid for victory and even anything not included in the rule book such as gamesmanship, a tool which any tradesman, any true "professional" in sport, must have in his tool kit.

[News Ltd.]
PAT NILAN . . . finesse to the game

RICK CHARLESWORTH . . . versatile sportsman, now Australian captain, in action against Pakistan

[News Ltd]

For who can forget the cliff-hanging drama of it all when India and Australia were locked 1-all and had to move into the tie-breaker of five penalty strokes each taken alternately.

And how Australian goalkeeper Robert Proctor's mind must have been ticking over as he reached deep into his bag of tricks for one little ploy which might swing the pendulum his team's way.

And how successful was that slight limp as he walked slowly to the net favouring his right leg. For penalty strokes in hockey, like penalty kicks in Soccer, really should be certain goals.

But that hapless little Indian had noticed Proctor was favouring his right leg and as surely as if it had been fired from a pre-aimed rifle, it was to the right that the shot came.

And just as surely it was Proctor who gained that split second he needed to bring off what will surely go down as the save of the century to put Australia through to the final.

So came the final and what a fitting thing it was for Australia and New Zealand to meet.

Here were the two most hockey-starved nations in the world overcoming all opposition to meet on the game's biggest stage.

The two nations who had met so many times over the years in friendly rivalry with first success to one and then to the other.

And all the time picking each other's brains, for those were the only hockey brains to be picked by either country for so long.

And what a triumph it turned out to be for the boys from the Shaky Isles.

Excuses? Naturally there were some offered by the sideline experts after the smoke had cleared.

Certainly the great Ron Riley was only a shadow of his former self in this match and it was so far out of character for him when inside-right Rick Charlesworth on a number of occasions produced beautifully controlled passes through the gap and Riley just couldn't capitalise on them.

There had to be something wrong, and there was. It came out later that Riley was carrying a painful knee injury, a legacy of the hard fought semi-final against Pakistan.

And it came out later that Charlesworth, that versatile sportsman who has also made a name for himself as a member of the successful Western Australian Sheffield Shield cricket side, had his problems.

Charlesworth, the Australian hero of these Olympics who has now taken over the mantle as Australia's hockey captain, received a long gash in his leg at the very beginning of the Games, and this had to be re-stitched after every time he played.

But that is only by way of explanation. It is only to point out that the way to the final had not been an easy one. Victories are hard to come by at this level and a certain price has to be paid. It is not an attempt to offer excuses. No excuses are necessary when a side has played so well to get to an Olympic final.

New Zealand, too, had to earn victories in just as hard a manner as the Australians and no doubt they had their share of tender spots.

No, this was a victory that was all New Zealand's. A triumph which they earned. One which they thoroughly deserved and one which no member of the Australian team and no true sport-loving Australian would begrudge.

For it was all there on the scoreboard . . . one goal to nil. New Zealand went into the game as underdogs, and came out without doubt the better team on the day.

But back to Australian hockey and its giant strides forward during the past 10 years.

Mind you, among those giant strides there has been quite a bit of marking time and also one or two little backward steps.

For mixed among those Olympic dramas of success and near success were some inexplicable moments when the taste of defeat has been a bitter pill to swallow indeed. There have been three World Cups during the past decade and by and large, apart from the experience gained, they were great disappointments.

A seventh placing was the best Australia could do at Barcelona, and there was no improvement from the team which competed in Amsterdam, while in the last World Cup in Kuala Lumpur the six points gained were not enough to get Australia to the semi-finals.

Perhaps some consolation could be taken there from the fact Australia scored 16 goals and allowed only six against, to come home with the best goal average for the series.

Explanations for those performances? Not really. Certainly it can be claimed some of our top players were not available at World Cup time.

But if that is going to be thrown in the ring it is a pretty poor look out. For surely in a sport as healthy as hockey, more than 15 or 16 world-class players can be produced at the one time?

Better perhaps to believe that a little of our indigenous people's tendency to go walk-about has rubbed off on the country's hockey sticks.

For among the string of successes have been some almost inexplicable failures.

Failures like the 3-1 loss to England in Kuala Lumpur in a game in which an almost unbelievable, and certainly inexcusable, four penalty strokes were missed.

And that is to say nothing of a mind-boggling 2-3 defeat by Argentina to force that famous play-off with India at Montreal.

But by and large it has been a success story decade and what is the reason behind it all?

Perhaps the greatest single contributory factor is the almost fanatical accent on fitness gradually built — and carried on from coach to coach.

Handed on till it reached Merv Adams and his preparation of the team for Montreal.

Adams and his accent on speed and endurance. An accent which saw him devise a special circuit of stress exercises against the clock.

A course which included specialised distance running, a thing unheard of in preparation by other countries. And with distances so great and finance so limited, all this had to be done by correspondence.

Yes, all done in the manner outback kids get their schooling, but carried out so loyally by each and every member of the team the Australian hockey contingent in Montreal earned the nickname of "The Mail Order Team."

It is a nickname they carry proudly as those "Originals" before them carried theirs, for they are certain, as dedicated men like Merv Adams are certain, that our finest hour is yet to come.

TWO AUSTRALIAN WORLD RECORD HOLDERS

DES RENFORD . . . the 'King of the Channel' has never failed to conquer the often awesome English Channel, with his tally currently standing at eleven crossings from as many attempts – the record. Renford, now 51, was a late starter on the marathon swimming scene at 39, yet he has stamped himself as a world champion, among his many feats including swimming Sydney to Wollongong non-stop, 38 miles down the Murray River and swimming the shark-infested waters around Alcatraz . . . a truly remarkable record in the most mind snapping of all endurance sports.

KEN WARBY . . . Australian Ken Warby hurtled across Blowering Dam near Tumut, New South Wales on November 20, 1977, to set a new world water speed record. Warby powered his home-built Westinghouse J34 auxiliary unit from a Neptune bomber over the two-way run to average the new mark of 464.457 kph (288.60 mph), breaking the previous record held by Lee Taylor Jnr. (USA) of 459.005 kph (285.20 mph) set in 1967 on Lake Guntersville, Alabama.